CATERING: HOUSEKEEPING AND HOTEL MANAGEMENT

CATERING: HOUSEKEEPING AND HOTELE MANAGEMENT

M. C. METTI

ANMOL PUBLICATIONS PVT. LTD.
NEW DELHI - 110 002 (INDIA)

ANMOL PUBLICATIONS PVT. LTD.

H.O.: 4374/4B, Ansari Road, Darya Ganj,
New Delhi-110 002 (India)
Ph.: 23278000, 23261597

B.O.: No. 1015, Ist Main Road, BSK IIIrd Stage
IIIrd Phase, IIIrd Block
Bangalore - 560 085 (India)
Visit us at: www.anmolpublications.com

Catering: Housekeeping and Hotel Management

ISBN 978-81-261-3249-2

PRINTED IN INDIA

Printed at Mehra Offset Press, Delhi.

Contents

Preface

Catering is the business of providing food service at a remote site. A mobile caterer serves food directly from a vehicle or cart that is designed for the purpose. Mobile catering is common at outdoor events (such as concerts), workplaces, and downtown business districts. An event caterer serves food with waiting staff at dining tables or sets up a self-serve buffet. The food may be prepared on site, made completely at the event, or the caterer may choose to bring prepared food and put the finishing touches on once they arrive. The event caterer staff isn't responsible for preparing the food but often help set up the dining area. This service is typically provided at banquets, conventions, and weddings. Any event where all the attenders are provided with food and drinks or sometimes only hors d'oeuvres is often called a catered event.

A catering company or specialist is expected to know not just food preparation, but how to make it attractive. Many events require working with the entire theme or color scheme. Catering companies have moved toward full-service taking charge of not only food preparation but also decorations, such as table settings or lighting. It's not that food is no longer a focal point, but rather that it is part of a broader mission. Many suggest that catering is about satisfying all the senses. A caterer and his or her staff should be friendly and coorperative because, after all, they are in the food service industry and should follow the motto "the customer is always right".

Catering is typically sold on a per-person basis, where adding additional people is a flat price per person. Keeping the cost of the food and supplies below this is required to make a profit on the catering. With the correct atmosphere, professional event caterers experience can bring clients satisfaction of all the senses in a way that makes an event special and memorable. Of course, beautifully prepared food can appeal to your sense of taste, smell and sight - perhaps even touch, but the decorations and ambiance should play a significant part in the clients enjoyment as well.

This book provides all necessary references required for catering and House keeping Management. Suggestions for the improvement of the book are highly soliciated.

Author

Chapter 1

Catering and Food Service

Catering is the business of providing food service at a remote site. Mobile catering is the business of selling prepared food from some sort of vehicle. It is a feature of urban culture in many countries.

The food service generally encompasses those places, institutions, and companies responsible for any meal eaten away from home. This industry includes restaurants, school and hospital cafeterias, catering operations, and many other formats. The companies that supply foodservice operators are called foodservice distributors. Foodservice hard goods like ovens and refrigerators are often sold by large buying groups.

Some companies manufacture products in both consumer and foodservice versions. The consumer version usually comes in individual-sized packages with elaborate label design for retail sale. The foodservice version is packaged in a much larger industrial size and often lacks the colourful label designs of the consumer version.

Foodservice sales to restaurants and institutions are estimated to be approximately $400 Billion, about equal with consumer sales of foods through grocery outlets.

A food cart is a motorless trailer that can be hauled by automobile, bicycle, or hand to the point of sale, often a public sidewalk or park. Carts typically have an onboard heating or refrigeration system to keep the food ready for consumption. Foods and beverages often served from carts include ...

- Halal food such as lamb or chicken over rice, or in a gyro
- Ice cream and other frozen treats
- Coffee, bagels, donuts, Egg sandwichs (ie. bacon, egg, and cheese) and other breakfast items

Food Truck is a mobile kitchen, known colliqually in some regions as a "X" Truck, is a mobile venue that sells food. Some, including ice cream trucks, sell mostly frozen or prepackaged food; others are more like restaurants-on-wheels. Food trucks make frequent appearances at carnivals, construction sites, and other temporary venues where large numbers of people gather.

Some college campuses and surrounding areas boast many food trucks with loyal followings; for example, visitors to Harvard University or MIT in Cambridge, Massachusetts or the campus of the University of Pennsylvania in Philadelphia may see some very popular trucks parked outside the main entrances to buildings at lunchtime. At Rutgers University, the Grease Trucks serve "fat sandwiches" that contain an ensemble of ingredients such as steak, cheese, chicken fingers, french fries, mozzarella sticks, jalapeño poppers, and more.

In the United Kingdom, these are known as burger vans and can be found on nearly all major trunk roads at the side of the road selling their food. A 1/4lb burger can be purchased for about £2 (approx. $3.5USD). Many people prefer to stop at one of these Burger vans when travelling due to the cheap price, rather than stop at a motorway service station where prices can be extremely high.

Sometimes also called "maggot wagon," "roach coach," or "gut truck," these rolling restaurants can frequently be found at or near construction sites.

An early version of the food truck was the US Army's mobile canteen and before that the old West's chuckwagon. A mobile kitchen is a modified van with a built-in grill, deep fryer, or other cooking equipment. It offers more flexibility in the menu since the vendor can prepare food to order. A vendor can choose to park the van in one place, as with a cart, or to broaden the business's reach by driving the van to several customer locations. Examples of mobile kitchens include taco trucks on the west coast of the United States, especially Southern California, and fish and chips vans in the United Kingdom.

A concession trailer has preparation equipment like a mobile kitchen, but it cannot move on its own. As such it is suited for events lasting several days, such as funfairs.

In addition to being operated as private businesses, mobile catering vehicles are also used after natural disasters to feed people in areas with damaged infrastructure. The Salvation Army has several mobile kitchens that it uses for this purpose.

An event caterer serves food with waiting staff at dining tables or sets up a self-serve buffet. The food may be prepared on site, made completely at the event, or the caterer may choose to bring prepared food and put the finishing touches on once they arrive. The event caterer staff isn't responsible for preparing the food but often help set up the dining area. This service is typically provided at banquets, conventions, and weddings. Any event where all the attenders are provided with food and drinks or sometimes only hors d'oeuvres is often called a catered event.

A catering company or specialist is expected to know not just food preparation, but how to make it attractive. Many events require working with the entire theme or colour scheme. Catering companies have moved toward full-service taking charge of not only food preparation but also decorations, such as table settings or lighting. It's not that food is no longer a focal point, but rather that it is part of a broader mission. Many suggest that catering is about satisfying all the senses. A caterer and his or her staff should be friendly and coorperative because, after all, they are in the food service industry and should follow the motto "the customer is always right".

Catering is typically sold on a per-person basis, where adding additional people is a flat price per person. Keeping the cost of the food and supplies below this is required to make a profit on the catering. With the correct atmosphere, professional event caterers experience can bring clients satisfaction of all the senses in a way that makes an event special and memorable. Of course, beautifully prepared food can appeal to your sense of taste, smell and sight - perhaps even touch, but the decorations and ambiance should play a significant part in the clients enjoyment as well.

Industrial catering includes providing food for airline passengers, schools, prisons and other institutional settings. It can include contract management of client foodservice facilities. Airlines often have divisions or hire third parties to provide food for passengers.

Catering is covered by two different groups. "Independent caterers and companies with a catering business on the side" is a phrase that could be combined with the previous sentence.

CATERING TIPS AND TRICKS

CHOOSINGRIGHT CATERING SERVICE

Food is an integral part of any party so one must choose a catering service wisely. But how does one choose the right caterer for an event? It is important to do a lot of research, check references, and often request a sampling to make your final decision.

List your catering needs In order for a caterer to provide an accurate estimate for your party or event, you must communicate your needs clearly. Do you have a location for your party/event reserved and is there a kitchen on site? How many guests are coming to your event? Find out if the potential caterer has a minimum guest requirement. Take into consideration that some of your guests may have special dietary needs and be certain to communicate this with your caterer. A great caterer will be ready for any surprise that may surface, but at what cost to you?

Discuss your budget with your caterer and what options are available. Ask yourself, do you prefer a buffet style or a silver-service sit down dinner for your guests? Be clear about your proposed menu, do you have a theme or style at the event that will be reflected in the cuisine? Your budget may or may not determine how flexible your caterer is to meet your needs. Keep in mind; it is the type of food that often determines the bulk price of the catering job. Find out, and possibly request, if the caterer will provide a detailed contract of service and outline what the payment terms will be.

Does the caterer use fresh or frozen food for recipes? Is the produce grown locally? Is it organic? Will any of the dishes be pre-made and then frozen until the party/event? Does anything come from a can?

Does the potential caterer supply decorations, linens, tables & chairs? Very often there will be a brochure catering services supply with examples of past event and table decorations. It is important to be very clear in what your event needs and what the caterer will be supplying. Is a menu board provided for the guests that describes the ingredients of the dishes being served?

Will the catering company provide a wait-staff? What is their required dress code? What is the ratio of servers to guests? A rule of thumb is one server for every 10 guests. Be certain to ask your potential caterer if taxes and gratuities are included in the final bid.

What happens to the leftovers? Often, upon request, a catering service will compile a food basket at no additional charge for the host or hostess of the event. Remember, it is critical that you communicate with your potential caterer exactly you want; the result, you get what you want and the caterer can provide an accurate bid for the job as well as the exceptional service your event deserves.

SERVING ALCOHOL AT YOUR EVENT

When one commits to planning an event or party, one must decide whether or not to serve alcohol to the guests. There are a few considerations to keep in mind and discuss with your caterer.

Where will your event or party be taking place? It is important to confirm that your event or party site will allow alcohol on its premises. Once you have made certain that you can serve alcohol at your chosen site, ask your caterer if he or she holds a liquor license. He or she must have a valid liquor license. If he or she does not hold a liquor license, then you must contact a liquor-licensed dealer.

Prepare to provide a guest estimate for your caterer to work with. The caterer in turn will supply you with a quote for the number of bartenders that must attend bar and the quantity of ice, glasses, and mixers necessary. The amount of bartenders depends on the number of guests. Your caterer or licensed liquor dealer will be responsible for setting up the bar.

You must now determine what you wish to be served from the bar as well as if you require your guests to pay for alcohol themselves.

A cash bar requires the guest to pay for their drinks. Guests tend to consume less alcohol when it isn't free. This is a basic bar with all the works and at no charge to the guests. The open bar includes hard liquor for mixing drinks, wine, beer, and soft drinks.

A limited bar will set boundaries on what will be served and in what moderation. An example of a limited bar is an event in which beer and wine is offered to the guests at no charge and hard liquor is offered at a pre-determined price.

Whatever you decide in regards to serving alcohol at your event or party is up to you. Be certain to discuss all the beverage details with your caterer beforehand. Cheers.

WEDDING CATERING

After watching the happy couple exchange vows and begin their married life together, your guests will be hungry. Many of the guests may have scaled back on eating in order to look good for pictures or just because they were so busy during the day.

When you're putting together such a large assortment of people, there are bound to be those that have certain ways or preferences of eating. You may find that there are vegetarians or those that can not eat dairy. You might have a diabetic in the crowd or some other health restriction.

You should certainly try to have options for any sort of eating arrangement. In the case of those that don't eat meat, you might want to have a cheese lasagne available or other pasta dish. This is becoming widely popular to have two options anyways, so why not offer them?

Another way to cope with varied needs is to serve dinner in a buffet style. This allows each person to pick only what they want or what they can eat.

A lot of wedding caterers rely on word of mouth (no pun intended) to get their services recognized. If you can, talk to other people that have gotten married in your town to see who they recommend. Of course, you will still want to see them for yourself, but this list can be a great starting point.

Another way to find good catering is to talk to the reception hall coordinators. Many times they will either require the use of a particular caterer or they have a list of those that they recommend. Of course, you will want to schedule an appointment with all of the catering candidates in order to do a taste test of their menu options. At that point, you can pick what you think your guests will enjoy.

A good meal is a great way to send your thanks to your guests for coming to your wedding. This is the part that shouldn't be skimped on for any reason. Of course, that doesn't mean that you can't find moderately priced options. Try your favourite restaurant, for example. If they're able to cater, then you may be able to get a better deal because you're buying food in bulk.

Having a friend who is a cook is even better—so long as they don't mind working through the wedding. So you've tasted the offerings of the caterer and you've selected your main menu options. What about drinks?

Much like selecting the menu options, you will need to factor in what kinds of drinks everyone would like to drink. The easiest way to take care of this is to offer a full service bar. In this way, guests can have mixed drinks of all varieties or they can stick to wine and beer.

You want to plan this option out carefully as you may end up paying more than you would like. Check with the provider as to how many drinks each guest can have, or can expect from the supply that will be brought. In most cases, there is no limit.

A word of advice: Don't ever have a cash bar. Making your guests pay for their drinks when they may also have paid for their outfits and transportation is just a lot to ask. In terms of wine and beer, tastes and varieties are enormous—how does someone choose?

The best advice is to select four to five different kinds of beer with each one having enough to fill everyone's glass. This may surprise you, but sometimes all of your guests will like the same thing and you may want to make sure that they can have it.

As for wine, you may want to have at least one of each a red varietal and a white varietal. This ensures a milder and more acidic selection. A way to make sure that everyone is happy is to find blends of each of these wines. By blends, this means to find a red that includes a merlot, syrah, and pinot noir, while the white might include a chardonnay, reisling, and zinfandel. These can be tricky to find, but they are crowd pleasers.

Toasts are just not toasts without a little glass (or two) of champagne. It's common sense to make sure that the new couple and their wedding party have the very finest in champagne (as determined by the budget), while the rest of the guests have another variety. In many reception halls or catering services, the champagne for the wedding party is provided. Of course, there will also be designated drivers at the wedding, so you will also want to have water, sodas, coffee, and juices available as well. When you're planned it thoroughly, everyone will be well-watered throughout the evening.

HOW TO START A CATERING BUSINESS

The catering industry in the United States is estimated to be worth $5 billion a year. Caterers are hired to perform an assorted number of jobs-everything from cooking to serving, mixing drinks, and whipping up delicious desserts. Functions range from dinner parties that serve a handful of guests to enormous events that serve thousands of guests. Normally a caterer will define their niche, meaning a caterer will choose what type of functions to specialize in as well as their job description. For example, you may offer the best fondue table for up to 100 guests, perhaps you would rather prepare meals for business catering parties that are held within banker's hours. There really are no limits in regards to catering styles.

Once you have arrived to the idea stage it is great to begin a business catering plan. Be meticulous when you detail how the catering business will be operated, managed and capitalized. The following checklist can help you organize your ideas into the beginning of a business catering plan:

- What services will your catering business offer? Will you run a full service catering business, corporate catering service, custom event catering service, or a scheduled events catering business?
- Research necessary permits and requirements your local government imposes on a catering business.

- Determine your start up costs of your catering business. Remember to include everything-permit fees, catering equipment, marketing, uniforms, catering supplies etc.
- Construct a budget, forecast and projection.
- How will you finance the start up of your catering business?
- Research liability insurance needed to protect your catering business.
- Where will you house your catering business office and how will you manage your business? Prepare to think about cancellations, payment policies, consultations, menu-planning as well as samples, contracts and the transportation of food.
- What food suppliers do you intend to work with?
- Will your catering service rent equipment for special requests?
- What will you name your catering business?

Owning a catering service not only includes cooking but also be prepared to wear many hats such as: accountant, manager, marketer, sales representative, and bill collector.

Additional questions to consider when constructing your catering business plan:

- Is my business idea practical and is it in demand?
- What is my competition?
- What is my advantage over existing services?
- Can I deliver a better quality service?
- Can I create a demand for my business?
- What will be my legal structure?
- How will I compensate myself?

Your answers to these questions will help you create a focused, well-researched catering business plan that can serve as a blueprint for your new catering service. Whatever you choose to specialize in, running a catering business offers creativity, flexibility, and growing opportunities.

Maybe you've got the details of the actual wedding ceremony worked out, but what about the reception? One of the major costs of the wedding reception will definitely be the food, so you'll want to make sure you'll have enough food for everyone without spending too much money. Here are some top ways to cut on your catering bill that will ensure that your guests enjoy your reception—and you save money.

Most couples want to order an extra tray or two of hors d'oeuvres in case extra guests show up. This is fine (and usually a smart idea), but you should still make sure that you're not order more appetizers than you actually need; use your discretion based on the guest list. For instance, if you know a number of your guests are vegetarian, you may not need to order as many appetizers with meat. Also, ordering two or three types of hors d'oeuvres will help to reduce your catering bill. If you buy more of the same dish, you can usually save money with most catering companies—different kinds of foods will increase the bill, so it's important to keep it classy but simple at the wedding—even when it comes to food.

Caterers will also try to encourage you to spend more than you may need to on the actual meal as well. You may not need a five course meal if you've already purchased three types of appetizers and a salad, or three extra desserts if you already have a pretty large wedding cake. The time of day that you hold your wedding will give you a good indication of how much food to serve; if you're having the ceremony in the afternoon or early evening, you may want to serve more food.

There are some foods that are always going to be expensive, even if you only order small amounts. So, since you have to order a considerable amount of food, ordering dishes that aren't so costly will help you to keep your catering bill reasonable. Certain seafood, like shrimp, lobster and salmon will definitely make your catering bill higher, so if you have to have them, try to use them as only one of the course choices for dinner, or purchase these foods as appetizers to save on costs.

Food stations are a unique way to serve a variety of foods at your wedding reception, and you can be sure that everyone will find something they like to eat. This way, you won't have to worry about people changing their minds about their meal choices once they arrive at the reception. A food station with different types of pasta is usually a hit with most guests, and can be very economical. You can also include food stations with other types of the ethnic foods, such as Mexican or Indian fare, to celebrate the cultures of the people who will be attending your wedding, or to acknowledge your backgrounds.

You may also be able to cut your catering bill by not requesting an elaborate setup for your food stations and tables. Using a single colour for tablecloths, usually white, will cut down on labour costs.

Chapter 2

Customer Focus

Some businesses fail because critical fundamentals have been ignored. Firms can ensure sustainable success for the long term if they conduct a rigorous analysis of their value-creating capabilities beginning with the fundamental question of "what business are we in?" Answering this question requires a firm first to define the value it is providing to the customer. Next, the firm needs to figure out how to create and deliver this customer value at a profit. To be able to sustain these profits, the firm needs to provide customer value that is superior to that provided by the competition. Firms that intuitively pay attention to customer value are also service oriented. Customer value analysis presupposes a customer-focused perspective. Customer-focused firms create and deliver superior customer value through unbeatable service.

Businesses fail when the fundamental question—what business are we in?—is either ignored or misunderstood. To answer this question appropriately, businesses have to be customer focused. What does being customer focused mean? Why is it that customer-focused firms achieve a sustainable competitive advantage? What does customer-focused management involve?

A January 2001 issue of the *Wall Street Journal* featured an article titled: "Can these dot-coms be saved?" The dot-com malaise was becoming widespread. The message in the article was simple, the question straightforward, but the answers were not readily evident. A closer look reveals that the answers are implicit in the questions within the article. "Is Priceline's vaunted name-your-own-price model good for anything but plane tickets?" "If traditional catalog retailers can make money selling clothing why can't a Web site like Bluefly?" "Can Webvan's net-fueled automation turn profits delivering cornflakes?" All three of these Internet examples represent a very typical situation that most if not all dot-coms, including that mainstay, Yahoo!, had been facing. The problem was endemic to the dot-com business. The technology was powerful, but in each case, the appropriate revenue model remained elusive.

The question on everyone's mind was: Where are the profits? And, when the profits arrive, would they be sustainable? The answer is in the question. If you asked the right questions, you could find the right answers. A Francis Bacon quote comes to mind: "A prudent question is one-half of wisdom." As the dot-com frenzy reached epidemic proportions, the right questions were not being asked, and the right answers were not available. All this may (yet again) seem simplistic, but many of the dot-com failures were at least partly attributable.

Customers buy solutions, not products. Every firm needs to understand what it is providing the customer in terms of customer value, not by focusing on the product but by focusing on the customer. In doing so, the firm is able to assess whether it is providing superior customer value and whether it has a sustainable competitive advantage. Competitive advantage cannot be sustained unless it can be protected from competitor matching. Any aspect of the product can be matched by the competition. What is most difficult for the competition to match is how the firm approaches and treats the customer. The firm *serves* the customer by providing product enhancements in the form of service. When other firms can provide the same service, the differentiator is in the service orientation of the firm.

Many firms focus on the product rather than on the customer. When the focus is on the customer, the business is defined in terms of customer value, not in terms of product. The product is viewed as a customer solution and experience. That is, for any firm, the most fundamental definition of its business.

Try this one. What business is Amazon in? That you can buy just about anything on Amazon may not be too much of an exaggeration. The company abandoned or at least cut back on its strategy of buying up companies, as it did with Drugstore.com in 1999. It now handles retail for such established brands as Toys 'R' Us, Target, and Circuit City. Amazon shocked everyone in early 2002, when they announced their first operations profit of $59 million and a net profit of $5 million in the previous quarter. What value does Amazon provide its customer?

Customers don't buy products. They buy solutions. If firms are focused on the customer, they ought to see themselves in the role of providing solutions, not products. The information technology sector has popularized the term "solutions providers, " with labels such as application service providers (ASPs, as they are called) or technology solutions providers. These labels may be appropriate at the very general level and allow people to gloss over and take for granted the real meaning of the term *solutions.* The label has no real meaning as a concept unless it can be translated into customer value terms. Customers buy value in the solutions. Thus, customer value defines the primary purpose of any business.

This chapter presents an approach to conducting a critical analysis of this fundamental question of "defining the business of a firm." In doing so, it defines "customer value" and redefines "products" in the customer-focused perspective. Finally, this chapter briefly indicates the fruits of a customer-focused organization providing superior customer value.

Management guru Peter Drucker said in his 1954 book, *The Practice of Management,* "to know what a business is we have to start with its purpose." He goes on to say: "There is only one valid definition of business purpose: *to create a customer.*" Drucker reiterates this concept in a number of different ways, always emphasizing that "it is the customer who determines what a business is." It is not important what the business thinks it is producing. The customer determines the value of what the business produces based on what the customer thinks he or she is buying. Such a perspective places the final result in focus—what the product *does* for the customer. Thus, the purpose of a business is what it creates for the customer. The first and foremost question for any firm to ask is, what business are we in? How many firms diligently confront this question? And, when they do encounter this question, whose perspective do they take? Taking the customer's perspective to answer this fundamental question forces a number of thought processes that benefit the firm in different ways.

In fact, businesses will find that approaching the question of *what business are we in?* in so fundamental a manner not only allows the firm to understand its existing customers, but will also help open up new market potential. It forces the analysis of value-creating assets, including the firm's skills and knowledge sets. The question also opens up the analysis of who the competition is. When firms strive to beat rivals, they typically end up competing within the confines of existing business. Firms sometimes do not realize that they compete with firms in other industries. They are able to see this if they articulate their business from the customer's perspective.

When customers consider their options in meeting a need, they don't limit themselves to one industry. Without realizing it as such, their solutions may involve different industries. Firms are forced to redefine their competitive landscape when they take the customer's perspective because they will find themselves competing outside their well-defined spaces. Kim and Mauborgne call it competing in a "market space."

They urge firms to expand their view of their business by looking "across substitute industries, across strategic groups, across buyer groups, across complementary product and service offerings, across the functional-emotional orientation of an industry and even across time." They argue this point with examples of how Home Depot cultivated the do-it-yourself market from homeowners using contractors, how Intuit saw that people managing personal finances using a pencil and paper calculation actually competed with their software, how overnight package delivery firms FedEx and UPS competed with telephones and fax machines, and how Southwest Airlines competed with driving. This argument illustrates the definition of a business from the perspective of the customer. Not only does it underscore the value that the customer places on what the firm delivers, but it also reveals that the customer's perspective redefines the business.

Well-known Harvard scholar Ted Levitt expanded on Drucker's thesis of defining a business from a customer's perspective when he popularized the concept "marketing myopia," where firms and entire industries (such as buggy-whip makers) could perish when inwardly focused. He used the example of railroads as an industry that suffered from marketing myopia because it did not see itself in the business of transportation, but rather in the railroad business. Contrast this with a firm like the Williams Companies, one of the world's largest pipeline builders. Until a few years ago, it built steel pipes to move oil and natural gas. Today, it also builds fiber-optic pipes for the big cable companies. Clearly, Williams did not see itself as being in the oil and gas business, but as being in the business of serving big companies that needed to move material (or data) through pipes. Would Williams have seen this opportunity if it had been focused on competing within the oil and gas industry? To expand your opportunities, you need to look beyond the product horizon and into the customer's space. For example, if a family was looking for something to do on a Saturday, consider their options: have some friends over for dinner, go out for dinner, go to a nearby mall, go to the movies, go to a play or a show, go bowling, go to a miniature golf course, go for a drive to the lake or the beach—and many other options. Now, look at these options in terms of all of the different industries that are competing with each other. If you were a firm in any one of these industries, you could be defining your business the same way as any of the other industries, depending on who your typical customer is. The customer's perspective broadens your own view of your product.

Taking the customer's perspective helps firms identify what they are about—their mission and their values. They are better able to understand their strengths and sources of competitive advantage. Firms are better positioned and more effective in allocating resources and efforts, both strategically and operationally. They are better situated to understand what would be considered superior customer value.

Where do you even begin when you want to define your business? Let us consider the basics. What *do* businesses sell, at the most general level? In what terms will your response be made? Do you see services and goods as solutions to a customer problem—a need to be met? Customer needs are problems searching for solutions and firms are providers of solutions to customer problems. When seen this way, firms draw focus away from products and orient themselves to the customer with the sole purpose of delivering solutions to problems. The business is defined in terms of customer solutions. Firms suffering from a product focus define their product by its capabilities in terms of product features and promptly lose sight of the customer. The solutions-to-problems approach emphasizes the customer rather than the product. It emphasizes product benefits rather than product features.

Firms must align processes, people, and their entire culture to serving the customer rather than on making and selling products. In customer-focused firms, processes are designed with customers in mind. The output of the processes, the product, is defined by the customer need it serves. In serving the customer, firms offer a combination of benefits or values. Are all products, therefore, a service to the customer?

In a sense, yes! The solution represents the value that the firm is providing customers by serving their needs.

Firms' activities produce solutions as value bundles that we call products. All products involve a mix of value producing components—tangibles and intangibles—in value bundles. The proportion of tangibles and intangibles in the entity that the customer takes title to prompts the artificial distinction between services and products. This unfortunate dichotomy detracts from the necessary customer focus in the conception of the product. Regardless of whether the total product is predominantly a packaged good or a service, in a business-to-business (B2B) or business-to-consumers (B2C) context, all solutions to customer problems can be seen as bundles of benefits or value bundles designed to deliver value by meeting customer problems or needs. This book adopts the approach that all products are a mix of physical goods and services in some proportion. Some solutions employ more tangibles (physical goods) than intangibles (services) in meeting customer needs, while others may provide an intangible (service) involving physical objects. The important question is, what is that total solution from the customer's perspective? It is more important to understand what the value bundle *does* for the customer than what the bundle *is*. To identify the value bundle, one needs to identify and understand the customer.

UNDERSTANDING THE CUSTOMER

To understand the customer is to understand your business. To understand the customer's perspective is basic to defining a business. The first obvious q7uestion is, who is the customer? If the firm defines the customer too narrowly or without context, any subsequent analysis is flawed. Firms either focus on their end users as packaged-goods firms tend to do, or as in the case of industrial firms, the focus is on the immediate customer. Both cases reflect a narrow view and a lack of understanding of the context. To determine who the customer is, the question to ask is, how does what we produce or provide add value to the client's value creating process? Most important, what do customers see as the value we are providing to their value creation process? This point is central to what we know as the "value chain" concept. An understanding of customers requires an understanding of the customers' value chain that includes the set of their value consumption activities. If the value created by the immediate customer creates value for a subsequent customer, that customer is also an indirect customer of the firm. We really need to identify the customer as a first step to determine whose perspective we should take and to understand the customer value that we are providing.

Performing the analysis of the customer sometimes forces the redefining of the customer. For Bright Horizons, a workplace child care and early education service company, it made a huge difference in how they went about their business when they viewed employers, and not parents, as their primary customers. The company could now tap into the financial and other resources of corporations and gain access to a much wider pool of parents. The value they were providing to the employer became the focus of the company. Chase Manhattan, for example, figured that its child care centre was yielding 110 percent return on investment through reduced absenteeism. Similarly, Merck found that its employee retention rate among those who were young parents went up dramatically.

The customer-focused perspective blurs the boundaries between entities in the value chain. Take the case of Aramark Corp., a firm that caters special events and runs cafeterias for big corporate clients. Nancy Naatz, resident district manager for business services for Aramark, has an office in the premises of her customer, Sears, in Chicago. Since Ms. Naatz is on location at her client's company, she is able to observe and interact with the local vendors Aramark has contracted to supply and serve Sears. Ms. Naatz is able to understand Sears executives' and employees' nutritional needs and interact with the vendors to ensure that the appropriate choices are made available. In this case, Aramark matches the food vendors' solution with the needs of the Sears employees who are the real customers.

So, who is the customer? The perspective of *which* customer I inspect and analyze, so as to help determine the business of my business, is the question. This question also raises the fundamental marketing decision of what or who our target market should be. It is a logical place to start before making any marketing or operations decision. Of all the potential customers that make up the market, which particular type of customer is most appropriate for our solution? The analysis involves segmentation, and the decision involved is one of targeting. We are able then to determine which particular type of customer from the universe of all customers for this product would find most value in what our value-creating assets can produce. We thus segment the market and target those segments for whom our value-creating assets can provide differentiation and a cost advantage. To know who the customer is necessitates an understanding of the typical customer in that segment at a general or aggregate level.

Traditionally, customer profiles have come out of the segmentation exercise. Segmentation variables in the B2C context have included demographic, psychographic, and behavioural variables. For customer-focused management we need information on all of the characteristics of the need or problem or use-situation that the customer is involved in, encompassing all of the activities of the customer that the product is a part of. Consequently, the question, who is the customer? takes on different shades and meanings. You want to know how the customer purchases and uses the product. Similarly, the profile of the customer in a B2B context involves understanding the business of the organizational customer. For either the B2C or the B2B context, an understanding of the customers requires analysis of their use-situations, and the contexts within which a product helps them in what they do. Of what value are you to them? Now we begin to hint at the notion of what customer value really is. The answers lie in the *consumption* of the product, not in its production.

CUSTOMER VALUE

Customer value is what the customer thinks he or she is getting in return for what the customer has to part with, reflecting an implicit comparison akin to "give and receive." It has been described as the quotient of quality over price. Understanding the customer is about understanding customer value. Customer value is a complex concept and measuring it is complicated. But in the exercise of trying to understand customer value, the manager benefits from a better understanding of the customer and of the opportunities for a superior solution. Here are some characteristics of customer value that any manager should examine in an analysis of the firm and its activities: Customer value

- Is what the customer believes that a product or service provides in a certain use situation.
- Is an implicit comparison between what the customer receives from the provider and what the customer provides in time, effort, and money. The frame of reference is not just the price tag on the product, but also the ease and convenience in the acquisition and use of the product and the whole interactive experience the customer has with the firm.
- Is the customer's rather than the provider's perspective. It has to do with customer perceptions of the product and the firm, and not the provider's perspective of what the firm is delivering.
- Is dynamic, in that it can change over time before, during, and after the purchase, use, over repeated use of the product, and during all the various stages in the relationship with the providing firm.
- Can vary over different use situations. Your automobile may provide less or more value in transporting a group of kids to the ballpark

compared to taking the spouse to the boss's house for a party.

- Can be shaped by attitudes, opinions, and behaviours of others, such as friends, family, media, the providing firm, and other competitors in the industry as well as in substitute industries.
- Determines customer satisfaction and the likelihood of brand or firm loyalty. This cause-effect relationship could be affected by comparisons with competitors and other substitutes.
- Is hard to measure and keep track of. Customers may find it hard to articulate all the different dimensions of customer value and firms may find it a rather onerous task to keep track of all the manifestations of customer value.

In order to determine what business a firm is in, therefore, the fundamental and imperative exercise is to understand customer value. Let us begin the analysis with the question, what exactly does customer value consist of? It is not easy to determine what the customer is getting as value from a product or service. To understand customer value, you really need to get into the customer's way of thinking about products. In a recent *Harvard Business Review* article, Chase and Dasu urge the use of behavioural science to get into the head of the customer, to understand their total experience with the product or service. Only then can you grasp all the components of customer value.

Examining the components and determinants of customer value is a critical step in the analysis. It requires analysis of the benefits as well as costs to the customer. The benefits seen are evident in the perceptions of the product performance. Perceptions of product performance are framed in the context of customer expectations. The expectations are shaped by past experience with the product and by messages about the product received from a variety of sources such as friends and family as well as from the marketer. From an analytical perspective, product performance comes from functional (core) benefits and supplemental benefits. Functional benefits arise from the core attributes of the product. For instance, you buy a set of golf clubs. How the golf clubs affect your game is a core and functional benefit, as in the primary benefit from the product. The prestige of the brand image, the product return policy, and other customer service features would translate into supplemental benefits. Every customer value analysis requires that we identify and examine core and supplemental benefits.

Similarly, we need to identify the costs to the customer—both monetary and non-monetary costs. Monetary costs include costs incurred in the acquisition, use, and disposition of the solution. Non-monetary costs could include the time and effort in acquiring and benefiting from the solution and the opportunity costs where the product failed. Tom Wright, Buy.com's vice president of operations called his company's old way of handling returns "almost embarrassing. To return a product that a customer bought from Buy.com, the customer had to telephone Buy.com to generate a return authorization, which led to a shipping label from the package delivery firm (UPS) to be mailed to the customer, who then used that label to send the product back to Buy.com. It was weeks before the customer got credit for the product return! Imagine the non-monetary cost of aggravation to that customer. Many firms that focus on acquiring customers do not retain customers because of their shallow understanding of customer value. Customer value includes interactions with the firm before, during, and after the consumption of the product. Smart firms are focusing on the whole customer and defining their business in terms of market spaces. The market space is the actual set of customer solutions defined by the consumption activities to which the firm caters.

In recognizing that customer value is dynamic, we need to place this analysis in the context of different use situations and how they are changed over time by various influences. Customers' concepts of what to expect from a provider change with each consumption experience. They learn from their own experiences with the product as well as vicariously from others. Competitor offerings and marketing messages continually shape their expectations. Therefore, implicit in the assessments made by the customer is a comparison with expectations based on the alternative—that is, the competition. Customer value analyses can be performed at a qualitative level and with some difficulty can be quantified as well.

Data-driven representations of monetary worth of what a firm does for a customer are what Anderson and Narus called "customer value models." Such models are useful in assessing the customer value of your product and comparing it with the competition to determine whether you are providing superior customer value or not. The next fundamental question is, Can you provide this superior customer value at a sustainable profit by commanding revenues to cover costs and profits?

Just as the customer value analysis requires an examination of the benefits versus the costs, the firm makes a similar analysis to determine the profit potential. In providing the customer value, what does the firm get in return? How do the monetary and no monetary benefits from the customer compare with what it cost the firm to provide that solution to that customer? Can we sustain these profits in the long term?

A firm creates value for itself by creating value for the customer. In many ways, the value of a firm is reflected in the profits it provides its investors and the value of the customer to the firm is reflected in the profits that the customer provides the firm. The greater the value of the customer to the firm, the greater are the profits. This means that the surplus from the revenues after costs is greater if you can attract and retain profitable customers in the long run. Part IV in this book covers the valuation of the customer by the firm. Firms can attract and retain customers if they can provide superior value. It could boil down to, Can we command a premium on our solution? If you can, it turns out that the margins are not in the commoditized part of the product, it is in the services provided by the firm. The margins increase when you are able to extend your role in the customer's space. This may come in the form of "cross-selling" or "up-selling." It may be the case that the total solution provides such value to the customer that the customer is better off with you than with the competition.

As the firm gets more valuable to the customer, the customer gets more valuable to the firm. The value from a customer is derived not only from purchases. Customers can become advocates for the firm, the benefits of which are frequently less understood. The value of the customer in terms of purchases and referrals over the lifetime of the customer should be an imperative calculation for firms who are focused on the customer. It appears that in the final analysis, it is the customer-focused firm that can provide a complete solution through a service orientation that succeeds in providing superior customer value and in return enjoys sustainable profits. So, how is it that a firm is able to provide superior customer value? What gives them a sustainable competitive advantage, such that the firm has sustainable profits?

What characterizes firms that can provide *superior* customer value? To answer this question, we have ample evidence from research on such firms. Every firm in any industry provides some customer value. The firm that provides superior customer value is the one that has a sustainable competitive advantage. Firms compete with each other on differentiable aspects of the total solution. If we can conceptualize that every product has parts that are commodities and parts that differentiate it from others, superior value is in the augmented product, not in the conceptual core. For example, all airlines provide transportation from point A to point B. But the total solution includes aspects other than the physical transportation of the person itself, such as amenities on the airplane. A firm must seek opportunities to differentiate itself from the competition in ways that are meaningful and relevant to the customer. How do firms find opportunities to differentiate themselves in a way that it is sustainable?

Consider how CDW creates superior customer value. CDW is the leading B2B e-commerce firm selling technology equipment to small and medium-sized firms. Wall Street analysts claim that the firm uses a "clicks and people" strategy. Supposedly, their competitive advantage is superior customer service and lower customer acquisition costs. The firm's Web site is tailored to each specific customer as a "custom extranet." How are they able to sustain this competitive advantage? Their own chief financial officer, Harry Harczak, notes that retaining people is key. In his experience, the productivity difference between an employee who has been at the firm six months versus one there three years is a factor of six. CDW values employee commitment.

What are the generalizable characteristics of firms that create superior customer value? A team of Harvard Business School researchers set out to discover exactly this and concluded that successful firms such as BancOne, Intuit, Southwest Airlines, ServiceMaster, USAA, Taco Bell, and MCI made employees and customers paramount. These researchers modeled the findings from their case studies into a framework they called "the service profit chain." Their cases provided data to establish powerful relationships between profitability, customer loyalty, and employee satisfaction, loyalty, and productivity. Evident in the whole model is the focus on the customer and the service orientation of satisfied employees, and the implications on investors and other stakeholders of the firm.

As firms focus on customer needs and become service oriented to deliver satisfaction, there are favourable ripple effects throughout the firm. Consistent delivery of customer satisfaction persuades customers to be loyal because perceived risk in buying a product from that firm is substantially reduced. When providers of solutions to customer needs are able to consistently deliver expected value, customers are more likely to be consistently satisfied. By way of their continued patronage, they become more valuable to the firm. When customers are loyal to the provider by choice, it is also in their best interest to support the provider because the prosperity and longevity of the provider is beneficial to the customer. Similarly, with regard to employees, research has shown that when employee satisfaction is high employees are more likely to be loyal to the company. When employee loyalty is high, employees are likely to be more productive and to be providing quality products and service. Neither employees nor customers are likely to be loyal unless their expectations are met and they are satisfied. Therefore, customer satisfaction and employee satisfaction are inherently tied to each other, in that, when employees are loyal to the firm, they provide superior performances driving customer loyalty. When employees are productive and customer loyalty is high, the firm is successful and can command a premium. With increased profitability and growth prospects, investors are attracted to the firm, which in turn makes more resources available to the firm. With more resources available to the firm, capital is available to continuously improve value-creating assets (people and processes) and to produce consistently superior customer value in its products and service. This sequence of events, presented as the "loyalty circle", contributes to profitability and growth and requires that people and processes are aligned to deliver superior customer value. Delivering superior value should be a relentless endeavor for the firm.

FOCUSED ANALYSIS IN PLANNING

The analytical frame to understand customer value consists first of identifying the customer and understanding the customer's problem and solution needs. The next issue is to focus on the options that the customer would consider appropriate in meeting the need and how the options compare with each other. Are there other options provided by other firms whose value-creating assets have a sustainable competitive advantage? This would dictate whether the firm should be in this business at all; if so, is there the potential for a sustainable competitive advantage? The following table presents the kinds of questions that need to be asked by the customer-focused firm as it examines its business and how it can provide superior customer value for a sustainable competitive advantage.

Framing the Customer-Focused Analysis: Customer Value

Analytical Frame	*Analytical Questions*
The Customer:	Who is the customer? Who is involved in the buying decision? How is the purchase decision made?
The Customer Value:	For what purpose/use does the customer buy the product? What are the activities associated with the use situation? What value does this customer expect in a solution for this purpose? What are the assoicated costs to the customer?
Define the Solution:	How does the customer perceive the solution that we are providing? What kind of business provides such a solution?
The Substitutes:	What are the various ways in which customers solve this need? What other value-creating asset combinations provide these other solutions? How do we compare with the customer's other choices?

The core of any product is essentially a commodity. Competitive advantage comes from services as product enhancements made to the core. To compete on service, firms need to understand the opportunities and challenges presented by the special nature of services. Sustainable competitive advantage comes from an ability of the firm to compete through service.

A common misconception is to view services as being synonymous with customer service. "Services" are not limited to customer service. Customer service is only one of the services that enhance products. Managers who are product focused and not customer focused usually see services as meaning customer service. They see service as something that is done when a product fails or invoked to prevent it from failing. Others who see service as "freebies" that you toss in with the product are probably sales focused. Firms with such a product or sales orientation actually do a disservice to the customer in the name of service. Their tendency is to offer a refund or return policy, which is often enough structured to favour the firm rather than the customer. These firms may offer a customer service toll-free telephone number, which is usually set up to be a frustrating encounter for the customer service personnel as well as the customer who may have been calling in for retribution. Such is often the unfortunate consequence in firms that are not customer focused. In customer-focused firms, customer service is not just an add-on, a little something extra to keep the customer happy. Customer service is an integral part of the total product.

Service is not what you *do to the product*, it is what you *do for the customer*. The customer-focused firm looks at the core product as an incomplete solution for customers. These firms supplement the core product with services that help customize or otherwise enhance solutions for customers. Such product enhancements add value for the customer. The Aramark employee being on location at Sears adds value to the core product of catering for Sears. It allows Aramark to be more customer focused by obtaining first-hand customer information and being able to deliver on it. By being on hand, Aramark can be immediately aware and responsive to the customers' needs. Service-based product enhancements are an imperative for the customer-focused firm.

You will see what the inherent characteristics of services are, and thus the challenges and opportunities you need to recognize when you incorporate services into the value you create and deliver to the customer.

The traditional view of services is to treat products dichotomously, in two categories—*either* services *or* (physical) goods. Sometimes the term *product* is even used interchangeably with packaged goods but not with service. Not only has this usage caused unnecessary confusion, but it has also encouraged the flawed approach that services and packaged goods are separate and mutually exclusive entities. Scholars have gone as far as to suggest that "most product manufacturers and service providers alike are largely service operations." They asserted that the role of services is critical for any organization in providing value in the form of "technological improvements, styling features, product image, and other attributes that only services can create." The fact is that all products come with some services. As a matter of degree some products have more services than others and are therefore more intangible than others.

Picture a continuum ranging from products that are most tangible (and least intangible in proportion) at one extreme to products that are most intangible (and least tangible in proportion) at the other extreme. At one end of the continuum, services such as education, consulting, and financial services have very few physical goods that customers take title to. At the other end, packaged goods such as a bar of soap or table salt come with no apparent service unless, for example, the customer initiates a customer service phone call. In the middle of the continuum are products such as fast food restaurants and custom-made clothing that have an almost equal proportion, with no real predominance of tangibles or intangibles. In products that are predominantly intangible, where the customers don't take title to anything physical, such as in banking services, the service provider might use tangibles such as documentation, statements, and billing. The value for the customer is in the information contained in them. As a proportion of what the customer is getting in the total product, the predominant source of customer value is from the intangibles in the total product. For physical goods, services enhance the core product and provide opportunities for competitive advantage. Thus, any product has some proportion of services attached to it, and this part of the product has a special nature that needs to be handled differently. If all firms provide some proportion of service components as part of the total product, it behooves them to have an understanding of the nature of services. Only with such an understanding can we truly get into the service-orientation frame of mind. Take for example, the table salt manufacturer, Morton's. For this firm to look at itself as a packaged goods firm and therefore not concerned with services is a mistake.

The fact that Morton's makes the product available at the retail store through the appropriate distribution channels is a service to the customer. Morton's has essentially outsourced its distribution and retailing to channel intermediaries. To be truly customer focused, Morton's needs to view all the value-added it provides the customer, over and above the product of the production process—the salt—as services it provides to the customer. Morton's cannot manage its service components in the same way that it manages the production of its table salt. Most B2B manufacturing firms intuitively recognize the importance of the service component in enhancing its product. Caterpillar, the earth-moving equipment manufacturer, recognizes that prompt and reliable service is critical to its success and organizes the whole firm around customer locations. You need a service orientation to see such product enhancements as service dimensions that add value to the core product. Service orientation is

- A philosophy or frame of mind reflected in the firm's culture
- An attitude to serve the customer reflected in the firm's treatment of its customers, and
- A view of services as necessary enhancements to any core product to make a complete solution.

To provide complete and competitive solutions to the customer, one needs to understand and adopt the service orientation. The service-oriented frame of mind requires a grasp of the fundamental nature of services (whether as the product or a component of a product). Once the inherent characteristics of services are clear, it becomes apparent that their implications for the customer and the provider offer a number of opportunities and pose a variety of challenges.

As a preface to a discussion of these issues, it would be useful to note the evolution of interest in the concept of service.

Prompted by the frustrations of practitioners in the service sector who were finding that marketing practices from the packaged goods world did not make sense for services, scholars began to get interested in the problem. In the late 1970s and early 1980s, for a number of reasons, the academic research community in business disciplines, particularly in marketing, operations, and human resources, began a serious intellectual debate as to whether products that were services, compared to products that were packaged goods, needed to be studied differently. For example, could you study the marketing of hospitality services the same way as you would the marketing of toothpaste? Some scholars maintained that marketing is marketing regardless of *what* you are marketing.

Either way, they argued, one had to go through the tasks of segmenting the market, positioning a product, and making product, pricing, distribution, or promotion decisions. Others argued that although that might be true, one would need to approach these tasks very differently; and they proceeded to offer the rationale for this argument. There was a great deal of interest in this effort, especially among those who recognized the tremendous growth of the services sector.

Around the same time there were environmental changes in the economy and in the competitive landscape. Services sectors such as airlines, telecommunications, and, later, banking and insurance were going through deregulation in the United States. Manufacturing was moving to cheaper labour markets in the Far East and in Latin America. Meanwhile, by the late 1980s in the United States, even professional services such as health care and legal services began to recognize the need to employ marketing practices. Not surprisingly, even manufacturing firms were being forced to add service components to their product offerings. As these changes occurred and services were being established as an integral aspect of doing business, the United States had become a service economy. Ultimately, the debate over whether services were really different from physical products produced the rationale that the skeptics demanded. The evidence and essence of this argument epitomizes the service orientation.

There are certain fundamental characteristics that are inherent in all service products and in the service components of any product. Let us begin by defining service as *a deed, performance, or action*. Thus, by definition, services are intangible. The product that is a service or that component of the product that is a service cannot be seen, touched, or felt. As a deed, performance or action, a service is consumed as it is produced, such that the acts of production and consumption are inseparable. Thus, services are also perishable, in that they cannot be inventoried or produced and stored for later use. Nor can they be produced without some level of customer interaction. Since services are produced and consumed in real time, they are inherently variable – from customer to customer, from provider to provider, and from time to time for the same customer and/or the same provider. These statements describe features that are fundamental and are inherent in products or components of products that are deeds, performances, or actions, and may sound very simplistic until you delve into the meanings and consequences of these inherent characteristics to the customer and to the provider.

It is generally accepted that services are different from physical goods along four fundamental characteristics labeled as intangibility, simultaneity or inseparability, perishability, and variability.These characteristics are conceptually inherent in all services or in the service component of any product. Although this framework is more useful as a pedagogical vehicle rather than a framework for research or practice, it is powerful in fully capturing the concept of service orientation and accomplishes the objective of placing the reader in the necessary frame of mind. This mindset is grounded in the appreciation of the fundamental nature of services necessitating appropriate managerial decisions and actions service orientation requires a thorough understanding of how these inherent characteristics of services are manifested for the customer and the manager.

PRODUCT AND SERVICE

Services are performances. Services cannot be seen but they can be experienced. The product is a process. As a service provider, you cannot show your product as you could if you were the marketer of a packaged good. Yes, services are the result of value-creating activities, just as physical products are, and may employ tangibles or physical products in producing the service. However, the product being purchased is an experience and not a physical good. Customers cannot take ownership or title to a service. For example, hotels provide the service of overnight stay as their core product. The customer does not take title to the room that is being rented. The hotel provides the use of the room for the duration of the time that the customer has paid for. Similarly, customers don't take title to anything in air travel or in entertainment. When office copiers come with service, there is no ownership involved with the service component unlike with the copier itself. When your automobile comes with free service under warranty, unlike the automobile itself there is no real ownership of the service component.

Now, as a manager, you might say: "All this is well and good, but if it doesn't change the way I manage the product, its production, or its marketing, whether it is a packaged good or service, why should I care? Services are intangible and service components in products are intangible—yes! But so what?" Let us examine this question from the customer's point of view. For customers, one immediate consequence of the intangibility is increased perceived risk. When you cannot see the product or what you are going to get before the purchase, customers have to acknowledge a certain amount of risk they are taking. While there is perceived risk in the purchase of a packaged or physical good, you cannot return a vacation as you can a defective lawn mower. Thus, you accept a certain amount of risk as unavoidable in the case of a service. When you book your vacation, do you really see the product? If you have previously been to the locations, you may have seen the facility, but your product was the experience. Complicating the perceived risk is the fact that the evaluation of services or the service component of the product is inherently subjective. Compared to packaged goods, customers find it harder to evaluate services before the purchase. In some cases, services are harder to evaluate even during and after their performances. In the case of health care, for instance, you use several proxy elements, such as the cleanliness of the facility, the medical professional's "bedside manner, " and the process you had to go through. What you are evaluating is a lot more than the core product, the medical treatment itself. Being intangible, services cannot be produced until you have purchased (whether you pay before, during, or after) the service.

Fundamental Issues Common to All Services

Fundamental Characteristics	*Managerial Implications*	*Managerial Actions*
Intangibility	Product is a process and difficult to evaluate; Perceived risk is high.	Find ways to reduce perceived risk, e.g., service sampling and guarantees.
Simultaneity	Customers are resources and co-producers; Customer participation needs to be managed.	Shape individual customer behaviour during consumption, e.g., diagnostic questions for service specifications.
Perishability	Product cannot be inventoried; demand management is key to profitable capacity utilization.	Smooth fluctuations with segmentation and marketing mix, e.g., discounts during low-demand periods.
Variability	Product varies across frontline providers, customers and over time. Quality control is difficult.	All frontline personnel are marketers as well, e.g., training in customer interaction skills.

The acts of production and consumption occur simultaneously in services. This is primarily because services are produced and consumed in real time. There is a great deal of interaction before, during, and/or after the service between provider and customer. Some sort of customer interaction is necessary even if customer physical presence is not. At the very least, customers have to specify their needs and their need situations. In most if not all cases, it can be argued that production and consumption cannot be temporally separated. Thus, this characteristic is also termed "inseparability" A related complication for services is that in services, the provider is part of the product. As a customer, the frontline personnel you interact with are a part of the product. In professional services, for instance, the lawyer is part of the (legal service) product, the doctor is part of the (medical care) product, the professor is part of the (education) product. Comparing this to packaged goods: Do you have to interact with Procter & Gamble and the shop floor employee who made your particular tube of Crest toothpaste? You do interact with the retailer of the toothpaste, but remember that the retail store that makes the toothpaste available to you is a service. What you are consuming from the retailer as it is produced by the retailer is a service. In fact, you interact with the provider of the service component of the packaged good. If you interacted with P&G, it was with customer service.

Once again, let us confront the question: "So what?" To understand what difference it makes for the manager, the customer-focused firm must examine the consequences to the customer from the customer's perspective. The customer has to interact with the provider at some stage or at all stages of the production process. The customer is in the service factory in the case of an amusement park. Sometimes the service factory comes to the customer, as in the case of the landscape contractor. Sometimes the interaction is at arm's length, such as in the case of an online travel agent like Expedia.com. In each case, there is some interaction that the customer usually initiates. Thus, there is some effort on the part of the customer for the product to be produced. The customer takes on a role in the production process. To perform the expected role, customers have to be educated and sometimes socialized into the process. For example, at a fast food restaurant, the customer needs to get familiar with the process of ordering and picking up the food. When you call your long distance phone company for a question on your bill, you need to have some information ready for the service to be performed. These days you have to be familiar with complex automated voice menus before you can get anything done over the telephone. Since consumption and production are simultaneous, the customer is consuming as the product is being produced. The product cannot be produced ahead of time and then consumed. This means that the product cannot be inventoried.

PERISHABILITY – SERVICES CANNOT BE STORED

Since services cannot be produced and stored for later use, as physical products can, services are said to be perishable products. What actually perishes? In fact, what perishes is the productive capacity of the service, or more precisely, the opportunity to produce a product. A hairdresser's time is wasted or unproductive when he or she is not serving a customer. The customer service personnel ready to handle customer enquiries is not producing a service unless there is a customer to serve. An empty airline seat perishes without a passenger in it on takeoff. The factors of production such as labour, facilities, equipment, and billable time are the value-creating assets for the service provider. The opportunity to produce the product from these assets perishes without the adequate number of customers for which the capacity is designed. And the service provider needs to maintain a certain level of capacity that is not easily adjustable. Some services are more capacity-constrained than others. A hotel cannot reduce the number of rooms in its facility when there are not enough guests. A management consulting firm with fulltime employees would be hard pressed to release its staff when there are not enough clients to fill the capacity.

For the customer, service products need to be available and accessible when and where they are needed. When the productive capacity is sometimes not able to meet the demand, customers are likely to have to wait in queues or find another provider. Whether it is on the phone for customer service, at the doctor's office, or in line for a ride in an amusement park, customers will have to get used to waiting. In some services, customers need to plan ahead of time and place reservations. That is how managers instinctively manage the utilization of capacity in the operation. Conversely, when there is more productive capacity than there are customers to be served, service providers have to look for other customer segment opportunities for their value-creating assets. Service providers have to manage that balance between capacity and demand. They employ methods to anticipate and manage the pattern of demand and to manage the capacity accordingly.

Service products as experiences vary from one experience to the next, from customer to customer, as well as for the same customer from one occasion to the next. In fact, this variability is compounded with differences among frontline personnel. When there are several steps in the service process where the customer interacts with several different personnel of the service provider, there could be variation from one interaction to another. In some cases, customers will prefer specific frontline personnel with whom they have become familiar and comfortable. Since services are produced and consumed in real time, it is clear that customers will likely see a great degree of variation in product quality. Customers can receive a different experience each time, even at a standardized operation like McDonald's. Service managers attempt to deliver consistently high quality with frontline training and technology and to customize where possible and standardize where necessary. Customers expect customization even when it is not feasible. Managers have to balance the economics of standardization with the quality issues around customization.

Thus, the fundamental characteristics of services force their implications on the customer. The manager of services and products that involve a significant degree of tangibles are forced to orient themselves to these implications. The complexity of managerial situations as a consequence of these characteristics is manifested as opportunities and challenges. Consequently, the services manager must analyze these consequences.

MANAGERIAL CHALLENGES IN PROVIDING SERVICE

The implications of the fundamental characteristics of services suggest that managers need to examine how they would adapt their business processes to take advantage of the opportunities and to address the challenges. The example presents a logical sequence of steps in fundamentally analyzing a service and addressing the ensuing implications. The following is a discussion of some of the key managerial challenges and opportunities.

Table: Managerial Challenges with Services

Impact of the Fundamental Nature of Services on the Customer	*Managerial Actions*
Intangibility - What aspects of the intangible product cause the customer to perceive risk in committing to a certain service provider? What do customers use to anticipate and evaluate what they are likely to receive from the service provider?	What are the risk levers for the customer? Are there risk relievers that we can provide to alleviate the customer's concern? What can we do to "tangibilize" our service?
Inseparability - Where, when and how do customers interact with the production and delivery process? What roles do or should the customer play in the production or consumption of the service?	How can we improve the customer's role so that the quality of the product can be improved? Are there opportunities for increased margins or reduced costs through customization or customer self-service?

Impact of the Fundamental Nature of Services on the Customer	*Managerial Actions*
Perishability - What are the demand patterns? What influences customers to purchase or use the service at the times that they do?	How can I influence demand patterns? Am I missing opportunities by not providing the service when and where customer wants it?
Variability - What aspects can be standardized and what needs to be customized in the customer interactions? What do the customers expect the frontline personnel to be able to do?	What kind of individual should we hire for those positions that interact with customers? What kinds of training should they have?

With products that contain a significant proportion of intangibles and where the core product is a service, managers of services need to continuously monitor and understand the risk customers feel when they purchase the service. What is the nature of the risk? How do you lower this risk? Professional services providers such as lawyers and doctors have certifications prominently displayed on their walls. Consulting firms provide lists of clients, mutual funds companies show off their performance charts. What would be most appropriate for you to do to reduce customer perceived risk? To determine this you begin by understanding what those risk levers might be. What is the source of the anxiety that customers feel? To what would you attribute the risk that they feel? Only when this is clearly understood can you think about the possible ways you might reduce their perceived risk. To understand the risk, you need to break down the service into the features that contribute value toward the total solution. Which service features produce benefits, and how can the risk associated with each feature-benefit connection be reduced? The degree to which the customer feels assured that expectations of these benefits will be met would depend on how you can instill confidence in the customer that you have the ability to deliver on those expectations. Christopher Hart is credited with the concept of service guarantees that works to reduce perceived risk. L.L. Bean's famed "100% satisfaction guaranteed" goes back to 1912, when the founder was marketing the Maine hunting shoe. Service providers who understand their customers' perceived risk seek to address it.

CUSTOMIZATION VERSUS STANDARDIZATION

One of the powerful implications of the fundamental characteristics of services is that they are not produced ahead of time. The service is designed, created, and delivered to customer specifications. While customization is possible, some standardized parameters are also necessary to derive economies of scale. There is opportunity to standardize as well as to customize. Where there is low margin from a service component and the volume provides the profits, perhaps ways to standardize the production process would be appropriate. On the other hand, if there is opportunity for high margin, customization and low volume is the way to go. Consider the difference between automated telephone-based customer service and a fee sometimes charged for customers who want individual attention. Professional or knowledge based services are generally customized and are high-margin, whereas drycleaning services are low-margin services and require considerable standardization and the required volume. The opportunity is to increase margins by providing customized experiences and the challenge is in standardizing the process to reduce costs and maintain consistent quality.

A related issue to the opportunity to customize is the accompanying challenge posed by the variability of the product. Since services are produced in real time, and they have a high degree of variability, the challenge is to ensure a consistent quality in the service. Managers must assess the sources of variation. Sources of the variability are typically associated with the people delivering the service. Every interaction with the customer provides or facilitates some aspect of the product bundle, and therefore the quality of the product is dependent on each and every interaction between the service provider and the customer. Therefore, selecting, training, and motivating frontline personnel become very critical. For example, service firms such as Walt Disney amusement parks and the Ritz-Carlton hotels have a specific profile in mind when they hire people for the front line. These firms provide extensive service training for their frontline employees, and they motivate employees to provide customer satisfaction. FedEx rewards employees who take care of customers in service failures. Empowered frontline personnel are more likely to deliver quality service.

DEMAND AND CAPACITY MANAGEMENT

Since services are perishable, productive factors that are in place may be idle at low demand times and stretched to capacity at high demand times. The demand is fluctuating, and it might be impossible or at best a serious challenge to stretch or contract capacity. Therefore, smoothing demand and managing capacity become a constant endeavor for the managers of services. The key to managing this challenge is to understand the demand patterns and to figure out the flexibilities in your capacity. To the extent that the demand patterns can be predicted with a good understanding of customer behaviour, service providers can manage demand as well as capacity. Pricing is commonly used in smoothing demand. Early bird specials, matinee prices, lower fares if you stay over Saturdays are all different ways by which service firms use pricing to manage demand.

Reservations and appointments are another way for service managers to smooth demand. Different segments and markets are served at different times and prices to fill capacity. Hotels depend to a great extent on the lucrative conferences and meetings market to ensure capacity utilization. Such capacity-constrained services rely more on managing demand than on managing capacity primarily because it is harder to adjust capacity. Product mix adjustments are another way of managing capacity, whereas the more versatile the value-creating assets are in producing different services with the same productive factors, the better the capacity management opportunities. For example, ski resorts turn into hiking or whitewater rafting facilities in the summer. Staffing and scheduling are typical capacity-side management options that the service firm employs. Creative use of value producing assets is critical for efficient and effective management of a firm's capacity.

MANAGING THE CUSTOMER

Since the customer is part of the process and some degree of interaction with the customer is necessary and inevitable, managers of services must find ways to educate customers on their roles. If the customer fails in playing the appropriate coproducer role, it could ruin the process and the outcome quality. A clear understanding of the steps in the process and how, where, and when customers interact with the process is a must. Doctors, nurses, and pharmacists provide directions and instructions for patient roles. Banks and other financial institutions have specific protocols for various financial transactions. A key question to ask is how the customer should participate in the process and whether you have the appropriate instructions for your customer. Differences in customer willingness and ability to participate in the production of the process force the issue of segmentation on the service delivery process. Thus, restaurants have self-service, take-out, or drive-through options. Automatic teller machines are an early example of self-service in banking services. Hotels have express check-in and check-out facilities. Airlines have electronic ticketing options. Self-service checkout facilities have become a standard option at grocery stores in the United States and elsewhere.

It is clear as we think about these issues that not all services are alike. While all services face all these challenges to some degree, the challenges manifest themselves differently in different services. In fact, the management solutions presented are more applicable in some and inappropriate or impossible in others. There is a systematic way of addressing these differences among services by examining characteristics that differentiate services from one another. A service that shares characteristics with another service exhibits similar challenges and opportunities.

In employing the service orientation, every manager needs to understand that there are different types of services in every product, each with its own manifestations of the fundamental characteristics of services. The nature of these manifestations in different services implies different situations for the customer and the manager. While all services are fundamentally intangible, inseparable, perishable, and variable, services differ from each other along dimensions peculiar to their category. These category characteristics provide the manager with an insight into the specific situations that they have to deal with in their particular service category.

Christopher Lovelock demonstrated that this sort of categorizing is necessary and powerful as a means of understanding the managerial situations specific to each type of service. Service managers should look toward other services that share similar characteristics and expect to find similar challenges and transferable solutions to those challenges. Consider for example that hospitals provide executive-style rooms for the businessperson who is a patient. They learned this from hotels that have executive-style suites for the businessperson. Now consider the service characteristics that are shared between hospitals and hotels. In both cases, the customer comes to the factory and frequently requires an overnight stay. In both situations, the executive is likely to be away from an office with all its business support for an extended period of time. Both services are similar in the type of customer interactions, even though they are in two completely different service sectors. An analysis as depicted earlier represents the benefits of learning from the successes of services that share certain specific service characteristics.

Managers of services can understand the specific challenges and opportunities presented by the characteristics of their product and corresponding situations by examining a number of characteristics that profile a service category. Here are a few characteristics to examine:

- Tangible or intangible act
- Person or thing as recipient of the act
- Type of interaction between provider and customer
- Service delivered by people or equipment
- Extent of customization or standardization

What are the tangible and intangible acts involved in the services that you are providing? Is the service act delivered on a person or a thing? For example, if you are an entertainment electronics repair and service provider, you perform tangible acts on a DVD player and intangible acts with the customer as you obtain information on what problems the customer has experienced with the DVD player. Now, examine the nature of the acts and the impact on the customer. When you are working on the DVD player, the customer needs not be present and the process that you employ need not be visible to the customer. However, you do interact with the customer at a number of points, from the initial customer call to the final interaction at delivery or pickup of the DVD player.

Similarly, you might analyze your service about the nature of interaction of with the customer. Is it face-to-face or arm's length, via telephone or the Internet? Do you visit the customer or does the customer visit your premises? How much technology is involved in the interface with the customer? Sometimes the customer does not even interact with a person. How much standardization is built into the service? Are there options provided to customers who require a customized interaction? What benefits does this analysis provide the manager?

The challenges and opportunities discussed earlier as fundamental are common to all service managers. By understanding the characteristics of their specific category of services, the manager can find ways to take advantage of the opportunities and address the challenges of their specific situation. Additionally, in understanding how the fundamental characteristic of intangibility manifests itself in their particular situation, managers can understand customers' perceived risk and use the tangibles in the customer experience to reduce the risk that customers perceive. By understanding the nature of the interaction, managers are in a better place to manage the roles of customers and recognize opportunities for customization and standardization to improve the customer experience and, therefore, customer value. What is most interesting is that you may find that service businesses in a different industry sharing certain characteristics may offer you innovative ideas to meet these challenges and capitalize on opportunities to better serve customers in your business.

In order to understand how the required service-oriented frame of mind needs to be handled in the customer-focused firm, the firm analyzes the various services with which it augments the product. Each service is analyzed from a fundamental and category perspective. The fundamental nature of services requires an analysis of the implications of the intangible, inseparable, perishable, and variable nature of services for managerial action. The analysis of category characteristics specific to each type of service should deal with how these consequences of these characteristics manifest themselves in that situation.

Table: Framing the Customer-Focused Analysis

Characteristic of Service	*Customer-Focused Analysis*
Nature of the Act	Is the act tangible or intangible? Who or what entity in the firm performs the acts? How does the nature of the act affect the perceived risk of the customer?
Who or What Is the Recipient	Which acts are directed at a tangible such as a person's body or a thing? Which acts are directed at the person's mind or intangible assets? How is the customer's perceived risk shaped by the recipient of the act?
Nature of the Interaction	What are the various ways in which the customer interacts with the firm? What are the roles of the customer and the firm in each interaction? Are there opportunities for economies of standardization or premium from customization? What other delivery options are feasible for the interactions?
Fluctuation in Demand	What is the impact of the fluctuation of demand on the value-creating assets and their revenue potential? What is the versatility of the value-creating assets in producing different solutions and catering to different segments?

Chapter 3

Managing Customer Information

Firms cannot claim a customer focus or attempt to satisfy customers unless they have customer knowledge—that is, a deep understanding of the needs of the customer. Customer-focused firms really understand their customers by proactively acquiring information on the entire consumption process, especially the consumption activities of the customer. Such information must be processed and used to guide each and every interaction with that customer. This information can be used not only to make changes and improvements in the value-creation and delivery processes of a firm but also in managing relationships with the right customers.

Managerial decisions and actions cannot be customer oriented when customer data is lacking. Do we know enough about the customer's consumption activities to enable us to create and deliver customer-focused value and manage relationships with the customer?

As Lew Platt, former CEO of Hewlett Packard, is widely quoted as saying: "If HP knew what HP knows, we would be three times as profitable" With the increasing ubiquity of information technology, there is an increasing focus on information—in a way, simply because it is there. Most managers understand the crucial role that good information plays in decision making. And here is a seemingly radical proposition: most data is underutilized in business. If you don't know what data is important, you may not recognize it when you see it. When there is an opportunity to obtain what may be valuable data, you will not access or gather, process, or utilize it.

Careful observation would reveal that as a norm, firms don't capitalize on opportunities to gather critical customer data. One reason may be that firms focus on the sort of data that is needed for a specific decision, such as in the development of a new product or an advertising campaign, especially in the B2C context, where there are no direct interactions with the customer. In the B2B context, where there is direct interaction with the customer, there is a greater amount of customer information being utilized for decision making. This is partly because formalized systems are in place to document customer information. The customer being a business is very likely to have formalized purchasing procedures. Information-age technology has very naturally developed in the B2B case earlier and faster than in the B2C case. In the B2C business, where there is direct interaction with the customer, this technology is opening new thinking about customer data. A basic question is, what information is needed and for what purpose?

The convergence of numerous information technologies in the gathering, storing, processing, disseminating, accessing, and using data has revolutionized the most generic of all business tasks—making informed business decisions. Communication, storage, and computational technologies have made this possible. Firms have found ways to deploy these technologies toward of increasing productivity. When the promise of technology is not delivered, as in many CRM and ERP projects, the focus has turned to how and why this data is useful for a business to support the investment in information technology. One of the primary information systems of a firm is the customer information system. Customer-focused firms have used their information technology to develop smart customer information systems and broaden the scope of this business function. The role of the Chief Knowledge Officer, a title that was unheard of just a few years ago, is to manage the creation, discovery, and dissemination of knowledge in firms. In the context of managing the knowledge resident with the firm about its business, customer information is one of the key pieces of the knowledge this person manages. The status given to this function is reflected in the seniority of the position and indicates the commitment of the firm to managing customer information that can be used to improve the value created and delivered by the firm.

The key issues discussed in this chapter are: what kinds of customer information are needed to perform as a customer-focused firm, what information is required to usefully profile a customer, and how such a customer profile helps a firm understand the customer.

We saw that delivering superior customer value is a prerequisite for sustainable competitive advantage and that to be able to deliver superior customer value, a firm requires a good understanding of what customers value. A good understanding of customer value presupposes good customer information. You cannot claim a customer focus, or seriously attempt to satisfy your customers, unless you understand their needs. An effective customer information system ensures that the appropriate knowledge of the customer is available for customer-focused decisions and actions. Without customer information, for example, it would be impossible to customize customer experiences, let alone manage customer relationships.

Knowledge of the customer is about being intimate with the customer. Customer intimacy is not just a cliché. Customer intimacy is a value discipline for firms that value and use an intimate knowledge of their customers to determine precisely which types of customers to serve and then align all their value-creation processes to create and deliver solutions to their specific type of customer. In a competitive landscape where competing products with little defensible product differentiation are becoming commodities, customization is one very powerful way to de-commoditize a product and build customer relationships. *Customization,* as a term, is used broadly here to denote making changes in value creation and delivery such that the customer value is adjusted to each customer when and where appropriate. To know when and where customization is appropriate, you need to know your customer. Customer-focused firms pay attention to their customers. They listen to their customers. They really know their customers. The more knowledge the firm has about its customers, the more poised and able the firm is to deliver superior customer value.

Ritz-Carlton is known for its ability to personalize its service encounters with its frequent guests by maintaining a detailed preference profile at the individual customer level. With smart customer information systems, Ritz-Carlton's frontline employees are empowered to address guests by their first names and with knowledge of the guest's specific preferences. CLASS (Customer Loyalty Anticipation and Satisfaction) is an example of the information technology backbone to the Ritz-Carlton's guest relationships management programme. Nadia Kyzer knows that having a database system is not enough, saying: "If our employees didn't put the information to real concrēte use, the system would be worthless" Many firms use their knowledge of the customer to tailor their products and messages, or to promote new services to their customers. For example, on the Internet, firms use knowledge gained from cookies to model patterns of customer behaviour on their Web sites so as to target promotions deemed appropriate for that customer. But good customer information management goes beyond targeting messages and promotions. QVC, the television-based retailer, uses a "daily activity report" to capture, monitor, and respond to customer perceptions of quality. Indeed, customer information should drive all business processes of the firm, including anticipating and meeting customer needs, creating and delivering services, and anticipating and recovering from service failure. Customer-focused firms must have good customer information to support the decisions and activities of the firm.

Customer-focused decisions affecting customer value require information on customers' needs, their product preference criteria leading to brand choice or loyalty and their perceptions and behaviour with regard to the product. This is true not only in the acquisition and use, but also in the disposition of products. Since service firms interact with the customer during consumption of the product there is ample opportunity to obtain and respond to customer information. For example, New England's largest bank, FleetBoston, recently instituted the "customer experience crusade." The firm hired new staff to be stationed in the lobbies of its large-volume banks to serve as "meeter-greeters" assisting customers with their banking problems. Ostensibly, the attempt was to reverse the lousy service reputation FleetBoston had acquired due to its preoccupation with challenges following its merger with BankBoston. With the knowledge gained from the activities of these customer service agents, the bank could be learning a lot about customer experiences and about how its customers actually use a number of the bank's services. This knowledge could then be used to drive all decisions about structuring and delivering the bank's services.

Good customer information is an asset of the firm. Logically, anything that contributes to sustainable competitive advantage is an asset to the firm. Since information on customers is useful in better matching a firm's products as solutions to customer needs, customer information is an asset that contributes to sustainable competitive advantage. For example, retailing has become so fiercely competitive that customer information assets are now seen as a competitive advantage. Customer loyalty programs in retailing are an attempt to link customer information to transaction data. Customer databases with purchase histories showing shopping preferences can be used in customercentric business decisions. Customer information is so valuable that firms who share customer information have to be careful about ownership of the database. At the end of a joint project, for example, Wells Fargo bank and Microsoft went to court to determine who owned a customer database that was created as part of that joint venture.

A good example of the power of customer information is on the Internet. Personalized Web pages use customer information "on-thefly" to customize the online customer experience. It is common knowledge now that firms have data that tells them who is visiting, how long they are staying on the site, and where on the site visitors are spending their time. Firms have knowledge of customer behaviour on their Web site with information on where visitors were entering the Web site (beyond the home page) and leaving the Web site, what keywords or links brought them to the site, and so on. All this is possible with data-warehousing and data-mining techniques. In the Internet age, entire new services, such as online investment brokerage firms, have sprung up with value propositions enabled by technology-powered databases of customer information. In the brave new investment world, such new business models have forced traditional investment brokerage houses to incorporate these added value propositions to their existing businesses. Other new financial service models have emerged. For example, a number of online firms offer instant mortgage or credit application and approval. Much of this is possible because rules-based algorithms created from studying databases allow firms first to offer conditional approval then then to be able to verify the credit risk because financial institutions have well-developed databases of an individual's financial history with them.

While the technology is a ailable to do more with information, it is unfortunate that the kinds of information that most firms obtain on a regular basis are usually limited to transactional data—such as what was purchased, when, and for how much. With this information, firms are able to use recency, frequency, and monetary data and conduct what is called RFM analysis. Patterns of relationships between the variables are used to determine the best prospects among the customers in the database—those that might be high-propensity targets for a promotion. Transactional data is important, but not adequate to make customer-focused decisions. In addition to being able to individualize interactions with the customer, with customer information that goes beyond transactional data a firm can derive knowledge to guide anything from cost-saving measures in operations to new product decisions. To really understand the customer, firms need information on a multitude of dimensions other than just transactions around their other actual consumption activities.

Customer-focused decisions and actions require customer information at two levels. At the aggregate level, customer information is about the market—or more specifically, about the typical customer in the segment(s)—and at the individual level, it is about a specific customer. When the number of customers for a firm is large and there is no opportunity to directly interact with the customer, it does not make economic sense to get down to the level of individual customer-specific profiles. For example, Procter & Gamble may not be able to interact with each and every Crest toothpaste user. In such a situation, the customer profile is aggregated and constructed at the market segment level. On the other hand, for firms that directly interact with the customer, it makes sense to profile specific individual customers. For example, General Electric interacts with individual customers of kitchen appliances who contract customer service agreements. GE can use their knowledge of each individual customer to target service contract renewal offers or offers for replacement products when the normal life of the appliance has passed. In general, it should become apparent that the more the aggregation, the less specific and accurate the information on individual customers. As seen the level of aggregation of the information will also determine whether that information is useful for individualized or segment-level decisions, processes, and activities. As the level of aggregation of customer information increases, the level of aggregation of the customer solution increases and the firm is working at the segment level. With lower levels of aggregation, the firm is working at the individual customer level.

Customer information, whether at the market segment level and/or at the individual level, provides a profile of the customer that guides a customer-focused firm's decisions and actions. A customer profile should be based on two broad categories of information: *Background profile* is general customer information not directly related to the product and is not product-specific; and *consumption profile* is directly related to the product and is product-specific, in that it is about behaviour related to the consumption of the specific product.

DEFINING CUSTOMER IDENTITY

The background profile helps to identify the customer and to understand the customer's product-related behaviour. Firms have been diligent about gathering demographic and psychographic data to establish the background profiles of customers in the B2C market. Customer-focused firms use this background profile to understand product-related consumption behaviour. Such information is managed on an ongoing basis. In the B2C context, "who the customer is" can be profiled along the dimensions of demographic, psychographic, and consumption behaviour. Of these three dimensions, the demographic and psychographic dimensions provide the background profile. Similarly, the background profile of the B2B customer needs to be in terms of their size, type of industry, their corporate culture, and other characteristics used to identify the firm.

In the B2C context, customers purchase and consume solutions for individual or household use. Consumers' consumption of products are determined to a great deal by their backgrounds. Their personality, family, economic, social, ethnic, and cultural profile influence the way they think, feel, and behave at home, with their friends and social circles and in society in general. This background profile helps us understand their consumption profile and the customer value they seek in specific product solutions for their needs in the context of their activities.

Similarly, in the B2B context, the background profile of customers helps us understand their consumption profile and the customer value they seek in product solutions in the context of their value chain activities. Business customers purchase and consume solutions for their own business activities. The type of industry they operate in, what value they create, their size, the skills and knowledge sets of their employees, and the "personality" of their firm (their corporate culture) affect the way firms think, feel, and behave in the marketplace with all their stakeholders, especially with their suppliers and their customers.

Whereas the background profile serves to identify the customer, to truly understand customer value one needs systematic information on the purchase and use of the product by the customer. This information is crucial to get a complete picture of benefits and costs to the customer. A consumption profile comprises information that provides a comprehensive view of the customer's knowledge, attitude, and behaviour with respect to a specific need and associated solutions. The consumption profile containing information on product-related behaviour helps profile a customer in terms of the how the product is acquired, consumed, and disposed. We have already discussed the comprehensive and systematic view of the customer's consumption activities and serves as a conceptual framework for the information on the product-related customer behaviours buy value in the solutions. Thus, customer value defines the primary purpose of any business.

Table: Customer Profile

Customer Profile	*B2C Dimensions*	*B2B Dimensions*
Background Profile	• *Demographics* - Age, Income, Gender, Social status, Household characteristics, etc.	• *Firm Characteristics* - Type of industry, Size of firm in revenues, Employees, Geographic location(s), etc.
	• Psychographics - Activities, Interests, Opinions, Cultural orientations, Lifestyle, etc.	• Organizational structure and culture - Management style, Employee personalities, Reward structure, etc.
Consumption Profile	• Consumption needs and expectations - Product preferences, Purchase decision-making process, Choice criteria, etc.	• Customer needs and expectations - Value-added sought, Purchase decision-making process, Buying (and usage) centre profile, etc.
	• Product purchase patterns - Where, when, how, and how often purchased	• Product purchase patterns - Where, when, how, and how often purchased
	• Product use patterns - Where, when, and how product is used	• Product use patterns - Where, when, and how product is used, etc.
	• Customer experience - Transaction and encounter satisfaction, Product failures and firm's response information	• Customer experience - Transaction and encounter satisfaction, Product failures and service recovery information
	• Loyalty status - Value of customer to firm, in revenues and word-of-mouth referrals	• Relationship status - Value of the buying firm as a customer

Management guru Peter Drucker said in his 1954 book, *The Practice of Management*, "to know what a business is we have to start with its purpose." He goes on to say: "There is only one valid definition of business purpose: *to create a customer.*" Drucker reiterates this concept in a number of different ways, always emphasizing that "it is the customer who determines what a business is." It is not important what the business thinks it is producing. The customer determines the value of what the business produces based on what the customer thinks he or she is buying. Such a perspective places the final result in focus—what the product *does* for the customer. Thus, the purpose of a business is what it creates for the customer. The first and foremost question for any firm to ask is, what business are we in? How many firms diligently confront this question? And, when they do encounter this question, whose perspective do they take? Taking the customer's perspective to answer this fundamental question forces a number of thought processes that benefit the firm in different ways.

In fact, businesses will find that approaching the question of *what business are we in?* in so fundamental a manner not only allows the firm to understand its existing customers, but will also help open up new market potential. It forces the analysis of value-creating assets, including the firm's skills and knowledge sets. The question also opens up the analysis of who the competition is. When firms strive to beat rivals, they typically end up competing within the confines of existing business. Firms sometimes do not realize that they compete with firms in other industries. They are able to see this if they articulate their business from the customer's perspective.

When customers consider their options in meeting a need, they don't limit themselves to one industry. Without realizing it as such, their solutions may involve different industries. Firms are forced to redefine their competitive landscape when they take the customer's perspective because they will find themselves competing outside their well-defined spaces. Kim and Mauborgne call it competing in a "market space."

Customer behaviour during this stage of the consumption cycle falls into three broad and sequential sets of activities: experiencing the need for a solution to a problem, identifying and analyzing the options to the problem, and deciding on a specific solution or way of meeting the need. For interactions with the customer during the preconsumption stage to be customer-focused, firms need to understand the perceptions, attitudes, and activities of customers as they go through their purchase decisions. Firms need to understand what customers expect from the solutions provider during this phase.

Since a product is a means to an end, to really know how the firm is doing with its products it is necessary to understand what the ends are. It becomes necessary to find out what role the firm's product plays in its use for the customer. It is also important to understand what those product roles might be in different usage situations. Often the customer's preferred solution can vary from one situation to another and yet the provider may not pay attention to that important change in the value that the customer is expecting from each customer experience.

The customer engages in accessing and assessing the relevant information on the ways in which a need can be met. Based on the information available to them, customers identify the various options and sort through information to determine the merits of each option. A number of complex issues about the customer experience in this stage are relevant for the firm. Where do customers get the information on the options – from what channels and in what form is the information sought? What are the firms, brands, or solution providers that are evoked in the customer's mind? What are the criteria that the customer uses to evaluate the choice of providers of solutions? What are their expectations from the solution? How do customers benefit from the products and services? When Nike introduced its slip-on sneaker Presto, teens could select designs for their shoes, attach matching music to them, and email them as music videos to friends. Nike was engaging itself in the preconsumption activities of the teen shopper. The firm acted on its understanding of how teens make and follow fads and fashion to introduce a new and innovative footwear design. If you can understand and reach into the customer's preconsumption activities, you can identify and attract the most appropriate customer for your firm's solution. Customer acquisition efforts can be more precise.

Customers make their choice after weighing all options against their criteria. Firms must learn how they make these vendor decisions. Who is involved in the purchase decision making? Who influences the customer's preferences and biases? Household (B2C) and organizational (B2B) consumption activities can involve several different individuals in a purchase decision. Individuals play roles of users, buyers, influencers, decision makers, and so on, in what are called "buying centres." What are the various perspectives of each of these individuals and units engaged in the process? What are their respective roles in the decision? How is the purchase decision made, and what process do the customers follow? When and how often is the decision made? What are the preferences on the method of payment? How do these customers evaluate you and your products before purchase? Who is involved in that evaluation? This kind of detail in the purchasing activities of the customer, if gathered and utilized, can improve the effectiveness of the firm's customer acquisition efforts.

When the firm can interact directly with the customer, as in the case of services, there is the opportunity to obtain answers to these questions and respond immediately. Where there is an intermediary involved, the firm has to rely on the intermediary to represent the firm during this stage because the customer interactions are with the intermediary, not the firm. In the hand-held ("pocket PC" or "PDA") market, the competition is so fierce that companies are constantly monitoring the retailer to ensure that their products and promotions are well displayed and that the salespeople are well informed about them. The personal digital assistant maker Palm sends its agents as mystery shoppers to retailers carrying their products. Microsoft, for example, gave a free Casio EM500

Pocket PC device to salespeople who completed a Pocket PC training.

In first-time experiences with a service provider, customers may want to obtain information from the provider; thus that interaction is required prior to the consumption of the product. In situations where prices and terms of sale are negotiated, quite often the case in services, there is a significant amount of interaction. In most cases of intangible-dominant products, there is some customer involvement at least in the specification of the needs of the customer so that the specific solution can be configured for each customer. Every firm should explore the opportunities it has for customer information to help in its acquisition efforts. The total solution includes the firm's contribution to the customer's preconsumption activities. Rich Hanks, Marriott's executive vice president of sales, recalls the early days of Marriott's Web presence. He says they did not even know that they had to put reservations on the first page.The way to design Web pages is to think like the customer and ask what the customer would like to do on the Web. Whatever prepurchase decision-making process the customer will be using should be used in Web site design. For example, at what stage of the consumption activity cycle should a Web site charge a visitor for a service? Some visitors balk when they are asked to pay up front for a service they haven't used—they mightn't want to pay member fees when they only want one transaction, for example.

THE CONSUMPTION STAGE

Firms that are not customer focused are focused on product and sales. They typically pay a great deal of attention to the sales and purchase process—the preconsumption stage, but not the consumption process. During the consumption stage, it is important to understand how the customer uses the product or service and what kinds of customer activities are associated with the value that your firm's product provides. To truly understand customer value, the firm needs to dig deeper into the consumption activities of its customers.

Who is involved in the use of the product? How do they use the product? Does the customer have all of the information it needs on your firm's product to fully benefit from its use? Will the customer want to interact with the firm during the consumption stage? Will customers need customer service assistance, and if so, what kinds of usage assistance would they need? What kinds of issues dictate the effectiveness of the solution from the perspective of a consumption process?

Understanding when, where, and how a product is used is often a powerful piece of information if used effectively. Consider the following examples of firms using the context of the consumption activities as they relate to their products: Starbucks gives out free Frappuccino samples on a hot day at a busy square in Manhattan. Unilever hands out free Lever 2000 handwipes at a food court in a shopping mall and body wash and deodorant to fitness class students at a Bally's Fitness Club. Schering-Plough provides blister treatment cushions to runners at a marathon. These firms are obtaining and using their knowledge of how their products are used at the point-of-use of the product. They are in a position to determine what customer education is necessary and what customer value improvement opportunities there may be.

Product-focused firms remain focused on the product and its sale and on not much after that. To these firms, most likely, a complaining customer is the cost of doing business and a necessary evil, and is frequently cast to the unwilling hands of a customer service person. Consider the example of the "easy to assemble yourself" products that come in a box with some assembly required by the consumer. The unsuspecting customer is frequently confronted by a confusing set of directions written by someone who doesn't need directions to assemble the product.

Procter & Gamble has been actively collecting first-hand information on how consumers use their packaged household products, just to understand how the customer uses the product—rather than depend on the pencil-and-paper survey method or focus group discussions. Those methods are fine for demographics and psychographics information, but are fraught with misinformation since they rely on the accuracy of memory and communication by the consumer as well as the interpretation and visualization on the part of the firm's researcher. In fact, P&G goes as far as to send ethnographer filmmakers who spend full days—from the time a family wakes up until bedtime—for several days, just to understand how the firm can create value for the lives of families—a way to look for new product opportunities.

In the case of service-dominant products, since production and consumption are simultaneous, the consumption phase involves the firm's production activities as well. There could be a significant degree of customer interaction and participation in the production of the solution. The customer is part of the production process, and the information regarding each interaction needs to be carefully documented and utilized to deliver customer-focused experiences. Customer roles need to be scripted and customer performances in these roles need to be monitored and managed. This information about customer interactions is critical in improving the processes involved in service delivery. Consider what package delivery staff have to do at some of their destinations. "Please place boxes in barrel. If they (it) don't fit, put on top of barrel—Dogs will rip up if left on ground, " is a set of instructions given to Land's End by a catalog customer for package delivery by a courier. Customer data must be collected, and the value creation and delivery system should be designed to obtain and use that information appropriately.

Here, customer evaluations and their disposition to be loyal to your firm is the main feature of the customer's experience. When the product is predominantly a service product, the customer might be in a formal membership relationship with the service provider, such as in the case of banking or financial services, or enrolled in an educational programme, or a fitness club, or a contractual obligation, as in a B2B context. At the end of each interaction in the case of service products, customers may assess their experience and determine their inclination toward the solution provider. In such cases, it would be important to collect customer reactions and impressions after each consumption experience so that the relationship is intact. With packaged goods, on the other hand, where there is no interaction during the use of the product, customer assessment of the provider is made during and after the use of the product.

What is the level of satisfaction with the features of your product and with the interactions they have had with your firm? They may be pointing out systematic failures in how you are creating and delivering customer solutions. Are there fail points in your value-creation processes that need more attention? It is possible to get some very critical process-improvement suggestions from the customer. How can the benefits to the customer be improved and costs to the customer reduced so that the net customer value is improved? Which aspects of your product are most and least useful for the customer?

This information would be useful in conducting a cost-benefit analysis of the service enhancements to your product. What is the value of each customer to your firm, by transaction and in the long-run? Can the value of the customer to the firm be increased? Are there opportunities to increase the role you are playing in meeting customer needs by providing a more complete solution either by adding products or adding features to the product? Are there ways to reduce the costs of serving the customer?

Although strictly speaking not part of the consumption profile, customers may have valuable information on how well your frontline personnel are providing value to the customer. Customers can provide you with an assessment of how well your intermediaries and resellers are representing you. For example, travel agents who represent hotels, airlines, and other travel-related services might need more information, attention or encouragement to represent you appropriately. All things being equal, retailers have no incentive to sell a particular brand in a nonexclusive retail store. As long as the customer purchases the item from their store, the retailer does not care which particular brand is purchased. Customers are the best judge of your suppliers and vendors as well. If there are aspects of your value-creation processes that are subcontracted out, customer feedback is critical in assessing whether these contracts are working as desired and whether there need to be any changes in how these processes are structured.

How will the customer want to convey feedback? Have you provided the avenues that customers are most likely to use to tell you what they think about the solution and your performance? Are your touchpoints able to solicit, record, and report customer information? The next chapter develops these issues around customer information management.

Understanding customer value is a prerequisite for being able to create and deliver superior customer solutions. Firms need to study customers' consumption profiles to understand their needs and what they seek in the best solution. The background profile of the customer is a useful context in which to analyze the information on the consumption activities of the customer. The consumption activity framework attempts to frame the information on the customer in the three stages of consumption activities. Companies focus attention on attracting and acquiring customers so that data collection is generally geared toward the preconsumption phase. Existing customers' transaction data is used to guide attempts to generate more sales from them. When data on consumption and postconsumption activities are gathered, a great deal more can be done to inform the entire range of the firm's decisions and activities in creating and delivering the product.

A high-involvement consumption context is one where customers face a purchase decision that requires more time, effort, and money than low-involvement consumption contexts. Compare the purchase of chewing gum, a low-involvement purchase, to that of an automobile, a high-involvement purchase.

Chapter 4

Customer Knowledge Management

Among other reasons firms have a low return on their information technology investments is that they only poorly understand what the technology makes possible. The objectives and role of information in customer-focused management must be understood. Customer-intelligent firms use their customer knowledge to drive all of the firm's activities and decisions.

When firms have so much opportunity to interact with their customers, why is it that they treat their customers like strangers? The reason is not lack of information on their customers, but a lack in a firm's managing of that information. Firms may have the ability to capture that information, but may not process and utilize the knowledge to manage relationships with their customers. Information technology has only placed this realization in sharp focus. On the other hand, the power of information technology has also raised the ugly specter of abuse of privacy when firms have access to a vast amount of customer information. Network Solutions, the first company that registered addresses on the. com,. org, and. net domains for the Internet, now a unit of VeriSign, raised eyebrows when it planned to sell names, street addresses, and other information gathered from businesses and individuals who signed up for an Internet address. There are several examples of Internet companies that have been reined in for their use of customer information. DoubleClick Inc., decided against combining Web-tracking data with offline databases. Toysmart was not allowed to sell its customer database when it shut down.

Hagel and Rayport suggest that customers will become savvy about their personal information and be reluctant to divulge it unless they receive some value for it. They predict that customers will win the battle over their information and firms they call "infomediaries" will "become custodians, agents and brokers of customer information, marketing it to businesses on consumers' behalf while protecting their privacy at the same time." Nevertheless, customer information is crucial for a customer focus because of the need to make and execute customer-focused decisions in all aspects of the business. Firms will continue to require customer information to do business. Information technology will continue to challenge a firm's judgment in obtaining and using customer information.

Traditionally, research on the customer has been at the aggregate level, most utilized during the new product development process, to test new product ideas, in test marketing, and to test new campaign concepts in the realm of advertising. Marketing research has been standard practice preceding the launch of new products or advertising campaigns. Most firms conduct regular market research activities to direct segmentation decisions such as targeting and to determine how to reach segments.

This chapter does not limit itself to data from market research studies, nor is it about how to conduct market research studies. Instead, this chapter is about the consolidation and utilization of information on the customer to align all the activities of the firm to meeting customer needs. The key issues discussed in this chapter are central to designing and implementing effective customer knowledge management: the sources and avenues from which customer information is available to the firm; in what form is it available; how this data can and should be analyzed and interpreted; and how the information should be utilized.

BENEFITS OF CUSTOMER KNOWLEDGE MANAGEMENT

Scholars have implored managers to "spend a day in the life of your customer" and to "get inside the lives of your customers, " so as to obtain a deeper understanding of customers. The quality of the knowledge on the customer is much greater because of direct observation. Obtaining that knowledge is only the first step. The basic skill of listening involves competence in sensing, evaluating *and* responding. A study of 500 new car buyers found customer perceptions of these three dimensions of listening to be strongly linked to trust in the salesperson. There are also benefits within the firm when the practice of listening to customers is emphasized by senior managers. Senior managers at First Chicago discovered that in emphasizing listening to the customer they found a cultural change within the organization. Customer knowledge gained from firsthand customer contact is very persuasive. Smart CEOs at firms like IBM, Cisco, and EMC intuitively realize this, and their senior managers contact their major customers on a regular basis. These firms also act on that information to improve relationships with those important customers.

The benefits of customer knowledge management have concentrated at the individual level. For example, Dreyfus, like other mutual fund firms, keeps track of client activity, claiming that they can predict when a client is going to shift money out of their mutual funds. Clients receive a call from a Dreyfus representative, who wants to know how the client feels about the investment and if his or her goals are being met. If Dreyfus is able to track clients at all stages of the consumption process, then the firm has a better chance of retaining the customer. A number of CRM- and ERP-type software programs allow companies to track processes in the life of a specific sales order from order entry all the way to delivery to customer. Of course, FedEx introducing package tracking is a well-known example from years ago. There are a number of benefits of information technology for firms of any size.

Siebel software allows Honeywell to spot problems and opportunities by tracking and analyzing all customer interactions; and at Marriott, Siebel empowers sales reps to respond more quickly to customer needs by integrating customer information from different departments. Lexmark International used Microstrategy software to help build what they call a data warehousing solution that accomplished a reduction in product delivery time by 70 percent, a threefold improvement in being able to deliver a customer's order on the desired date, and a 60 percent reduction in the information costs. Package delivery firm UPS's selfservice tracking system, built by IBM, saved the company $450,000 a day in customer service expenses; and, the Clarify call centre software helped payroll-processing firm ADP improve customer retention rate by 5 percent and increase revenues by $100 million in 1999 simply by providing its customer service reps with customer information on its 8000 clients. There are numerous such examples of technology-based customer information management systems having a profound impact on a firm's productivity and in customer retention. Both outcomes are the basis for achieving and sustaining profits.

The marketing research practice has undergone a major transformation in recent years. A primary function of marketing research activities is to collect and analyze customer information. Technology has enabled all phases of the marketing research process ranging from sampling and data collection to analysis and reporting. With newer technologies and faster cycle times, firms conduct research at all stages of the product life cycle and not just at the product development stage or the test marketing stage. This is at the aggregate level, whereas there is another change in research on the customer at the individual level, where technology is enabling customers to interact with the firm in a multitude of different ways not previously possible. These interactions can now occur during all stages of consumption. At every interaction with the customer, a firm has the opportunity to acquire valuable customer information, as well as to process and utilize the information for creating and delivering superior customer value.

Once the data is available, the challenge is to provide the user of the information and decision maker with targeted information. Enter rulesbased approaches, which are simply programs that make sense of data using preconceived models. Sadly, the majority of CRM and ERP packages fail the firm not for lack of data, but simply because the firm does not have the appropriate understanding and appreciation of the fundamentals of customer-focused management. The rules for decision-making should be founded on customer-focused management principles. The better the understanding of the customer and the utilization of that knowledge, the more customer focused the rules are. The best technology is only as good as what you tell it to do. CRM and ERP packages are really knowledge management software, tools to manage knowledge of the customer and enable the processes within the firm that are working to meet specific customer needs. To be more effective with these tools, firms need to gather the information, analyze and process it to obtain a good understanding of the customer, and utilize it at every opportunity in the value-creation and delivery process. Therefore, for a thorough understanding on how to manage customer information, it is important to understand the principles of knowledge management, in general.

What is knowledge management? To answer this question, we have first to deal with a more fundamental question: what is the difference between data, information, and knowledge? Are these terms just synonyms that are interchangeable? No, they are not! The simplest way to understand the differences among these terms is to picture a continuum. As we add value to data, it becomes information; and as we add value to information, information becomes knowledge. When we interpret data in a context, we convert that data into information that has some meaning. When we categorize and elaborate on that information with explanations, then we have added more value and the information can now be considered knowledge. Thus, *knowledge management* is the management of data and information so that a firm can optimally capture, process, and utilize its knowledge for effective decision-making and operation. *Customer knowledge management* is the management of the acquisition, processing, and utilization of customer information for effective customer-focused decision making. Knowledge management practice has been studied in the context of how organizations learn. Before we discuss the methods of managing customer knowledge, it would be useful to understand knowledge management and, specifically, information processing from the perspective of organizational learning. Organizational learning can be broadly depicted as a three-stage process:

- Information acquisition or generation
- Information transmission or dissemination
- Information analysis or interpretation

Studies have demonstrated that a customer-focused firm has a formal and systematic method for gathering, interpreting and using customer information. To be customer-focused, therefore, firms need to be committed to the importance and value of customer information and to the use of customer information in guiding the creation and delivery of customer value. Thus, recognizing information's value to the firm and realizing when and where it is accessible is a prerequisite for knowledge management.

Richard Schulze, CEO of Bestbuy, the runaway success in electronics retailing, says: The best way to find out whether a store is running smoothly is by asking the cashier. "The cashier really understands where the problems lie. They're the last people to see the customer. "To consider all of the sources of customer information we also need to first identify the natural state of the information. Customer information is available as tacit and as explicit knowledge. The explicit knowledge is present in the databases of the firm or as documented information. Customer information files in databases are usually quantitative data. More and more firms are also using qualitative data when the technology is used to accommodate that type of data. Otherwise, most of this rich information remains as hidden knowledge. This information that is not recorded is the tacit knowledge that is usually resident with the employees and managers of the firm. For example, records of customer service interactions capture the actual transaction, complaint, or feedback from the customer. At the same time, employees, based on their prior experience, will unconsciously record and bring to bear their judgments of the situation, which are not necessarily documented. The knowledge that employees have that is not recorded anywhere is deemed the tacit knowledge of the firm.

While at the individual level information is available from customer information files in the firm's databases, other types of information at the aggregate level may be gathered during the course of product development activities and other specific projects and reside in research reports. There is information on the customer at several locations within the firm, from sales to customer service, to name the most obvious areas. As we know besides this explicit knowledge, there is a wealth of information at both the aggregate and the individual levels. Wherever the firm has interfaced with the customer, the "touch-points, " there is information on the customer. It immediately becomes apparent that several product and service delivery contact points within the firm have access to customer information, but not all are part of the customer information management system.

CRM software packages enable the firm to capture all of the information gathered at each touch-point into a central database and make it available at any touch point. To determine all of the opportunities for gathering information on the customer, firms can develop a blueprint of the order delivery or customer service processes depicting all of the touch-points from the consumption cycle when the customer interacts with the firm. Knowledge gained on the customer from each and every customer interaction when recorded and made available can be valuable in improving the customer focus of any of the firm's decisions or actions. The major sources for customer knowledge are discussed below.

Table: States and Forms of Customer Information

	Individual level	*Aggregate level*
Explicit - Documented knowledge	Customer Information Files	Research Reports
Implicit - Tacit knowledge	Knowledge held by employees and intermediaries about individual customers that are not recorded	Knowledge held by employees and intermediaries about groups of customers that are not recorded

Table Customer Information Sources Based on Consumption Stages

	Sources of Information Salespeople
Preconsumption	Channel intermediaries Referral data Frontline service personnel
Consumption	Service delivery personnel Service failure and recovery data Customer satisfaction surveys
Postconsumption	Customer complaints Customer service logs Frequent user profiles

Customer Information Files are typically transaction-related and purchase-related individual-level customer data found in sales records, customer interaction records, and customer service incident records. What is perhaps not in these files, which needs to be considered as a necessary component of individual customer profiles where available, is information related to the activities of preconsumption, consumption, and postconsumption.

Research Reports have segment-level aggregate data that are found in product development reports, advertising research reports, sales and marketing reports, and customer service reports. What needs to be seen is whether research on market segments is an ongoing pursuit of the firm—to indicate that the firm is proactively assessing customer value being delivered by the firm.

Knowledge held by employees and managers: Tacit knowledge of the customers—is by definition not completely identified and its utility not realized. If there is no formal process to regularly capture and utilize this information, a wealth of knowledge resident in the firm is being ignored.

Upstream and downstream sources: When suppliers and intermediaries are regularly included in discussions of value-creation and delivery decisions, there is an opportunity to discover information on market trends, technology, ideas for product improvement, and so on that are useful at the aggregate level. At the individual level, where there are (downstream) intermediaries, if it is possible, it would be highly valuable to obtain individual customer level information.

Now let us look at opportunities that may be missed by firms that are not proactive in looking for customer information. For example, how many firms capture and utilize data on referrals? If it is appropriately captured and analyzed, firms can use this information to proactively stimulate referrals. Firms can identify customers who could be bringing in new customers. Firms can determine what incentives would be effective in stimulating referrals. From the referring and referred customers, firms can learn what messages are being conveyed about the firm and which messages are most effective in stimulating product trial from new customers. Firms can learn what types of customers are most liable to switch from their current patronage based on word of mouth.

Firms can track and follow the patronage behaviour of these new customers and nurture their loyalty and referral behaviour. Firms can also find out from these new customers valuable information on the competition as well. Similarly, what about prospective customer queries? How well is this information captured and utilized? What would such information contain? They are a good source of what customers look for in a product, a reflection of their choice criteria. How many firms systematically record information on complaints and praises? This type of information would be very helpful in understanding how the firm is faring on creating and delivering customer value. It could highlight failpoints in the value-creating processes and provide input into frontline evaluation and motivation activities.

Many firms have loyalty programs to reward the frequent user. What sort of frequent-user data do these firms maintain? How many firms really use the frequent-purchase data? Some firms who know their customers well recognize the importance of sorting out the most profitable customers from their customer base and treating them differently. Some customers are indeed more equal than others! Most firms use frequent-purchaser data for targeting specials and promotions. However, this data can also provide invaluable information on customer value and customer profile information to align the firm's value-creation and delivery processes.

Traditionally, firms have gathered routine customer information only at purchase and when a customer returns a product for a refund or mechanisms. Feedback forms and customer surveys are administered on a regular basis in some firms. However, most often the information gathered from these efforts is worthless because of faulty designs and worse, sometimes even result in misdirected decisions because of flawed survey methodology. More often than not, the surveys are neither reliable nor valid. While reliability and validity as statistical measures of the psychometric stability of a scale are important for a scientific, unbiased study, management can improve the utility of customer surveys with a rather simple analysis. Examine the design, administration, and use of any survey along the dimensions of structure, content, and process. Structural features such as length and the time it would take the respondent to fill out the survey, the layout of the various questions in the survey, and the response format for the questions affect the effectiveness of the survey. Content decisions, such as the categories of information sought from the respondent and information identifying the type of respondent filling out the survey, affect the utility of the survey, which will only be as good as the effectiveness of its administration and its usability. Thus, the process of survey delivery, customer response delivery mechanisms, and the customization of the reports to the decision maker and user of the information in their value-creating and delivery roles is critical to the success of the customer feedback exercise.

There are other sources of customer information that the firm has access to and may not fully utilize. The systematic way of determining what these sources might be is to list all the possible touch-points where customers interact with the firm and placing them in sequence in the three phases of consumption. In the preconsumption phase, customers may interact with salespeople or customer service or other frontline personnel. Recognizing what these touch-points are and what kinds of information is shared between the firm and the customer is an important step. Firms must decide what data needs to be captured at the touch-points and how it is to be used in guiding decisions and activities.

How many firms systematically utilize frontline operations personnel for gathering customer information? Frontline operations personnel are in an ideal position to gather customer information. They can be trained on when, what, and how to observe or elicit information from customers. They need to be motivated and recognized for their ability to obtain, process, and disseminate such information. Similarly, there are also the intermediaries or resellers of the firm's products and services that represent the firm in different ways. These intermediaries might perform functions of delivery and distribution, promotion, or customer service on behalf of the firm. Walmart recognized and wielded the power it held with such customer information in negotiating terms with powerful packaged goods manufacturers, including Procter & Gamble.

Table: Guidelines for Customer Information Surveys

Elements	*Analysis*
Structure	• *Length* - What are the research objectives; recognize the trade-off between amount of information needed and impact on response rate
	• *Layout* - Examine the construction of the survey in terms of appearance and feel
	• *Format* - Examine question construction and response format; open-ended questions invite top-of-mind issues from customer, whereas close-ended questions focus on issues that are of specific concern; in close-ended questions, avoid a "yes or no" and adopt at least a 5-point scale if you want to do any serious statistical analysis
Content	• *Categories* - Compare the types of information solicited with the research objectives; recognize which aspects in the customer's consumption activity cycle are covered or not covered
	• *Profile* - Examine whether there is adequate and appropriate information obtained from the respondent to allow for some segment-based analysis of the responses
	• *Identity* - Examine whether it is appropriate to ask for the identity of the respondent to allow for response to customer inquiries or customer complaints
Process	• *Input* - Ensure that the appropriate users of the information have contributed to the research design; examine also whether the customer's perspective has been incorporated into the design of the survey
	• *Administration* - Examine how the survey is being distributed as well as returned, and the impact on who will be responding (for a representative sample) and who is receiving the completed surveys (for a nonbiased information)
	• *Output* - For what purposes will the information gathered be used; determine the best reporting format and procedure for maximum benefit to the user

In the consumption phase, customers may call for assistance in using the product or on some aspect of how the solution works. This information needs to be captured and incorporated into customer education activities such as product directions-for-use instructions, or used in product development and improvement efforts. There is also a wealth of information within the firm available from customer complaints and suggestions. Service failures and recovery situations provide valuable information on customers and their experiences with the firm and its solutions. If these are recorded and maintained on a systematic basis, they can be "mined" for patterns that yield insights not otherwise available. For example, recurrent complaints about customer service response time might suggest that the customer service process needs redesigning.

Often when the data is not available on which to base a decision, the firm has to collect that information. For example, say the firm has received several complaints about customer service access and wants to determine what changes need to be made to the customer service operation. In this case, the firm may want to conduct some research in order to determine the customer needs and preferences with regard to customer service. For each decision that directly relates to a customer, the firm has first to determine what kind of information is needed to make the most effective customer-focused decision. Some of this information is available in existing databases, while some may have to be gathered. To gather information, the firm needs to set up a method of determining what information needs to be gathered, how it can be obtained, and in what form it will be available.

When the information is not available from the day-to-day activities of the firm, then research needs to be conducted on the customer on a project-by-project basis. There are a number of choices and decisions to be made regarding the methods available in researching the customer. For example, to determine what changes are needed to improve customer satisfaction, there are formal and informal customer satisfaction measures. There are qualitative and quantitative methods to obtain the information. For unique project-based decisions, there are several datacollection methods. Among the quantitative methods typically used are paper and pencil surveys administered over the telephone or by mail. On the other hand, qualitative methods typically utilize structured and unstructured interviews, focus groups, or observation methods. A number of innovative qualitative approaches are being introduced. For example, Kimberly Clark for its diaper market, Intuit with its personal finance software, and Patagonia for its outdoor gear have used the method of "story-telling" by getting customers to tell real-life stories expressing how they use the product and feel about it.

Customer case research is another method that conducts chronological case studies of actual purchases to discover previously unknown purchase drivers by systematically capturing all events leading up to the purchase decision. These approaches can uncover customer experiences and thought processes that may not be accessible through a pencil-and-paper survey approach. Any research project should take a systematic approach for maximum benefit and to reduce errors (such as measurement and sampling errors) and biases and follow the following approach...

- *Framing the research*—Management needs for the decision or objective
- *Examining existing and available information*—For hypotheses, specific research questions and to guide research design
- Specifying the research questions
- *Determining the research design*—Questionnaire construction, sampling frame, data collection method, and plan of analysis
- Administering the research and collecting and analyzing the data
- Reporting the results and findings

First, the research objective frames the management decision to be made. Information already available is used to guide the research design. The research is then designed by making decisions on what information is needed and how and where to collect the information. The research design includes determining the questions to solicit the information, the method for administering these questions, the sample of subjects, and a plan of analysis. Qualitative research designs are appropriate when there is a need to generate ideas on what to focus on, or to get in-depth information on specific issues. Qualitative research, such as focus-group methods, can complement quantitative research, such as surveys.

Quantitative research designs are useful when a broader cross-section of the customers needs to be polled about a broad range of issues. Sampling techniques are used when it is not possible or necessary to contact all the sources of information. Statistical techniques allow for generalizing inferences and conclusions on the entire population of interest based on data from a representative sample of that population. The research instrument or questions and response format are constructed and pretested on a small subset of the population for validity and reliability before obtaining responses from the final sample. The responses are tabulated and statistical procedures applied to the data for analysis. The findings generated are then made available to guide the decision maker. The appropriate format of tables and the report are predetermined in the plan of analysis, so that the data is collected and analyzed according to the needs of the user of that information.

Especially in service firms and in the service component of manufacturing firms, where there is a significant opportunity to interact with the customer and to customize value, firms have used customer information in a number of ways. Observe any service encounter and you will see tacit or explicit customer knowledge being used. When the data from these interactions are systematically documented and analyzed, patterns in customer data can detect the dynamics in consumption behaviour. When aggregated, customer data provides an opportunity to analyze customer segments for anything from price sensitivity to demand patterns to why, when, and how customers behave in the various activities within each of the consumption stages. Firms can divide their customer base into segments based on profitability. When customer purchase information is mapped onto capacity utilization data, for example, a deeper analysis of the firm's value-creation and delivery processes can help determine which of the firm's marketing and operations practices contribute to its profitability. Which frequent customer promotion programs are most/least effective? Where are the low and peak demand periods? A yield analysis of the utilization levels at the various price levels would help determine the most effective pricing decisions.

Each customer has a value to the firm, and that information is also valuable to the firm to determine the right customer. The lifetime value of the customer to the firm is a function of what they bring to the firm as revenues over the lifetime of the customer. By the same token, it is also important to know what it costs the firm to serve that customer. Loyal customers with a favourable disposition toward the service provider are also likely to engage in favourable word-of-mouth behaviour. They are valuable in trying new products being offered by the firm. They are also less costly to serve because they are familiar with the firm and are socialized into the procedures of the firm that they encounter in their consumption. As customers' loyalty with the firm grows over time, the firm also has a better knowledge of the customer and is more efficient and effective in serving that customer.

Firms that have the data on their customers are able to engage their best resources for their best customers. For example, firms have used information on a customer's profitability to the firm to determine the level of service appropriate for each customer. A *Business Week* (October 23, 2000) special report titled "Why Service Stinks" cites several examples of firms pampering their premium customers. Charles Schwab's premium customer waits no longer than 15 seconds for a phone call to be answered, while others could wait as long as 10 minutes. Centura Bank's most profitable customers – rated 5 on a scale of 1 to 5 – get an annual call from the CEO; customer retention in this group improved by 50 percent in five years. Even utility companies, believed to be less sophisticated in their marketing than the consumer packaged goods firms, have a higher proportion of service representatives per customer for their higher-revenue customer groups. In each example, unless the firm knew what each customer was worth to the firm, it would not be able to proportionally allocate its resources to the "right" customers.

A grid guided by the three consumption stages can be a useful framework for determining what decisions need to be based on what customer information. All the functions and processes that affect the creation and delivery of customer value in each of the stages need to be aligned with customer information.

Technology has revolutionized customer information management. Information technologies allow firms to gather, store, and interpret demographic and behavioural data so that each subsequent interaction with the customer is customized, based on historical data gathered from each customer interaction. Digitized purchase transactions in commerce have enabled numerous opportunities to track customer interactions. Chip technology has progressed so rapidly that soon there could be a computer chip in just about any product that would enable mindboggling links to improve customer value and the customer-firm relationship. For example, take the Internet and e-commerce. Most Web sites will ask simple unobtrusive questions of customers when they browse the site. This information identifies the customer and tracks the customer's activities or "clickstreams" on the Web site. Subsequently, software can use this information to personalize the Web site and the experience for the customer.

A number of firms have emerged that provide customer information management software. Such software can customize Web pages for each customer depending on the customer's profile, which is created based on the customer's previous interactions with the firm and the Web site. Vignette's software allows Web sites to dynamically generate pages that are custom-made for each customer. Silknet's virtual sales assistant guides customers through a series of questions about their need situations and then makes product recommendations. Marriott has an enterprise-wide software that integrates information on customers from different departments so that its sales reps can anticipate and respond more quickly to customer needs. Similarly, H&R Block uses software from Clarify to combine and coordinate customer records from its tax offices, discount brokerages, its customer service centre, and its Web site so that customer interaction personnel in each department have access to all of the information on the customer.

There are a variety of methods for analyzing data. Data mining techniques attempt to discern patterns in the data where one set of characteristics affects another set in a certain way. SAS Enterprise Dataminer software helps detect patterns in databases and construct models to predict customer response to the firm's actions. Software from iMarket looks at customers' most recent or most frequent purchase decisions and the monetary value of these purchases for the firm and helps decision makers select a subset of customers for targeting specific promotions or new product introductions. Epiphany and Digimine are examples of firms that use a set of their own proprietary algorithms to analyze customer data for their clients. Early clients of Epiphany included Charles Schwab and Hewlett Packard, and for Digimine include Nordstrom. Edify has software that will link customer feedback such as survey responses to individual customer profiles for anlaysis. There is also software such as Nudist available for the analysis of qualitative data. When firms are able to sort through their customer databases and group customers by the relevant characteristics with such datamining software, the power of segmentation and targeting is fully realized with such datamining software.

In general, data is useless for decision making unless it is organized for interpretation. When organized appropriately, data can be contextualized so as to be transformed into information. Displaying and disseminating information is critical to the firm's success. Without proper reporting procedures, decision makers do not benefit from the information that the firm has. For example, ESRI has a programme called Arcview that allows the user to spatially display numerical data. The user can view the data in his or her preferred format to match individual cognitive styles. As Peter Drucker notes, no two executives organize the same information in the same way. Therefore, software that allows the users to display information in their own preferred formats is valuable in customer information management.

The task of the customer information management system is to generate intelligence on the customer so that firm can be more customer-focused in its serving the customer. Intelligence generation capability has been shown to be positively correlated to superior customer value. In a study that involved hour-long in-depth interviews and surveys of sixty-six of the largest one thousand electronic firms by scholars interested in the characteristics of the market-oriented firm, firms are urged to treat learning about the customer as an investment.

Ultimately, customer information is useless unless it is available to the user. Scholars researching the value of information have called this the "value in use" metric. The more the information is used, the more value it has! Customer information management, therefore, involves determining how the information needs to be made available, to whom, when, and in what form. The focus here is on who needs the information. In the spirit of customer focus, the information system serves an internal customer — the decision maker. What will the user need the information for? What specific information is needed for the firm's decisions and activities?

Is the user of the information able to enhance customer value with the information? At what level of aggregation is the information used: policy level and customer level, segment level, and individual level? Such decisions need to be made so as to priorïtize the customer information according to its impact on customer value. In making judgments about committing resources to managing and leveraging customer information, the firm should consider the worth of the information in terms of how it would help the firm provide superior customer value at a reasonable profit.

Table: Framing the Customer-Focused Analysis: Using Customer Information

Business Process	*Customer Information*	*Strategic Decisions Needs*
Core Value Creation	What are the specifics of the customer value in terms of core product?	Keep core of customer solution ahead of competitive offerings.
Delivery of Solution	What are the specifics of customer value in terms of augmentation to the core product?	Keep augmented customer solution ahead of competitive offerings.
Customer Service	What are the customer identity, background, and consumption profiles?	Personalize customer interactions with recognition, acknowledgement, and gratitude for patronage by caring for the customer and serving customer needs based on potential and long term value to the firm.
Communi-cations		What types of information are relevant and important for updating customers? Keep customer informed about firm's activities regarding customer solution.

Customer information must drive any business process and activity, as suggested in Table Customer-focused management requires a customer-focused analysis of the information necessary for designing processes and making decisions regarding value creation in the firm. These run the gamut of decisions regarding creating and delivering customer solutions, product improvements, attracting and retaining customers, customer service, recovering from product failures, hiring and motivating employees, and ensuring a customer-oriented climate and culture.

Chapter 5

Creating and Delivering Superior Customer Value

Firms create and deliver customer value as a bundle of benefits contained in a core and supplementary product. Since the core of any product is a commodity, the competitive advantage comes from the supplementary product. Designing and delivering superior customer value is all about adding value to the customer's value chain and doing it better than the competition. Paying careful attention to the details in each and every encounter with the customer ensures a customer-focused delivery of the value created by the firm. Since the customer-focused firm competes on service, it also faces the classic challenge of any service firm—matching demand and supply. In order to maximize the profitability from its value-creating assets, firms have to determine the most profitable mix of segments for its customer portfolio.

How do you design customer-focused solutions that compete on service? Let customer information drive the decision on how best to leverage the productive assets of the firm. Market-based as well as asset-based assessments are necessary to configure value-creating assets into core and supplementary product benefits that provide a sustainable competitive advantage.

How does a small startup bank beat the big boys of the banking industry in their own backyard? Commerce Bancorp in New Jersey is not your standard bank. You will find their branches open at 8:00 AM and at 8:00 PM, and for most of the day on weekends. Vernon Hill, founding CEO of the bank, who also owns Burger King franchises, has embraced retailing practices in successful firms such as Walmart, Home Depot, and Starbuck's. The core product at Commerce Bancorp is the business of banking, of course. But the total solution includes access and convenience benefits for the customer that most definitely distinguish it from other banks. There are even bathrooms for patrons in each branch at Commerce Bancorp. The total solution for any product includes a core product with supplementary features that in combination present a resultant value to the customer. Product differentiation and superior customer value is not in its core product, but in that total solution. The total solution for Commerce Bancorp is not just banking delivered by human or automated tellers in physical branches, it is banking at the customer's convenience when, where, and how the customer wants it.

Indeed, the difference in a customer-oriented firm is very evident at any Commerce Bancorp branch. Commerce bank has found powerful ways of differentiating itself by being customer focused and then it has been able to execute its customer-focused value creation and delivery.

Firms create and deliver value from their assets. Firms must determine how they might be able to create customer value that is superior to the alternatives available to the customer. With a customer focus, the firm seeks to design a superior solution that will provide the firm with sustainable profits. This chapter covers issues and decisions involved in conceiving, designing, and delivering the customer-focused product offering. What must happen to ensure that the productive assets of the firm, facilities, processes, and people, are set up to create and deliver customer-focused value?

TRANSLATING CUSTOMER NEEDS TO PRODUCT CONCEPT

We have already said that a firm must be able to assess what its customer value is—what its customers perceive as benefits received from the firm, versus what it cost the customers to access and receive those benefits. This assessment must be done both at the aggregate, segment level and at the individual, customer level, where appropriate. The aggregate, segment-level assessment orients the firm's thinking about overall product strategy. When a firm directly interacts with its customer, the individual, customer-level assessment helps the firm configure the product within that strategy to the individual customer.

In keeping with the view that a product is really a bundle of benefits, the core value in any product for any firm is the primary benefit that the firm provides. The supplementary product includes as parts of the solution additional benefits that augment the core product. Typically, a large part of the supplementary product is comprised of services. The example presents in a graphic this view of any product offering. For the most part, the core product is a commodity, as in the example of Commerce Bancorp. All banks offer deposits, withdrawals, and investments and banking products such as checking and savings accounts, and fixed and variable income securities, and today most banks offer mutual funds. These products comprise the core product for banks. How these products are different from bank to bank is represented in the supplementary components of the total product. Commerce Bancorp offers free checking and money orders and does not compete on its lower interest on its savings accounts and CDs. Thus, Commerce Bancorp differentiates itself on a number of different supplementary benefits to the customer, ranging from the quality of its customer interactions to a number of facilitating services such as bathrooms in its branches. Similarly, most if not all banks have an online presence, but customers at banks like Allfirst Financial can talk with bank personnel via their home personal computer.

The hotel industry is one that grew out of its room-and-board days to a total product offering that today includes a multitude of facilitating services. "Room and board" was the commodity. As all hotels in a certain level, competitors in the same segment, began offering the same set of supplementary services, such as room service, meeting and conference rooms, a swimming pool, a gift shop, personal grooming salon service, business services, cable, or Internet service in each room, these became commodity and part of the core product. By March 2001, 78 precent of all Ritz-Carlton hotels offered highspeed Internet. While only two hotel chains—Omni and Westin hotels—have laptops available for guests, most hotels in that class offer two phone lines. Thus, over time, as competing firms add supplementary services, these previously differentiating value components become a commodity and lose their differentiating ability.

Consider the recent "advances" in the form of supplementary services in the hotel industry. Electronic kiosks can not only check you in with your room key and print your bill at checkout, but can also be an electronic concierge providing a guest with directions or maps to locations of interest. Human butlers are back in the hotel industry. A growing number of hotels at the top end will provide a bath butler to prepare your luxury bath, a technology butler to solve your gadget problems, a private butler to pack your clothes or make your plans.

If you are traveling with a baby or young child, you can find a hotel that offers a room for a nanny and kiddie perks such as baby-sitting, some one to read a bedtime story with live actors, or toys and activities for the child. If you are bringing a pet along, some hotels will even offer you special pet services for a fee! Over time, hotels in the premium category will all be offering some or all of these supplementary features. These features become part of the standard offering and reduce themselves into a commodity for that category of hotels. You can expect that the "technology butler" service will be adopted by hotels for the business traveller segment, briefly providing a differentiating feature only very quickly to become standard fare. In designing superior customer value, a firm must translate customer needs to the specifications of a solution in terms of core and supplementary benefits.

All hotels need not have the same core product. That statement might seem confusing. Consider the Station Inn, in Pennsylvania, between Pittsburgh, and Harrisburg. It sits 125 feet from the railroad tracks. Railroading buffs sleep at the hotel just to see the freight trains, about 60 of them in a space of 24 hours. Same industry as hotels—but a somewhat different core product. Precise definition of a product can only emerge from deep inspection of the "What business are we in?" analysis.

If product differentiation is derived from the enhancement that the supplementary product provides the core benefit, what constitutes supplementary product? Starting with the familiar: customer service is a common supplementary product (sometimes mistaken as the only element in the supplementary product). There are elements of the supplementary product, such as billing and payment that are also common to all firms. They are required to facilitate the core product. These must also be viewed as part of the supplementary product to the extent that they affect customer value. A firm can add to the customer value when its billing and payment process is customer focused or can detract from customer value if it is unpleasant in the customer's experience. Thus, there are some supplementary features that are found in all products that may not necessarily be recognized as such. Services marketing scholar Christopher Lovelock visualized this concept as a flower with petals. Think of the supplementary product as composed of elements of the total value bundle that facilitate and enhance (or detract from) the primary benefit sought in a product. Visualize these elements in three broad categories: facilitating services, quality of customer experience, and brand image.

FACILITATING SERVICES

Facilitating services are all those features of the product and activities of the firm that serve to facilitate the consumption of the core product. All firms have to provide some of these services at some level. Large retailers such as Sears, Walmart, and Lowe's will provide assembly and installation services for a fee and sometimes for no charge.

Table outlines the four broad categories of facilitating services—complementary services, customer education, customer access, and customer service. Customer-focused firms differentiate themselves by excelling in these facilitating services.

Complementary services are those related to the consumption of the core product. Some are almost necessary, like the waiting area in a physician's clinic or parking facilities at a hotel. Passengers on long international flights enjoy a wide range of inflight entertainment activities such as films, TV channels, and even casino-style gambling or electronic shopping and services such as being able to rent a car or book hotel rooms from the technology at their seats. Some complementary services are product differentiators. For example, recognizing that some of its customers were coming in to the bank to conduct their business bringing little children with them, some Wells Fargo branches have a play area with television cartoons, Nintendo, and the like—and even sells toys to children. Washington Mutual offers calculators, pens, and piggy banks for a small fee. To compete for advertising within its *Mutual Funds* magazine for instance, the publisher, Time, Inc. offers its advertising customers anything from primary research and use of its subscriber list to assistance in customizing gifts and promotions to readers or sponsorship featured on special cover-wraps. These are examples of complementary services that help differentiate value created by different providers.

Table: Categories of Supplementary Product

Supplementary Feature	*Description and Examples*	
1.	Facilitating services	
	a. Complementary services	Services that are bundled with the core product such as the insurance feature for purchases made with an American Express card, or services such as free parking that facilitate the consumption of the core product

Supplementary Feature	*Description and Examples*	
	b. Customer education Information	and assistance to the customer, for example, on the use of the product or about customer role in the service interaction
	c. Customer access	Convenient locations and hours of the service such as, for example, a wide variety of customer touch points and 24/7 access to customer service
	d. Customer service	Problem resolution that requires personal attention as in product failures, refunds or special customer situations
2.	Quality	Quality of the product (core and supplementary) as well as the quality of customer interactions—including such things as professionalism, courtesy, understanding and general empathy shown to the customer during all interactions
3.	Brand image	The image of the firm or the brand contributes to the value of the product such as the reputation and status of the firm, as well as any customer relationship benefits that might be accrued as a source of customer value

Only with an intimate understanding of the customer's value chain consumption (and creation) activities can firms begin to see what opportunities there might be to facilitate the consumption of the core product. Sometimes complementary products are outsourced and provided directly to the customer by the supplier, as Wells Fargo did when it invited Starbuck's to open locations at some of its branches. Ultimately, these complementary products ought to be consistent with the positioning strategy for the product. When a complementary feature is offered by all competitors in a particular product category, it becomes a commodity and part of the core product for that category and ceases to be a product differentiator.

Customer education is a form of facilitating service in that it provides information to the customer about the firm or the product in such a way that it facilitates the acquisition and consumption of the product. Instruction manuals and product support via telephone, fax, or the Internet are examples of customer education. Consider what some banks are doing to be more accessible for customers looking for assistance. Tellers and managers are dressed in khakis and casual shirts to appear approachable and friendly. Bank of America has tested concierges in their lobby to help direct customer questions. Home Depot provides free classes on home improvement projects. Once again, the service feature might be a necessary component of the total product, but how it is designed and delivered may be a source of product differentiation.

Customer access has to do with everything that the firm does to make its products available to the customer and to facilitate the acquisition and consumption of the product. The hours of operation and location are a simple example of customer access for a service. The various touch points that are available to the customer to access the services of the firm or to reach someone within the firm would be a measure of the customer access. The methods of billing and payment for the product would relate to access to the product and can be a product differentiator. For example, the convenience of payment by credit card was once a source of competitive advantage. Convenience and ease of use is a critical component of customer value for any product. Services such as financing options are also related to this idea of customer access. If these are not customer-focused, they will fail the customer and the firm.

Customer service is a key facilitating service and includes the commonly understood activity of businesses related to product complaints or failures, product returns, refunds, and such. The accommodation of special requests or adapting to unusual or irregular customer situations would be an example of customer service as well. Poor customer service reduces customer value and risks losing the customer.

QUALITY OF CUSTOMER EXPERIENCE

When the total product provided by all firms contains the same set of facilitating services, the product is not necessarily a commodity. The quality of the service offered remains a source of differentiation and therefore a supplementary feature of the product. Perceived quality enhances, and lack thereof reduces, the value of the core product. For example, even when Internet service is offered by all hotels, the quality of the customer experience with the Internet service is still a differentiator. One hotel may require you to get into a closet, fish out the cables and force you to shape yourself into a yoga pose to hook up those cables to your laptop, while another hotel may offer wireless Internet access from anywhere on the property. All airlines provide seating and, depending on distance and class, also provide meals and entertainment while transporting you from point A to point B. Differentiation in seating can come in legroom and comfort. First-class services can offer six and a half feet of seat length, single seats, pajamas, and privacy partitions between seats. The quality of the entire customer experience is most definitely a source of differentiation. In Chapter 10 we will look in more depth at customers' perception of quality.

Brand image is a supplementary feature of the product in that it adds to customer value. Brand image is the sum total of all the perceptions and attitudes about a brand. The image of the firm in the general media as well as for each individual customer provides a measure of the perceived quality of the product. The reputation of a firm is usually a result of the firm's product and actions. Where there is very little tangible evidence of the product, as in the case of Web-based services, an entire industry of so-called "reputation managers" has emerged. These reputation managers are Web sites that rate the reputation of others! A firm's image is an implicit source of differentiation in the market. Brand image is the ultimate differentiator. When all else can be seen as equal, the brand image captures the essence of the difference in customer value among the alternatives available to the customer.

Firms have to determine what their total product offering is and what it should be. The value bundle of core and supplementary product needs to be designed based on what the customers expect as standard from all providers of a solution in a product category. The supplementary product might also contain features that are sources of differentiation among solution providers reflecting the positioning strategy of the firm. Firms must constantly watch the various solutions that are being offered. Sometimes the threat of competition comes from newer business models. For example, online broker ETrade surprised the banking business when it began to open ATMs with new services. A deep and broad analysis of customer needs could reveal value-creating opportunities.

To determine how best to match the total product as the superior solution to fit customer need, the firm must understand the customer's value chain. This is an integral part of the product concept development of the customer-focused firm. A thorough understanding of the customer needs and the customer value chain will help the firm conceive its product from the customer's point of view. Firms that best relate their own value chain to the buyer's value chain, said Michael Porter, will enjoy a sustainable differentiation strategy.

The value chain is essentially a chain of value-creating and value-consuming activities, where the value created as output from one activity becomes the input to another value-creating activity that in turn creates value as input for another activity, and so on. Thus, any activity can be assessed by the value it creates versus the value it consumes. This is why activity-based costing practices make a lot of sense. As already said the value creating activities *within a firm* are those that contribute to the creation of either the core product or the supplementary product. The value created by these activities is derived by the processing of the productive factors of the firm—its people, facilities, and equipment. There may be assets or value components sourced from external suppliers or intermediaries that contribute toward producing either the core or the supplementary product. Some outsourced services may even be delivered directly to the customer. When any value component of the total product is outsourced, as in the case of a retailer offering customers outsourced financing options for purchases, or airlines outsourcing catering services, there is the obvious issue of quality assurance in the value creation that is outside the control of the firm.

Externally (to the firm) when you relate other firms' value-creation activities into a value chain, you see that the value created by one entity contributes to the value created by the next entity in the value chain. The same idea is referred to by economists, in the context of forecasting, as "derived demand." The demand for a product is dependent on the market for another product, such as aluminum and aircraft sales for example. We know a homeowner who gets a home improvement job done receives (customer) value from the home contractor who in turn is receiving value from the retailer who in turn receives value in the form of products and services from the supplier or manufacturer.

LOOKING FOR CUSTOMER VALUE OPPORTUNITIES

An understanding of the role that the firm's product plays in the customer's value chain could open up value-creating opportunities. A customer-focused firm has a detailed picture of the customer's consumption domain. When a firm views value consumption activities, it can see if there are other value creating opportunities that it can leverage from its assets. The watchmaker Swatch, for example, offers wrist watches with the technology that allows them to function as electronic passes at ski resorts in Switzerland or for public transportation in Finland. Wrist gadgets can now serve not only the function of telling time, but also making phone calls, playing music and videos, browsing the Internet, or sending email.

This example defies categorization of product. What is the product? It is a wallet or a pocketbook, as well as a telephone, a personal stereo, a personal VCR, and an Internet communications device! The exercise of determining what revenue opportunities Swatch's value-creating assets would offer forces a complete redefinition of the product. As we saw the (product) solution is conceived to take advantage of opportunities to meet the needs in the customer's life with the assets that the firm has. Swatch has found a way to provide value to a recreational activity—skiing—and a functional activity—public transportation. It is contributing to the "customer access" components of the ski resort's and public transportation's product. By enabling customer access, information technology provides a whole range of supplementary benefits to a variety of products.

Contrast this with the example of a firm that does not understand the value of complementary product components and the customer's value chain. A customer came out of a movie theater in Kendall Square, Cambridge, and experienced a 40-minute ordeal trying to leave the theater's parking lot. She spent 30 minutes standing in line in frigid weather to pay the $2.50 parking fee and a further 15 minutes to exit the parking lot. When complaining to the management of the movie theater, she asked if she could pay the parking fee as she bought the movie ticket. She was told that the parking lot was owned by a different company and the theater would not take responsibility for the customer's bad experience at the parking lot. In contrast, the airline SAS has been known to provide an annual dinner to taxicab drivers in Stockholm because the SAS management wants the drivers to treat passengers on the way to and from the airport with professional courtesy and respect. Clearly, firms that are customer-focused conceive their product differently from other firms, because of their intimate knowledge of the customer's consumption activities.

Information about the customer's consumption cycle, therefore, is a key prerequisite to exploring the opportunities that might be tapped. As we saw in Chapter 4, an understanding of how the customer actually benefits from the solution and the information of how, when, where, and with whom the customer consumes the product should provide some interesting revelations of what the firm is doing and can be doing in the composition of the total product solution for customers. Thus, Procter & Gamble sends its researchers to homes to observe how people actually use laundry detergent. When Samsung was trying to break into the microwave business in the late 1970s and early 1980s, their design engineers observed homemakers shopping for microwaves at the retail store. You can stay ahead of the curve by offering value through supplementary product that your customer information tells you customers will be willing to pay for. Even if the value-producing feature or activity cannot be priced separately, you may be able to command a premium for your superior customer value. Being customer-focused is critical in identifying opportunities for establishing superiority in customer value.

All decisions about the product and, therefore, the value-creating activities of the firm are based on an understanding of the value-consumption activities of its customers. What are the decisions and what are the issues to be considered in determining the total product by a firm? The three major decisions constituting the product strategy are: the product concept, the operations design, and the value creation and delivery process alredy—displayed. The product concept defines the customer to be served and what value is to be provided. The operations design defines the productive assets of the firm required to create and deliver that value for that customer. Together, the product concept and the operations design define the scope and configuration of the productive assets that can be leveraged to produce the specific customer value that maximizes profits to the firm. The *value creation and delivery process* executes the product concept with the operations design. In developing the product strategy, the firm makes a fundamental decision in answering the question of how the product will be positioned among all potential solutions to the customer's need. This positioning question poses an asset- and market-based decision that comprises two perspectives.

- The *market-based perspective* looks outward at the market and asks what customer needs can be most profitably served by the firm.
- The *asset-based perspective* looks inward, at the firm's assets, and asks what assets of the firm can be most profitably leveraged by the firm.

The market-based perspective drives the product concept and the asset-based perspective drives the operations design. Thus, the initial step in developing product strategy involves two critical analyses. The product concept requires analyses of the various segments in the marketspace, while the operations design requires analyses of the firm's productive factors. These two sets of analyses are essential to determining what value-creating activities the firm should engage in to generate the maximum revenue from its assets.

A market analysis to determine what would be the most profitable segment mix for a configuration of the productive assets of the firm is the foundation for product strategy. First you need to identify the segments and the solutions that are currently available to the segments. The target market selection or the selected market segments to be served can be based on the profitability and size of each segment that the firm's assets are best positioned to serve. Here, a formal comparison of all the current solutions from the customer's perspective is necessary. Based on this analysis, the firm is able to determine what it can provide better than the alternative available to the appropriate target market, thus framing the firm's competitive advantage. Only after such customer needs analysis is it possible to specify what would be the desired customer value in the product offering.

The intended customer value in the product offering can now be translated into a detailed picture of the product concept—what the core and supplementary product ought to be. Remember that the customer value also reflects the customer's implicit assessment of the firm's solution compared to competitive offerings and, indeed, all solutions that are available to customers in the segment. To ensure that the product concept can effectively be superior customer value, the core product should combine the imperatives that have become commodities in the product category with the appropriate features in the supplementary product to reflect superiority in customer value. Thus, the product concept embodies the product differentiation and the superiority in customer value.

The operations design decision rests on how best the assets of the firm can be most profitably leveraged and follows a sequence of questions that pertain to the productive assets and capabilities of the firm and how they should be deployed: What people, facilities, equipment assets are needed to create and deliver the product? Which employees' skills and knowledge would be needed? When and where would specific human capital be needed and for how much time? Similar questions are asked about the facilities and equipment of the firm. Of course, when the asset or resource is not available within the firm, it seeks suppliers or outsources that part of the value creation. Ultimately, the question is what competitive advantage the firm is capable of and how the assets needed should be configured.

The process decisions are about determining the specific activities of the value creation and delivery. The process of making the product and delivering it to the customer must be detailed. The value creation and delivery activities required are set in a specific sequence as discussed in the next chapter. The firm must deliberate on the structure, content, and process of creating and delivering the product to the customer.

No product differentiation from supplementary product can be seen in isolation. If the total benefits from the product are not worth the costs that the customer incurs in acquiring and using the product, the product is likely to fail. The more carefully the firm designs the process with the customer in mind, the more likely the process ensures ease, convenience and quality for the customer. Thus, the customer-focused firm designs the creation and delivery process with the customer's percep tion of benefits and costs in the value consumption process.

Firms must also recognize that since customer value is dynamic, they need to continually monitor and improve this customer value. Ignorance of the need to innovate to sustain competitive advantage is a common mistake committed by the complacent firm. The argument is sometimes made that the firm's priority of customer focus minimizes the attention to innovation. Customer focus and innovation are not contradictory, an either/or strategic decision. Indeed, to be customer-focused would mean that the firm is continually looking for new ways and solutions to meet customer needs—and to be aware that customer needs evolve as well. Now we can know what the firm needs to do to ensure that it is creating and delivering customer-focused value that can be sustained. To sustain superiority in customer value the firm must ensure that management continually assess its market and its assets to ensure that the choice of customer and the value being created and delivered by the firm maximizes the profit goals of the firm. How well is the customer value in the product concept translated to the operations design and the value creation and delivery process? Is the superiority in customer value being executed. The answer lies in the customer's judgment. Customer-focused firms will let the customer decide whether the firm's value creation and delivery is customer-focused.

Continual customer satisfaction assessment information needs to be available for the customer-focused firm to improve by changing the product concept, the operations design, and the value creation and delivery process, or to continually reassess whether its assets and capabilities are being leveraged to realize the maximum profit potential. To ensure customer-focused value creation and delivery, firms must assess customers' perceptions of the benefits they receive as well as the costs incurred by them.

As an ongoing assessment of customer value, firms must continually assess customer needs and customer satisfaction. As customer needs change, the value bundle needs to be reviewed in terms of its product concept, operations design and delivery. An assessment of customer satisfaction presents an opportunity to improve customer value. The smart firm will continually monitor customer satisfaction to understand what customers perceive as the benefits they are getting from product compared to the costs that they incur. Based on customer satisfaction, does the value bundle need to be modified and redesigned? Are the assets and capabilities of the firm being leveraged for maximum sustainable profits? If the expected customer value cannot be delivered with the existing value-creating assets, then the firm has two choices. Either it acquires or outsources the required value-creating assets and capabilities, or it determines that the target market decision needs revisiting.

MANAGING CUSTOMER INTERACTIONS

The process of delivering value is a tricky and detail-rich exercise; it requires careful planning, using techniques such as blueprinting to visualize the entire customer experience. From the customer perspective, some service encounters are critical incidents requiring more attention than others. All service encounters must be staged for a customer-focused experience just as in the production of theater.

Why does Kimberly-Clark manage the discount retailer Costco's inventory of its diapers? The firm has a salesperson live near the Costco headquarters, and a data analyst responsible for overseeing stock at 155 Costco stores in the western United States. Similarly, Procter & Gamble stations 250 people near Wal-mart's headquarters in Bentonville, Arkansas. Large retailers are asking suppliers to more actively manage the movement of products from factory to retail store shelves. P&G estimates that stock-outs amount to 11 percent of an average retailer's annual sales. When firms like Kimberly-Clark pay more attention to how its immediate customers—the retailers—create value to their customers, they demonstrate that they are being customer focused. In fact, the Kimberly-Clark salesperson passed on information on how customers place packages in their shopping cart that played into package design for diapers. Wayne Sanders, chairman and CEO of Kimberly-Clark, attributes this change to the information age.

Prior to the industrial revolution, a service orientation and the individual-to-individual interaction was the predominant mode of competitiveness. Assembly-line production distanced the firm from the customer due to the sheer number of customers and the physical distance between the customers and the firm brought about by the wonders of modern transportation. Manufacturing goods became the engine of individual and collective (national) economic growth. Mechanization far outpaced services and replaced producer-customer interaction, relying instead on intermediary institutions to provide a specialized set of competencies that the producing firm lacked. Businesses lost sight of the customer. Now, information technology has brought this full circle, back to the customer.

We call it the information age because what has changed in our time is that new technology has revolutionized the way information is handled. Another equally significant revolution is the change in the customer's domain. Customers not only have access to more information on products and service offerings, they also have the ability to interact with the providers of products and services in ways not previously possible. Providers can also present enhancements to customer experiences from the functionalities presented by technology. Service providers must, however, also manage customer participation when they utilize technology. When firms take advantage of online marketplaces, it might be necessary to make changes in organizational structure so that value creation and delivery processes are adjusted to the addition of the online delivery. Two key technologies underlie this information age technology phenomenon: the Internet and wireless communications. What customer access to these technologies has done is to bring customer interactions to a new level and to the front and centre in how a firm deals with the customer. These interactions are essentially service encounters with the customer.

Much has been said about the service encounter—customer interactions with the firm. In a way, all customer relationship management (CRM) solutions are basically technology support to ensure that the firm maximizes returns from customers by enabling customer-focused interactions. The service encounter is truly "where the rubber hits the road"—where the prospects of customer loyalty are materialized or lost. It is where promises made in advertising are honored or reneged on, and where expectations of customers are disappointed or met. It is where all the assets of the firm need to be brought to bear. Service encounters with the customers are also laden with the challenges of a product that is produced and consumed in real time, where failures are bound to happen. When the firm designs the value creation process with the customer in mind, it will be prepared for all predictable eventualities. When the service fails, smart firms have smart processes, that recover and learn from the failure. They have service recovery and knowledge management processes in place. As firms compete more and more on services, the management of the customer interaction becomes critical to ensure superiority in customer value. As the core product is a commodity, and most facilitating services approach the commodity state, the competitiveness comes from how the customer is treated by the firm at each and every encounter. This chapter discusses a method for designing the value delivery process with special attention paid to the service encounter and the critical incidents in the value creation and delivery process. A framework for designing the service encounter based on the theatrical metaphor is offered as a way to examine the customer focus of value creation and delivery.

Analyzing customer interactions can be very rewarding. Amazon constantly tracks the reasons for every customer contact. It has made numerous changes to its value creation and delivery process based on customer input. The customer service function at Amazon is considered a research lab for ways to improve the Amazon customer experience. We can turn to the unique characteristics of services to obtain a clear understanding of what is involved in a customer interaction. Something intangible is always exchanged in the interaction (intangibility). Without a customer, there is no interaction and the separation of production and consumption is irrelevant (inseparability). To conduct the interaction, the firm has the resources and infrastructure in place that "perish" when not utilized (perishability). Each interaction is unique (variability). From these characteristics, as we saw in Chapter 3, emerge situations that are challenges and opportunities typical to the service firm. We need to keep these in mind as we design the process of creating and delivering customer value. At the most general level, all customer interactions occur in a certain place (or space), at a certain time, for a certain duration, between certain entities, in a certain manner for a certain purpose. Consider these as ingredients in a customer interaction and categorize them into elements of structure, content, and process. When the customer interaction is mapped onto the consumption activity cycle, the objective of the interaction becomes the driving force behind the design of the interaction in terms of its structure, content, and process.

- Structure relates to who or what entities are involved in the interaction.
- Content relates to the subject, the task, and its significance in the interaction.
- Process relates to the sequence of steps in the interaction.

The primary decisions that would configure the structure of the interaction involve the nature of the interaction—what entity should represent the firm, should the interaction be face-to-face or not, what technology can be utilized, where should it occur, and so forth. As a complementary question about the customer: What entities from the customer's domain are involved in the interaction? Similarly, decisions determining the content of the interaction should centre around the task and include what information should be required in the interaction, what should transpire between the parties, and what value should be created and consumed in the interaction. Decisions about process would include a script of the interaction and the roles of both parties in the interaction. Any of these decisions must be based on the information that the firm has about the customer's consumption cycle and on preferences regarding these dimensions of the interaction. For example, technology may provide the firm with scale economies, but the customer may want to disengage from the script and interact with a person instead. Ultimately, the important question is what value is being created in the interaction.

As we saw earlier the execution of the product concept as the delivery of the product involves a process, a sequence of activities. Therefore, designing the product must necessarily include a design of the delivery process. Lynn Shostack proposed a technique called "blueprinting" to detail the process design in the delivery of services. The service blueprint is a map or flowchart as a visual representation of the process of service delivery. Essentially, the blueprint design is diagramed in three steps. In the first step, all types of customer interactions with the firm are listed. Next, these interactions are arranged in sequence of occurrence. In the final step, processes within the firm that are required to create and provide each customer interaction are mapped. How and what information, materials, facilities and equipment, and people are processed must be included in the service blueprint.

The customer-focused blueprint is one that is designed with the customer in mind. With the activities in the customer's consumption cycle in mind, processes within the firm need to be designed in such a way that the desired value added in the solution is reflected at each and every encounter with the customer. Commerce Bancorp, for example, encourages its employees to make suggestions in streamlining the service delivery process. Commerce Bancorp employees receive a fifty-dollar reward for finding something about a process that does not contribute to customer value and instead is an impediment to serving the customer; the bank immediately adjusts its operations.

Even as a simple representation of the value creation and delivery process, the service blueprint has a variety of important strategic, analytical, and diagnostic uses. In designing the delivery of the product, it can be used to determine the uniqueness of the service process. When compared with competitive blueprints, where and at which points in the process the firm derives its competitive advantage and superiority in customer value become evident. Thus, the service blueprint can be used in a strategic analysis of the differentiating features and benefits of the service delivered by the firm. Only with such comparative analysis of the service blueprint is it possible to ensure that the value creation and delivery processes are commensurate with the superior customer value planned in the product concept and operations design.

The service blueprint has two major dimensions that characterize the nature and scope of the service delivery process: complexity and divergence. The complexity dimension reflects the number of steps or activities in the process. A highly complex service process has a great variety of activities during the series of customer interactions. Some of these activities occur in the front stage and some in the back stage, away from the customer's view. A so-called line of visibility determines what the customer sees or does not see. The customer-focused firm will need to examine everything that the customer sees and experiences to determine whether the service delivery at the service encounter is contributing to or detracting from customer value. The divergence dimension reflects the degree of flexibility at each customer interaction. The greater the divergence, the greater the customization built into the service—the greater the number of options the customer is given to choose from at each interaction. Therefore, supplementary product benefits such as customization must be mapped into the service delivery process. Complexity and divergence decisions will determine the position of the firm's offering compared to competitive offerings. Competitive blueprints can be compared to determine how competitive value bundles differ from each other. It becomes clear that the positioning of each competitive offering is reflected in the service blueprints.

The patient experience is very carefully orchestrated to support the entire concept of the "Shouldice Method." The surgical procedure itself is probably the least sophisticated element of the whole process. The recovery process is more important than the surgery. Every step in the blueprint is designed for a speedy recovery and an overall "enjoyable" experience—despite the anxiety and pain of the surgery. The method is known for a very low recurrence rate and high customer satisfaction. The hospital even has patient reunion parties each year that are sometimes attended by as many as a thousand former patients. For this service, its critical steps are not in the surgical procedure but in in the recovery process and the total customer experience.

All customer interactions depicted in the blueprint are not of equal importance in terms of criticality toward customer value—some are more important to the customer than others. It is imperative that the firm employ its knowledge of customer expectations so that the critical interactions are highlighted for priority when allocating resources of the firm. This is the primary application of the blueprint technique.

Jan Carlson, CEO of the SAS airline, popularized the notion of the "moment of truth" in services. While each customer interaction is a moment of truth, those product features and customer encounters with the firm that are considered critical to the satisfaction of the customer are considered *critical incidents.* The critical incident technique has been applied in the managing of services to understand what can make or break the customer's experience. The method was initially developed for the U.S. Air Force in simulations to help in cockpit design and pilot training.

A simple question to the customer soliciting a verbal description of a typically satisfying and a typically dissatisfying experience with the product and firm would yield valuable information on what might constitute a critical incident. The incidents to which the customer attributes a satisfying or dissatisfying experience are those that are critical to customer satisfaction. When a particular point in the service delivery process keeps recurring in customer descriptions of satisfying and dissatisfying experiences, it becomes clear that it is a critical incident. These incidents can also uncover "failpoints"—points in the process that are especially likely to fail to perform as desired. Some are internal to the firm and cannot be obvious to the customer, while others occur during direct interactions with the customer. For each of these, the design of the process should ensure "fail-safe" methods and have a system recovery process in place. Fail-safe processes require a metric that triggers the recovery processes. Thus, benchmarking the performance at the failpoints is critical to the successful implementation of the product concept and operations design to deliver the desired customer value.

For firms that rely on intermediaries to bring the product to the customer, critical incidents may lie outside the firm's control. Consider, for example, what Handspring, Inc. does to make sure the customers of its products are served well at the retailer. The firm sends its employees from channel marketing posing as customers to retailers such as CompUSA and ensures that its product is stocked and well displayed and that the floor salespeople are presenting the product to the customer in the way Handspring had instructed them to do.

Microsoft hands out a free Casio pocketPC to every sales rep who completes its training. These examples show an awareness that customer interactions at these intermediaries are failpoints and need to be monitored.

Critical incidents help in assigning the appropriate level of resources within the firm. Thus, the service blueprint is useful from a quality control perspective. Customer evaluations of a firm's service can be linked to specific customer encounters in the blueprints and all processes directly affecting or affected by the critical incidents must be monitored for quality. Customer-focused quality control efforts can be focused on critical variables that can be controlled. Service recovery procedures must be designed into the process at these points.

Interactive technologies provided by the information age revolution are now an integral part of the design of the value creation and delivery process. These technologies work through the three primary productive components of customer value – the people, the infrastructure in facilities and equipment, and processes and systems of value creation and delivery. Consider all the ways in which the customer can interact with a firm. Each touch-point can be made by the converging technologies of today. For example, in some interactions the location of either buyer or seller becomes irrelevant. Customers can interact by wireless or wired means, which can be by voice, video, or text, initiated by either party; they are constantly getting cheaper and better in features and functionality. The basic difficulty with any of this newer interactive technology is that the objective and role of the technology can be lost sight of and the technology itself become the focus. The final measure is whether the technology is contributing toward sustainable profits for the firm by improving customer value.

The benefits of interactive technology come in the form of efficiency and efficacy. Efficiency is reflected in increasing productivity and efficacy is reflected in improved customer value. Both of these outcomes contribute to the bottom line of the firm. For a firm competing on service, interactive technology is critical to sustain profits because of what it can do to customer value. Maximize the return from interactive technologies by deploying it at the critical points; prioritized by its customer value-creating power. For example, a common source of dissatisfaction and irritation to the customer is the length of waiting time before being served. Any point in the process where there is likely to be a wait is a potential critical incident requiring the firm's express attention. If there are interactive technologies that can be used to effectively manage the customer in these situations, customer value is not threatened.

All the service components in the total product, being susceptible to the inherent characteristic of being produced and consumed in real time, force customers to the experience of "wait." As we will see in the next chapter, demand and supply need to be matched as closely as possible. To avoid idle capacity, services adopt the queuing (and scheduling) apprcach to processing customers, resulting in a certain amount of wait before the process begins. In multi-stage processes, which many services are, in-process waits are common as well. The problem of course is that no one wants to wait. Customers will wait for a certain amount of time that is reasonable to them as per their expectations. What is reasonable is a very subjective judgment, of course—one that requires analysis of the factors that determine the perception of waits.

Maister's work on the psychological cause and effects of wait suggests a way to reduce the negative consequences where wait is a given.

- Preprocess waits feel longer than in-process waits. Allow the customer to begin the process by completing the first step in the value delivery process.

- Unoccupied waits feel longer. Keep the customer in wait occupied with activities, preferably related to the product or service.
- Uncertain waits feel longer. Keep the customer informed about how long the expected wait is to likely to be.
- Unexplained waits feel longer. Keep the customer informed about why they are having to wait.
- Inequitable waits feel longer. Serve customer based on priority, determined by what is considered just in the ambient society.
- Value of the service. Ensure that the customer value you are providing is clearly superior to any alternative.

The most important common thread through all of these suggestions is that they all have to do with managing the customer perceptions. The firm is better placed if the customer perceptions can be influenced favourably by managing customer role and expectations in the value creation and delivery.

To varying degrees, customers play a role in the production of products and not just in the consumption. Firms that realize this have paid serious attention to how the customer fits in the organization. In services, the role of the customer is abundantly evident. Customers engage in a coproduction role. In services or in the service component of the product, customers are coproducers in self-service configurations. All services as we saw earlier involve some kind of customer participation, as in the case of providing required information to the tax preparer, for example. Even when placing the order with the provider, the customer is essentially contributing to the production of the product by providing input into product specifications. When the customer is interacting with the firm and this interaction has some relevance to the production of the product, by definition we have the customer engaging in coproducing the product.

Service firms instinctively manage the role of the customers in their participation in the service. Restaurants have menus, professors have syllabi, airlines have their method of emplaning passengers according to a certain priority, etc. Sometimes managing customer roles may be in the form of a complementary service. For example, Universal is experimenting with a calming zone adjunct to its roller-coaster rides, for people who need help with coaster-phobia before they get on the ride. UPS and other package delivery firms instinctively accommodate special customer requests as to where their packages should be deposited if the customer is not at the location of delivery.

It is a matter of perspective. If we take the notion of value creation a step further, we could argue that even in the case of packaged goods, the value hasn't really been created to the customer until the customer actually begins to use the product. Value creation and value consumption are both inextricably interwoven into a continuous and overlapping set of activities. This is an important issue in a service orientation. In the case of services, customer interaction is a given. And the firm must include the customer in the design of its operations. The customer-focused firm by always keeping the customer in central view manages the role of the customer in the value creation and the value consumption activities. For example, providing excellent product assembly instructions improves the value created for the customer in an "easy to assemble yourself" product. Conversely, even with a well-engineered product, poor instructions reduce customer value. Recent product innovation studies have shown that some firms are equipping customers with the tools to design and develop their own products, ranging from minor modifications to major new innovations. PTC (formerly Parametric Technology) is a world leader in computer-assisted-design (CAD) technology, whose software solutions bring suppliers and customers together so that a client can use the software during product development to virtually interface with upstream and downstream players.

Ultimately, anything that the firm can do to manage the customer's role in the value creation as well as value consumption process is an imperative for the customer-focused firm. As mentioned earlier, Procter & Gamble is recruiting families to allow a team of their ethnographer-filmmakers to observe their daily routines to get a better sense for how their customers use household products. The actual use situation says a lot about how a product should be designed. It would also be a way to learn how the customers should be instructed in the appropriate use of the product.

How does a firm take a systematic approach to managing the customer? First, the firm identifies all the activities that the customer enacts in the value creation as well as value consumption blueprint. Next, the firm scripts the role for the customer at each activity. Firms then have to determine how best to communicate and educate the customer in playing the appropriate role. Customers' performance of their roles will depend on their ability and inclination to perform those roles. The consumer's ability will depend on consumption skills that the customer's past experience may have provided. The customer's inclination will depend on the personal characteristics of the customer. Familiarity with the service and service provider could affect the ability and the inclination of the customer in the role performance.

In the case of services and the service components of a product, customer role is managed by the service provider. The service provider's production skills and motivation could affect the way in which the service provider manages the customer's role. The service provider's familiarity with the segment and the specific customer will influence the service provider's skills and motivation in managing the customer's role performance. The service provider's production skills are reflected in its operations and customer interaction skills. The personal characteristics of the service provider can affect the service provider's motivation. When designing the service delivery process, it is important that the firm incorporate these factors on the customer's role performance.

CUSTOMER INTERACTION

The essence of customer-focused design of the value delivery process is in the design of the customer interactions that make up the blueprint.

Customer interactions have gone by various names in research on services—service encounters and moments of truth, for example. Designing the customer interaction requires analysis and decisions regarding three of the structural dimensions of the value delivery process: the process itself, the participants, and the physical facilities and equipment. Customer roles have to be defined so that customer participation can be designed into the delivery process as appropriate.

One useful framework that has utility in managing customer interactions is to view service encounters metaphorically as "drama." When firms and customers interact, firms try to put on the best performance—like theater. The firm's *actors* perform their roles for the *audience*, the customer. In any service, there are actors and audiences involved in producing *performances* in a *setting*. For example, restaurant customers are audiences with hosts and waitstaff as actors in the physical setting of the restaurant. Just as in theatrical production, there is a stage (the dining area) and a backstage (the kitchen); there are acts (welcome and seating, appetizers, main course, and dessert), scripts (menu and specials), props, and costumes. Each element is carefully choreographed to produce the intended impression on the audience. Any service provider can examine each of these elements and determine the exact impression that would be appropriate for each customer segment. The "drive-thru" or take-out type of fast-food restaurant confronts different impression management challenges compared to the sit-down type of restaurant.

Different types of services would require a different combination of these theatrical elements for the desired impression. Services rendered at arm's length over the telephone or by mail, such as in investment brokerage services or credit card services, would see these elements differently from the face-to-face setting of hotels or airlines. Internet "clicks" retailers would find a different set of issues compared to the "bricks" retailers. Hybrid retailers have to approach the issues differently for the two different settings.

In some cases, the performance is shared by a number of customers, as in a restaurant or a hotel or airline where customers share many aspects of the firm's productive factors—employees, facilities, and equipment. The setting dictates a shared product, and some aspects of the setting are visible (onstage) to the customer and some are invisible (backstage). Performers or actors (frontline employees) utilize scripts, costumes, and props in their performances. Every feature or theatrical element is carefully choreographed for the intended impression. Therefore, just as in theater, managers can focus on impression management for customer-focused business activities. World-class service firms like Disney employ a service orientation profile (personality and skills) in their hiring; they call their employees the cast and carefully train them in both operations and customer interaction skills. Disney's "guests" are treated in a customer-focused manner evident in the culture, in the way the cast is empowered and motivated to provide customer-focused performances.

What is the type of setting where the customer value is delivered? There could be no interaction necessary with the value provider at certain phases in the consumption cycle, and there could be phases of physical, face-to-face interaction, or electronics-mediated interactions. At each interaction, the value provider must determine the line of visibility between onstage and backstage, what is or should be visible to the customer. What is the process and duration of the various steps in the interaction, and what kinds of orientation must there be for the participants? What is the customer role in each setting, and are there other customers in shared experience? The following table presents the analytical questions based on the theater metaphor to determine whether the value delivery process is customer-focused.

Table: Framing the Customer-Focused Analysis

Role of Theatrical Elements	*Customer-Focused Analysis for Managerial Actions*
Actors – who the actors are and how they play a role in creating the performance for the audiences with their respective scripts	What profile of each employee would What are appropriate criteria in selecting and hiring and training employees? What kinds of scripts are appropriate for each employee? Are the employees motivated to be customer-focused?
Audiences -who the audiences are, their preferences and biases and how they derive value from the various elements in the theatrical production	What is the profile of the appropriate customer? Are the needs of the customers and how the product works in the customer's consumption activity cycle clearly understood?
Setting – the constituent elements of each setting including costumes, props, décor, ambience, etc., and how they create the desired impression for the performance	What is the configuration of the setting? Are all of the tangibles that make up the setting carefully examined for the appropriate value it must add for the customer?
Performances – the various acts and scenes that make up the entire performance and how they create the desired impression for the audience	What are the various steps in the process of serving the customer? Are the acts and scripts customer-focused? Are the actors wellrehearsed and supported for their performances from backstage? Is the customer given the necessary instructions to get the most out of the solution?

Ultimately, all of the theatrical elements need to be carefully directed and choreographed to provide the appropriate impression. *Servicescape* is a term that refers to the immediate physical and social environments containing a service experience, transaction, or event. The servicescape plays a number of different roles such as packaging the value bundle, facilitating the value delivery activities, socializing the employee and the customer, and differentiating the product. Managers must understand which servicescape elements can be controlled for the desired behaviours from both employees and customers.

What is the role of each process in the value creation and delivery as seen by a firm with a customer focus? What should the structure and content of the process include by way of design? What are the critical points in the process for its meeting customer needs and preferences? The firm should have in place metrics and customer-determined benchmarks that will trigger recovery procedures, anticipating that the firm will sometimes fail the customer. Using the theatrical metaphor, any impression that the actor, the audience, the setting, or the performance imparts must be examined and managed by the firm. The focus is on the effect each customer interaction or service encounter has on customer value from the customer's point of view. Customer-focused firms design the value creation and delivery process with the customer in mind.

Value-creating assets are perishable in that when idle they incur costs without generating revenues. Demand and supply management is an imperative for any firm, especially those that produce services or whose products have a significant proportion of service components. Analysis of demand patterns and capacity utilization should drive yield management in a customer-focused firm.

Following the dot-com crash, four-star hotels and other premium services in the hospitality industry found themselves losing business as corporate expense accounts became slim. By mid-2001, in some locations, you could get a room at the Biltmore, the Ritz, and others like the Waldorf-Astoria and the Plaza in New York for less than at such budget hotels as Holiday Inn, Comfort Inn, or Best Western. In the previous year, hotel overbuilding had prompted analysts to warn of lowered revenue from lower prices. The dot-com boom had hotels already committed to expansion. Similarly, key players in the cruise industry, also "over-built" following an ambitious expansion spree, found themselves in a quandary. The number of berths among cruise ships worldwide was scheduled to increase by about 12 percent over a couple of years from the year 2000. Vacations on cruise ships could be had for bargain basement prices. Why are firms better off selling their product for such low prices? If your assets are idle, you are still incurring fixed costs. As long as the variable costs are covered, every additional revenue dollar contributes to the fixed costs and profits as contribution margin. This situation is especially common to service firms and to firms whose assets are being used to provide services directly to the customer. Every firm must continually assess whether its value-creating assets are producing maximum value at minimum costs.

Most firms instinctively reduce capacity during low demand periods and increase capacity during peak periods. The airline industry uses sophisticated methods to get customers committed early so that a certain level of demand is ensured for any given period. The 21-day and 14-day airfares ensure that airlines have a certain amount of capacity filled before prices are raised. Idle capacity is too expensive to carry. Hotels will charge you if you are a no-show and some will charge you a fee for a late checkout. Upscale restaurants, too, will charge for no-shows and require cancellations to be made 24 hours in advance, just as hotels do. Underutilized capacity could be disastrous for any firm, especially for assets that produce services. The hospitality industry is a perfect example of capacity-constrained services that have to address the challenge of perishable revenue opportunity from their productive assets. An important consequence of the inherent characteristics of services and of service components in products is that the product cannot be produced without customer interaction—production and delivery processes of services are idle unless a customer is being served.

For a number of reasons, fluctuating demand is an inevitable fact of life for businesses. There are times when demand exceeds supply and at other times supply exceeds demand. For firms that produce services, the demand-supply mismatch results in situations where revenues and profits are not maximized. Every firm seeks to generate the maximum profits from its assets; this goal requires yield management for long-term profit maximization. The firm needs to manage demand and supply such that it attracts and serves the segment mix that provides the maximum total profitability.

This chapter is about managing demand and supply so as to maximize the returns from value-creating assets. Patronage and capacity of productive assets must be managed for maximum profitability. The pattern of the flow of customers dictates the utilization of the productive factors of the services. Thus, the firm should attempt to smooth peaks and fill valleys of fluctuating demand patterns. The first section is about how to understand the demand patterns and to study the capacity of the value-creating assets. Next, a method for assessment of the revenue-generating utilization of the firm's assets is presented. Finally, ways in which the firm can improve the profitability of its value-creating assets are suggested.

The task for the firm with perishable assets is not just increasing demand, but increasing demand during low-demand periods. The key is in the timing of demand as much as in volume. The task may be more one of shifting rather than building demand. This is a daunting task, especially when the causes for demand patterns may be uncontrollable, such as weather or the school year and other institutionally imposed events such as filing taxes or reporting quarterly earnings. When the demand is predictable and some behaviour can be modified, firms must find a way to shift demand when and where possible. Before you attempt that, you need to have a sense for the profit implications of shifting demand, because the quality of demand is just as, if not more, important than its quantity. Quality of demand refers to how desirable the customers are. A firm should be relentless in making sure that the profitability of the mix of segments making up demand is maximized. Segments are selected to be served based on the long-term profitability of the customer. Therefore, demand management should consider the timing of the demand as well as the profitability of the demand being served at all times.

A measure of how well a firm is doing is the profits generated from its assets. In service firms, this is yield management, plain and simple. Yield management is practiced extensively by airlines and hotels in the service sector, for example, as they seek to maximize the returns from assets by maximizing the utilization of capacity at maximum margins. Customer-focused firms base their yield management techniques of demand and capacity management on their knowledge of the customer behaviour without losing sight of creating and delivering superior customer value and sustaining profits for the long term.

Demand management should aim to manage volume and revenues generated by the firm for maximum long-term profits. Capacity management, at the same time, should aim to minimize the costs of production along with maximizing utilization for maximum profits. When competing through service, the analysis required for customer-focused yield management is discussed. Customer-focused firms will seek to understand customer behaviour to manage customer demand. They will also seek to cost-effectively adapt capacity to the demand level without affecting the customer experience. The objective of yield management is to manage customer behaviour and the capacity utiization of the firm such that returns from assets are maximized.

DEMAND ANALYSIS

Demand analysis is a critical review of the profitability of customers being served at any given time so that demand management methods. Creative financing skills and practices by the firm can provide cost efficiencies in raising capital and purchase conveniences.

Demand analysis begins with detecting and identifying the demand patterns. Are there discernible nonrandom fluctuations in demand? Firms must first establish the cycles of demand in terms of the time frame across which demand fluctuations occur. Take the example of customer call centres. Utilization patterns may reveal that there are peaks and valleys during the day as well as across the days of the week, weeks of the month, and months of the year. By mapping customer interactions over a demand period, firms can identify all of these peaks and valleys in customer demand patterns. Since each time frame has a different pattern of fluctuation, firms must identify when they occur in each time frame. What is the extent of the fluctuation—how high are the peaks and how low are the valleys? Firms might want to focus on those peaks and valleys that display the highest variance from the desired levels of capacity utilization.

As the timing and patterns of the fluctuations are determined, it is also important to establish at which points in the firm customers interact and to identify the utilization patterns at each point of customer interaction. Managers must look at their blueprints and determine the demand patterns, particularly at the failpoints, for all of the appropriate time frames. The variation in significance of the failpoints makes it imperative to prioritize capacity allocation decisions according to their significance in affecting customer value.

It is necessary to identify the customers or the segments that interact at the different times and to determine their prospects for profitability. Different segment-mixes are likely to patronize the services at different times. Further, the proportion of each segment within the total number of customers served at any given time could be different. To enable prioritizing capacity allocation, the size and profitability of each segment need to be examined. The size relates to the volume of revenues received from the customer, whereas profitability includes the revenues as well as the costs associated with serving that customer.

Yield management objectives cannot be met unless the firm understands customer behaviour in interaction patterns over the relevant time frames. Firms must use their understanding of customers to determine what causes the fluctuation in their demand patterns. Why do these patterns occur? What factors affect not just the customers' purchasing patterns but also their consumption patterns? When customers' consumption activities require interaction with the firm, it would require identifying the demand patterns in each interaction activity and its effect on the firm's capacity. This is where customer knowledge is critical. Without an understanding of the customer's purchasing and consumption decisions, it would be impossible to attempt effective demand management. Why do customers in each segment interact with the firm at the times that they do? Can that behaviour be changed and if so, what will change that behaviour? Once that is determined, it becomes apparent that the next question is: Are the costs of changing that behaviour worth the incremental effect it has on total profits? The answers to these questions lead to possible avenues for the firm to explore in its attempt to change customer behaviour.

Capacity analysis complements demand analysis and begins with identifying the processes in the blueprint that relate to each customer interaction. Very simply, the capacity in terms of servable customers for each value-creating process supporting each point of customer interaction needs to be calculated. The firm must identify what productive factors can be profitably adjusted to demand patterns by increasing or reducing capacity without affecting the quality of the customer experience. The alignment of the firm's assets and resources to demand fluctuations will require an analysis of the capacity of the productive factors of the firm.

The productive factors of employees, equipment, and facilities, allocated over a period of time, determine the capacity of a firm. The amount of time that the productive factors are available divided by the average time it takes to serve a customer gives the number of customers that could be served. Since the capacity for a service depends on the various steps in the process, the weakest link in the process, or the bottleneck, determines the capacity of the whole process. Capacity for a multistep process is said to be balanced if all the steps in the process are about equal in the number of customers they can serve in the same amount of time.

As we saw in the previous chapter, not all customer interactions with the firm are likely to be of critical importance in the customer experience. In order to prioritize the attention of capacity management practices, it is important to focus on those customer interactions that are likely to be critical incidents—the failpoints. Next, the cost of the productive factors for the value-creating processes for those critical incidents needs to be ascertained. The key question is: What is the feasibility of stretching or shrinking the productive factors? For each capacity-determining productive factor, an important input into capacity management decisions is how costs and customer value are affected by its shrinking or stretching.

There are several implementation considerations in determining which capacity management practice is appropriate in a situation. For example, what is the minimum capacity at which the firm must operate? The minimum capacity at which a firm must operate takes into account the volume of customers required to cover fixed costs (assuming variable costs are already covered in the pricing). The maximum capacity is, of course, the maximum number of customers that can be served. The optimum level of operation is not at the maximum capacity. Within this minimum-to-maximum range of capacity, there is an optimum capacity level at which both profits and customer satisfaction are maximized. Handling more customers than that could result in deteriorating quality. For example, there is a maximum tolerable waiting time at each interaction for most customers. When wait is inevitable, as we saw in the preceding chapter, there are considerations to be made. The main consideration is how these waits affect customer value. For example, in-process waiting is a less significant contributor to customer dissatisfaction than preprocess waiting. Adjusting capacity requires an analysis of wait time and its effect on customer experience.

Service firms must determine their optimum capacity based on frontline employee-customer ratio, such that quality is not compromised. For example, in airlines, the ratio of airport agents to passengers ranged from 15 to 1 at Continental to 68 to 1 at Southwest. Of course, the ratio should make sense based on the service design. As Southwest does not issue traditional boarding passes, they require fewer ticket agents at the airport. Similarly, frontline-to-customer ratios are commonly used as benchmarks in industries such as health care, education, and the hospitality among others. At every customer interaction point in the value creation and delivery process, firms must judge the desirable ratio of frontline capacity to customers.

Many operations optimization techniques seeking to minimize costs allow firms to ignore customer satisfaction unless specifically built into the algorithm. These yield management techniques ought to be designed and implemented with the primary

The objective for any firm is to maximize the return from its assets. To accomplish this, firms are naturally inclined to garner the most profitable segment of the market for which they are best suited. Firms need also to analyze the profitability of segments being served with the timing of their interactions with the firm. Which type of customer makes the interactions at what point in the demand period/cycle? The firm can then allocate its resources according to that profitability analysis.

It is possible to calculate a yield index to indicate how well a firm is doing in the realization of its profit potential— not revenues, but profits. The difference between the average price actually charged and the cost to serve the customer is the average profit per customer. Multiplying average profit per customer by number of customers should approximate the total profit of the service firm, which can also be seen as, simply, total revenues minus total costs. From an efficiency point of view, actual realized profits should be compared to the maximum potential profit. Equation A depicts this total profitability index as *revenue efficiency* (actual versus maximum possible revenues) minus *cost efficiency* (actual costs versus targeted costs). Since revenue is price times volume, Equation B translates the total revenue efficiency into price efficiency and volume efficiency. *Price efficiency* is the average price charged divided by the maximum price that could have been charged. *Volume efficiency* is the number of customers served compared to the number of customers that could have been served at full (optimum) capacity. The total cost efficiency can be similarly translated in the equation. Target costing, a technique used to determine the lifecycle cost at which a company must produce the product for a customer, would be very useful in ensuring that the profitability of the value produced by the assets is feasible.

If profit efficiency can be seen as price efficiency minus cost efficiency, Equation C reveals that the *yield index* for the firm is the profit efficiency multiplied by the volume efficiency. Equation D suggests that you could calculate these efficiencies for each segment to arrive at the yield index of each segment. Segments with the highest yield are served so that the total lifetime profitability of the segment mix is maximized.

Calculating the profitability efficiencies for different segments would reveal that not all customers cost the same to serve, just as not all customers bring the same revenues. Thus all segments are not equally profitable. Some cost less to serve and some bring more revenues than others. But, there maybe cyclical periods when you need the relatively less profitable customers to help generate revenue from idle capacity, as long as price charged can cover the variable costs and have some profit left over to help cover fixed costs. Firms need to examine the size and profitability of all of the customers/segments that are being served by the firm. Only then can firms pick the segment mix with maximum total profitability across a demand cycle.

They must also get the specific customers to interact with the firm at specific points in the demand cycle according to their profit contribution to the firm. In a hypothetical case : the proportion of the segments in the segment-mix must be such that the firm is maximizing the sale of its most profitable value bundles as well as maximizing serving the most profitable customers. The most profitable customers are gauged by their lifetime value.Thus, if value bundle I is the most profitable product for the firm, the firm should attempt to increase the percentage of this value bundle sold during any given time period. Further, assume that there are two segments A and B in this example. For each value bundle during a given demand period, the firm should maximize the proportion of the high-profitability segment being served.

Any yield management approach seeks to improve price efficiencies or cost efficiencies and at the same time attempts to maintain the demand at optimum levels. This is a challenge because of the inherent trade-off between price and quantity demanded. If you lower price, you could increase volume, but that does not automatically convert to profits because you may have sacrificed revenues and you could be spending more to attract and serve these customers. In other words, when you lower the price, you may improve volume efficiencies but lose price efficiencies and cost efficiencies as well. Therefore, a systematic approach to determine the most effective way to match demand and supply requires simultaneously measuring price, cost, and volume efficiencies.

Productive factors of the process are represented by capacity in the number of customers that can be served by the people, equipment, and facility. With activity-based costing methods, their costs can be assessed against their contribution to customer value. Firms attempt to keep costs down based solely on financial criteria. Indeed, any adjustments to capacity that must be made to keep costs down must be based on their impact on customer value. Consider how some common practices to adjust capacity might effect customer value. Firms attempt to shrink capacity during low periods of demand. Practically speaking there is a limit to this—hotels cannot shrink or expand the number of rooms, for example. But it can close off rooms and other physical facilities and equipment for maintenance and reduce the staff during low periods. Customer-focused managers will consider the impact of these actions on customer value for patrons being served during that period.

During peak periods, firms increase staff and bring all equipment and physical facilities into the operation. When other opportunities to increase capacity are utilized, such as outsourcing, then quality control is the issue that has to be traded off with the cost and volume benefits. Firms may also investigate other customer value opportunities if it can put its value-creating assets to a different use. When the margins are attractive and the value-creating assets during low periods can be reconfigured to produce a different solution, firms might consider acquiring more capacity. In general, capacity management is about expanding capacity during peak times and decreasing it during periods of low demand so that cost and volume efficiencies can be maximized. Demand management involves smoothing the peaks and valleys so that revenue and volume efficiencies are maximized; the most common techniques are pricing and promotions tactics. An important question in this whole exercise is to determine whether the service lends itself to the various capacity management techniques. Ultimately, the customer-focused firm will maintain a caveat in adjusting capacity: how will it affect customer value?

When different segments must inevitably be handled at different times of the demand cycle, an important consideration to be made is availability of alternate segments. For example, Bermuda began targeting younger travellers, under the age of 49, to boost its offseason visitor revenues.

With a resident population only one-tenth the size of the number of annual visitors, Bermuda's local economy depends on tourism. About a third of Bermuda's visitors are passengers on cruise ships. These cruise ship arrivals being seasonal, Bermuda is looking to attract younger vacationers year round instead of just the spring and summer high season. Bermuda used a guarantee to support perceptions of off-season weather—at least 68 degrees or a 10 percent discount in any hotel, dining, shopping, or ground transportation service! Segments can be mixed by their time of use or time of purchase. As a demand management tool, the timing of various consumption process activities such as purchase and use are levers that the firm can use to make its demand more predictable and to manage the utilization of its assets. For example, the time of purchase, use, and cancellation in travel, entertainment, hotels, and conferences, must all be considered in managing demand in service firms and in firms where assets are being used to produce services.

Group business is a savior for the hospitality business. It ensures a large volume of committed demand from one customer—but groups are usually booked far in advance and the price is discounted. The firm has to leave itself the appropriate amount of capacity for the anticipated "full-rated" customers for the same time period to be purchased closer to the time of use. When the anticipated demand is low, firms are forced to look for segments such as trade shows, business conferences, and executive seminars and the like. The Royal Caribbean Cruises positioned one of its new ships as "the first million dollar conference centre at sea." Segments to be served at any given time can be selected based on their lifetime value and their responsiveness or sensitivity to customer value changes.

Managing segments for maximum profitability by shifting demand involves understanding the sensitivity of the segments to the product bundle. Adjustments to the product can change customer value and shift demand. The productive factors can be aligned by the sensitivity of the segments to changes in customer value in such a way as to shift segments to other points in the demand cycle. But first, the firm must understand: What are the service preferences (value), sensitivity to price, and promotion specials? Will changing the customer value by changing either the benefits or costs of the value bundle change customer behaviour or shift demand to low-demand periods?

MODIFYING CUSTOMER BEHAVIOUR

Why do customers perform those interactions when they do? What will it take to change their behaviour to perform those interactions during other times? In other words, what is their behaviour sensitive to? Essentially, this analysis is reflected in a change in customer value. Segments differ in price sensitivity; different segments will switch their interaction times at different price levels. Insofar as customer value is affected by price, pricing is a powerful tool to modify customer behaviour.

Firms can do this with adjustments to the value bundle, by manipulating elements in the supplementary product. Adjustments to benefits and costs as reflected in customer value can be analyzed for its effect on customer behaviour. In how it affects customer value, the amount of customer participation sometimes allows flexible pricing. Automation versus personalized service can be used to provide varying degrees of levels of service to the customer. Customers may choose the technology during peak periods such as in the case of the self-service checkout counters in many stores. Standardized versus tailored versions can be used to shift demand. Different versions of the product with different combinations of features using product bundling are effective demandshifting mechanisms. Firms in some industries do this instinctively without much sophistication while others such as airlines and hotels use very sophisticated methods. Firms that have a good customer understanding are better equipped to adjust customer value without losing superiority among its competitors.

Price promotions are powerful demand-shifting tactics. There are numerous examples of price promotions, from early bird specials to discounts during low periods. The problem with most price promotions is that they are not aligned with demand fluctuations, so that the effect on the customer is random—where the firm is simply hoping to build demand without a sense of timing and how it would affect demand fluctuation patterns. Unless the firm's assets always operate at the same level of capacity, every firm should be offering price promotions to bring in customers during periods when the assets are idle. Anything from customer convenience in payment such as interest-free deferred payment schedules to outright price bargains are common uses of pricing for this purpose.

Customer behaviour can be modified to the benefit of both the customer and firm with customer education on how demand fluctuations can affect their own customer experience. Different industries have different norms in the attempt to inform the customer about peak times so that those customers who would not want to be subjected to long lines and wait times can choose to interact with the firm during lowdemand periods. Most customer service phone lines will inform you of the expected wait times after you are greeted and logged in to their system. When there is an exaggerated peak and valley pattern, firms must find ways to educate customers to move their patronage to a different time or access point to help with the strain on capacity while reducing the risk of a poor customer experience that could be detrimental to customer loyalty and sustainable profits.

Customer lifetime value and customer preferences and priorities can and must be kept in mind when attempting to manage demand by changing customer value. Any type of membership benefits and loyalty programs can be designed to essentially manage demand. The terms of the membership programme need to ensure that the firm is managing the use of its productive resources according to the lifetime value of the mix of customers being served. Any change in customer value with demand and supply management technique should be monitored for its impact on brand loyalty and customers' lifetime value to the firm.

Managers of firms competing on service will find that demand fluctuations are a definite predominant challenge. Demand must be managed by smoothing the demand fluctuations and making capacity adjustments in value-creating assets. The smoothing of demand requires building demand during low and shoulder periods and moving excess demand from the peak times to the low or shoulder demand periods.

When and why do the customers' consumption activities and demand fluctuate as they do? Demand analysis must include an understanding of customer behaviour and the profitability of the various customers and segments being served at different times during a demand period. Thus, their sensitivity to various customer value changes would determine the appropriate demand-shifting actions that the firm might attempt. Capacity management requires a cost-revenue analysis of the productive factors or the value-creating assets. That analysis should focus on capacity utilization. What is the profitability of the value bundle created by capacity (assets) that was being utilized? Are the value-creating assets being used to serve the maximum profitable customer mix at any given time?

Table: Customer-Focused Analysis: Yield Management

Elements for Analysis	*Analytical Questions*
Susceptibility to Fluctuating Demand:	What is the extent of variation in actual demand around the mean level of optimal customer demand levels?
Demand Analysis:	What are the patterns of demand? What is the segment mix in these patterns? Why do they interact when they do? What are the sensitivities of each customer/ segment toward demand management techniques that essentially change customer value? What is the profitability of the customer/segment?

Capacity Analysis: At what points in the blueprint do the customer interactions occur in the blueprint? What is capacity of processes and resource allocation serving each customer interaction? What is the profitability of the value bundle or the contribution of the specific process toward cus tomer value? What should the priority of resource allocation be for the customer interaction processes and productive factors of the firm? What is the elasticity of the capacity for these productive factors?

MANAGING CUSTOMER RELATIONSHIPS

The task of creating and delivering superior customer value must be complemented with the selection of the appropriate customers and the effective management of relationships with those customers. Managing customer relationships should be guided by an understanding of what the customer's equity is to the firm. Customer equity, the value of customer to the firm, improves as superiority in customer value improves. Since customer equity is perhaps the firm's most valuable asset, the firm must continually seek to improve customer value for it best customers. A firm's potential return on customer equity should determine the investment it makes in customers. For its most valuable customers, the firm must guarantee superior service quality and customer service, with special attention to recovering from inevitable product failures when they occur.

Maximizing long-term profitability comes from maximizing customer equity—firms must maximize the lifetime value of the customer, including revenues, referrals as well as costs of serving the customer. Customer acquisition and retention efforts must be guided by the worth of the customer to the firm.

Maytag provides premium service to its premium customers—those who purchase the Neptune line of laundry machines. Neptune customers get a dedicated staff, a separate toll-free number and fast response on service calls. This is an example of the common business practice where firms allocate resources by the profitability and value of the customer. They utilize the opportunity in directly interacting with individual customers to determine customer profitability and allocate assets accordingly. And what are the benefits of the practice of differentiating among your customers?

Broadly referring to the practice as CRM can sometimes defeat its purpose by losing sight of the basic meaning of the term: managing customer relationships. Managing customer relationships would mean actively planning, organizing, directing, and controlling a firm's business relationships with its customers. The term might be "new" in its current usage, but the business practice of managing relationships with customers is certainly not new. What has prompted the increased attention to CRM is new technology: how well firms can practice CRM has been advanced by information technology in the new economy. Technology brings with it the risk of missing the benefits of huge investment costs if used inappropriately, however. The benefits can seem so attractive that the costs are rationalized until the technology fails to deliver. The American Customer Satisfaction Index, a measure of customer attitudes toward about 200 companies from over 30 different industries, has actually shown a decline, while at the same time CRM technology investments had grown about five times. When used with a fundamental understanding of CRM's purpose, the benefits of CRM technology enabling the business practice of managing customer relationships are clearly powerful. Siebel, Peoplesoft, Oracle, and other CRM technologies are really customer information management or customer knowledge management systems. These systems gather data and convert it to knowledge that will help firms in their customer relationship management activities.

The most significant contribution of CRM technology to the practice of business is not the technology itself, of course. It is in what the technology does to the practice of managing customer relationships. Because technology has now made it easy to do all the tasks of gathering and analyzing customer information, firms have been able to discover and realize the incredible benefits in proactively managing customer relationships. For example, Continental Airlines' customer information system allows its staff to mine data on passenger profitability and is also able to suggest remedies and perks for special requests or complaining customers.

Customer benefits from relationships with firms have been conceptualized under three categories: social, psychological, and customization benefits, in a two-part study using interviews and surveys. Financial services such as brokerage and banking are heavy users of CRM technology. Deregulation and information technology have effectively blurred the boundaries between those two once-different financial institutions. They have had a heavy reliance on information because these are primarily knowledge businesses. "Signature"-level customers at Charles Schwab wait no longer than fifteen seconds to reach a customer service person, whereas other customers can wait ten minutes or more. Some banks have coded their customers so that customer service reps can decide on rates and fees depending on the customer's profitability code. Centura Banks rates its customers on a profitability scale of 1 to 5. The most profitable customers get service calls from staff and an annual call from the CEO.

Attrition rate at the bank is down 50 percent in four years, and—more interesting—the percentage of unprofitable customers has gone down from 27 percent to 21 percent. The hospitality industry was able to slash 50 percent of its promotion programs and increase response rates by 20 percent with a good database of response behaviour from its mailing list. CRM systems have provided firms with the data they need to determine the revenues and costs to serve at the individual customer level, allowing firms to prioritize their allocations of value-creating assets and resources to the more profitable customers. According to AMR research, the CRM market grew from $200 milllion to $1.1 billion between 1994 and 1997, and is expected to reach as much as $16 billion—an indication of how much firms want this technology to manage customer relationships. A firm's knowledge about its customers has allowed it to adjust customer value based on the profitability of the individual customer.

Just as with power, information technology has to be used judiciously. Discriminating against less profitable customers can seem unreasonable to all paying customers and could backfire with publicity. AT&T withdrew its minimum usage charges for its basic-plan customers who were unprofitable. GE Capital tried to charge credit-card users who were not accruing a minimum level of interest charges and ended up having to sell its credit card business. When used appropriately at the individual level, information technology can be very rewarding. Capital One's senior vice-president for domestic card operations, Marge Connelly, says, "We look at every single customer contact as an opportunity to make an unprofitable customer more profitable."

CRM systems are not just about profiling customers and loyalty programs. To derive maximum benefits, one must broaden the thinking about CRM technology. The technology should be viewed as knowledge-based systems that seek to prioritize commitment of a firm's assets and resources to the more profitable customers while enhancing the relationships with ALL (right) customers. Pricing may not be the appropriate means to deal with the unprofitable customer. CRM systems give the firm access to information that may reveal other ways to manage the unprofitable customer. *Enabling* the managing of customer relationships is the goal of the CRM system. Managing customer relationships is about selecting, acquiring, retaining, and enhancing relationships with customers by using an intimate knowledge of the customer's consumption domain to maximize the return on the firm's assets. With CRM systems, firms have the knowledge and the technological capability to identify, retain and enhance more desirable customer relationships.

This chapter covers issues regarding which customers to acquire and retain for maximum sustainable profits. How do you assign value to customers and what is involved in that evaluation? Who is the right customer? Who should be in your customer portfolio? Firms look at customers as investments. How do you value these investments? Or, What is the equity of your customers?

SELECTING THE RIGHT CUSTOMER

Markets consist of customers with diverse needs and differences in customer profitability. When serving multiple groups of customers, the goal must be to maximize the profitability of the combination of segments. When different segments are targeted, the firm essentially has a portfolio of customer segments—just as investors have an investment portfolio that maximizes returns at a certain level of risk, firms manage customer portfolios for maximum profits. In other words, this is the selection of customers at any point in time, compared to other segments, from which the firm can generate maximum profits. Firms must attract these most profitable customers and then must establish systems and procedures to retain them.

Most firms serve different segments depending on how the definition of segment is aggregated. The "segment-of-one" used in common business parlance to refer to customization at the individual level is really a maximum disaggregation of a market segment. As we saw in the preceding chapter, most firms facing fluctuating demand and experiencing peak, shoulder and low periods of demand find it inevitable that, at different times, different segments must be served. Of course, each of these segments must have a compatible fit with the overall corporate image as well as a compatible fit with the products, services, employees and other customers. The question is, are they selected based on their combined long term value to the firm?

Most firms forecast the volume and revenues from various segments at certain price points at different times in the purchase cycle. In the typical firm, sales and communications efforts follow these underlying assumptions in pricing and in messages targeting sales prospects. The typical firm then attempts to formalize advertising campaigns to reach as many people as possible in the case of packaged goods. In the case of business-to-business services, the salespeople focus on making a sale. Most firms then struggle to orchestrate all these messages for acquisition of the customer in a coordinated fashion. Much less attention is paid to the retention of the customer. Barring the well-run operation, common business practice for many firms is short-term oriented. On the contrary, a customer-focused firm begins by approaching sales as acquiring the right customer. The customer-focused firm also approaches the acquisition of customers as only the first step in managing the relationships with its customers. Once acquired, the customer must be retained. But, not always retained at any cost—a necessary condition is that the benefits outweigh the costs of acquiring *and* retaining that customer.

Customer-focused firms align all their activities and processes in acquiring and retaining the right customer. They see their value-creating assets as most profitably leveraged by focusing on the most valuable customers. In principle, the value of the customer is determined by contribution to the firm's objectives over the lifetime of the customer.

The right customer is that customer whose inclusion in the firm's target market helps maximize returns on the firm's assets.

A FIRM'S MOST PRECIOUS ASSET—CUSTOMER EQUITY

Ask a manager, "What is your firm's most valuable asset?" Chances are that you will not get the response, "my customers." You will find even fewer firms that actually make an assessment of this value in any real sense. The valuation of the customer is implicit in sales figures—essentially, the revenues generated by customers of the firm. What is the flaw in using sales as a proxy in valuing a firm's customers? Consider this. Two customers with the same cash value of purchases may not be of the same value to the firm. There may be differences in the cost of serving these two customers. The true value of the customer to the firm, or the equity that the firm has in that customer, must include all revenues and also all costs related to that customer, as in financial investments.

A recent framework by a team of researchers defines customer equity as the "total of the discounted lifetime value of all the firm's customers." They articulate three drivers of customer equity: value equity, brand equity, and relationship equity. They define value equity as the objective assessment of the utility of the brand, and value equity is driven by quality, price, and convenience; brand equity as the subjective assessment of the brand above and beyond the perceived value, and brand equity is driven by brand awareness, attitude toward the brand, and corporate ethics; and relationship equity as the tendency of the customer to stick with the brand, and relationship equity is driven by loyalty programs, special recognition and treatment, affinity programs, community-building programs, and knowledge-building programs. Their framework—the customer equity diagnostic—is offered as a way to determine which customers to acquire as well as what will enable their retention.

If we define customer value as the value of the firm or a product as perceived by the customer, customer equity is the converse and refers to the value of the customer to the firm. If the objective is to maximize the returns from your investments—the customer portfolio—you must maximize customer equity. This makes sense because you can maximize sustainable return on assets by maximizing customer equity for the long term. To maximize customer equity, we must be able to measure it. If customer equity is simply the value of a customer to the firm, we can articulate that value in the same way that customers articulate our value to them. Just as customer value is the difference between benefits and costs to the customer, conversely, customer equity is the difference between the benefits and costs to the firm in serving a customer. One team of researchers describes their method of measuring customer equity as follows: "[we] first measure each customer's expected contributions toward offsetting the company's fixed costs over the expected life of that customer. Then we discount the expected contributions to a net present value at the company's target rate of return for marketing investments. Finally, we add together the discounted expected contributions of all current customers." Evident in their metric are the following important points about customer equity:

- It is the sum of the equity of all of a firm's customers.
- It summates the gross contribution of each customer, taking into account benefits as well as costs of serving a customer.
- It includes consideration of future revenues and variable costs from each customer.
- It is a time-discounted present value of future benefits to the firm.

It becomes evident that the customer equity concept when disaggregated to the individual customer level allows us to look at the revenues and costs of serving an individual customer. It helps answer the question, which customer should we serve? The ideal customer to the firm is the one that gives it the maximum long-term customer equity, which theoretically you want as a brand-loyal customer. However, as we will see in the next section, the converse is not true, because not all brandloyal customers provide maximum customer equity.

The concept of brand loyalty is a well-researched topic. The notion of a customer having a lifetime value and the prominence of database systems in managing customers have spawned a renewed interest in relationship marketing. Just making repurchases doesn't make a customer brand loyal. There must be some commitment by the customer to the firm for relational continuity reflecting a positive patronage bias. Not all brand-loyal customers have a positive disposition to the provider—some relationships may be forced because of a lack of choice. Brand loyalty reflects a financial, social, or structural bonding with the customer. Relationship marketing seeks to enhance the mutual benefits from the relationship with the right customer—seeking brand loyalty from the right customer. To determine who the right customer is, we need to understand what benefits the firm expects from an ideal customer.

At the outset, it is clear that the stream of purchases from the brandloyal customer is the primary benefit. In truth, the value of a brand-loyal customer to the firm must go beyond the purchases made over the lifetime of the relationship with that customer. As we know, revenues can be direct and indirect. Direct revenues are all of the customer's purchases, and indirect revenues are the cash value of all of the other benefits the customer accrues to the firm, in the form of direct revenues from referred customers. Costs to serve are drastically reduced, as brand-loyal customers are generally easier to serve. The argument is that as customers get familiar with the firm, its processes and products, customers will require less costly assistance from the firm in purchasing and using the product. Loyal customers may even be able to open up ways in which to reduce the costs of serving the customer. Other benefits of brand loyalty would include product improvement contributions, new product opportunities, ideal sources for market information, and favourable word of mouth. At an overall level, all these benefits add up to a degree of stability and potential growth for the firms. Those brand-loyal customers who are committed in their patronage recognize their benefits from the firm and show commitment in the provider firm.

To select the right customer, the firm must be able to measure the value of the loyal customer from all these benefits as well as the costs of acquiring and retaining that customer. It is not easy to quantify all of these benefits. But it is possible to calculate the direct and indirect revenues from each customer. It is also possible to calculate the acquisition costs and relationship maintenance costs. Information technology has allowed us to obtain that data and made it easy to calculate the lifetime value of a customer.

A commonly used practice inherited from the direct marketing industry experience is called RFM (referring to "recency, frequency, and monetary data")—a method to determine whom to send promotions from among your customers. It takes into account the value of a customer's purchases, how recent they were, and how often they were purchased. As with the danger of any one approach, RFM has been used without much consideration for other important dimensions of the most valuable customer, such as how profitable the customer really is. RFM is therefore not a proxy measure for the lifetime value of a customer. Indeed, if the costs of serving different customers show a variance, then the RFM method could attract the wrong customer. As we know, there are three main factors in calculating the lifetime value of a customer. It is not just a simple product of the value of each purchase and the number of times the customer will purchase the product over that customer's lifetime. The lifetime value of a customer should also include referral value. And, it should include the lifetime costs as well. CRM technology has made it possible to do this, but, how many firms actually use this understanding in how they design and implement their CRM solutions?

Lifetime revenues is the sum of all purchases that the customer will make. An assessment of the progression of purchases over the lifecycle of the customer is a key point to be made here. For instance, consider what a college student's financial lifecycle would mean to a bank. First, it is a savings or checking account with a debit card and perhaps even a credit card. The college student may also be a good candidate for an education loan. Once graduated, this ex-student is now in the market for a car loan, and quite soon a home mortgage. Once other life events such as marriage and children occur, there are more car loans, mortgages, home equity loans, trusts, custody accounts, education loans for children, and associated financial products that a typical family would need. USAA, the life insurance and financial services company, follows marriages, births, and other life events so that it can advise customers on changing needs. Every firm should attempt to develop such a long-term consumption profile for the typical customer in each segment, charting their potential purchases over a lifetime to take into account the life events of the customer—a customer lifecycle analysis. A similar case may be made for business customers based on an assessment of growth potential, so that any B2B firm has to project the growth of its customers and factor that into a lifetime value calculation.

Not all customers become brand loyal. We have seen that superior customer value is a prerequisite for brand loyalty. What percentage of new customers find the firm's customer value to be superior? The lifetime value of a customer must also factor the probability of the acquired customer becoming brand loyal. The probability consideration takes into account that a customer may not be a good fit, that a competitor may have been able to provide a better fit, or that the need situation changed for the customer, such as in the case of relocation of the consuming unit.

LIFETIME COSTS

An activity-based costing approach allows a firm to account for direct costs that the firm incurs in the relationship with a specific customer. Once again, with information technology it is possible, where it makes sense, to attribute marketing and operating costs to individual customers. To obtain the full benefit from CRM investments, it is important to track costs at the individual customer level as well. Costs include acquiring and remarketing to the customer over the lifetime of the customer. Costs also include value creation and delivery costs of serving the customer. Thus, the costs after acquisition include not only the costs of serving the customer, but also relationship maintenance and development costs such as the costs of cross-selling or upselling, called remarketing costs. Once again, as in Equation B, the costs related to the first purchase are separated from that of lifetime purchases so that the probability of repeat purchase is taken into account when calculating lifetime costs.

The indirect revenue of referrals from a loyal customer is an often overlooked aspect of customer equity. The typical CRM solution and database marketing approaches ignore the referral power of a customer in calculating the lifetime value of a customer. Most firms do not even capture this data, partly because it is difficult to obtain information when knowledge systems in a firm are not configured to obtain it. The other reason may be that firms are not proactively looking for referrals from their loyal customers in any systematic way.

How is the value of referrals from a customer calculated? To answer this question requires looking at the process and mechanics of how referrals work. Who provides a referral? Customers who are satisfied and who have a certain degree of loyalty are the ones who are likely to convey favourable messages about a firm and its products and services. A key piece of information needed here is what level of satisfaction a brand-loyal customer needs to have before being likely to refer a customer. The next obvious question is, who receives the referral? Customers are likely to convey this information to family, friends, and colleagues. However, not all who receive the referrals are appropriate customers for the firm. What proportion of the customers who received the referral are good candidates for the firm? Out of the ones that are appropriate for the firm, not all are likely to be suitably influenced by the referral to make the first purchase. Finally, if a purchase is actually made, what proportion of referred customers makes repeat purchases? Those that are moved to try the product may not all turn into loyal customers, but if they do, then their lifetime purchases add to the value of the customer making the initial referral. Equation C reflects these fractional outcomes in the mechanics of calculating referral value.

Maximizing the collective lifetime value of its customers should be the goal in managing customer relations. By increasing the number of customers *and* by increasing the lifetime value of each customer, firms can maximize their long-term profitability. From earlier study it becomes clear that to maximize the lifetime value of customers, you need to:

- Maximize lifetime revenues
- Maximize lifetime referrals
- Minimize lifetime costs

Potential customers in a target market are by definition not yet customers. They may or may not be aware of or inclined to purchase from the firm. Firms have to nurture customers' dispositions to the firm through a number of stages before they can benefit from the loyalty of those customers. The acquisition process of customers could begin at any of the different stages on the road to loyalty. Customers may or not be aware or have an understanding of the features and benefits of the product. If the knowledge of the product is favourable, customers may have a liking or preference for the product. Some customers may even have purchased the product but may not be repeat purchasers, may not be loyal to the product, or may have switched to a competitor. The right customers from any stage need to be moved toward a state of loyalty to the firm and its products. Can CRM technology be configured to capture information about the customer's stage in this process?

Once the appropriate customers are acquired, firms must look for increased usage and frequency, cross-selling opportunities, and trading up to premium versions. Retaining customers requires proactive customer management. If not, as indicated earlier customers are likely to be indifferent to the firm, and a heavy user may become impatient and switch to the competition. Proactive customer management seeks to increase interest in the light user and treat the heavy user with appreciation and respect. Thus, in keeping with equation A the goal of maximizing lifetime revenues is achieved by maximizing the average purchase per year as well as the duration of the customer's relationship with the firm.

Referral customers have very low acquisition costs, since your brandloyal customers did the marketing for you. Following the mechanics of the process of word of mouth, it is clear from equation C that maximizing lifetime referral value requires maximizing the number of referrals from each customer and maximizing the lifetime value of each referred customer. To maximize the number of referrals, one must maximize the drivers of referrals from a customer. In other words, firms must attempt to increase the probability of a customer making a referral of profitable customers. Firms must move loyal customers to become advocates of the firm.

When word of mouth is seen as a powerful customer acquisition tool, firms will find a way to stimulate referrals. Many firms are not proactive in stimulating referrals, assuming simply that "good word of mouth will happen if we do a good job." What must firms do to increase the value from referrals?

First, firms must identify the current and potential advocates of the firm. Firms must proactively look for individuals and organizations that are likely sources of referrals and stimulate and reward them for the right kind of referrals. Satisfied and loyal customers are not the only ones who can stimulate positive word of mouth. There are opinion leaders: such individuals and organizations as consumer reports, firms such as Gartner and Forrester, who might be considered experts in the field, and most important, the general and trade media. Other ambassadors for the firm include players in often overlooked sources such as suppliers, resellers, employees, and other stakeholders such as investors. Community chat rooms on the Web are rich sources of information for the firm about what word of mouth is transpiring among its stakeholders.

Second, firms must attempt to stimulate referrals. Any new customer acquisition activity should record information on how the customer was moved to deal with the firm. When the firm obtains and records this information in the consumption profile of any customer, it is able to use it to calculate the average number of customer referrals made by each current customer of the firm. Customers and advocates with similar profiles need to be approached about playing a referral role. Since some customers may be amenable and others not, firms must explore what it would take to move suitable customers to play an advocate role.

Finally, from Equation C it is also clear that the better the fit between the referred customer and the firm's products, the greater the lifetime referral value. Research has also shown that the customers referred to by satisfied customers tend to be a particularly good fit with the firm and its products and services. The fit is better than with those customers attracted and acquired through marketing messages such as advertisements and coupon mailers. Brand-loyal advocates bring in like-minded customers. To get referrals to actually make a purchase or try the firm's offerings, it is necessary to get some incentives into the hands of the referred customers.

Reducing the costs of acquisition, costs of serving, and the cost of remarketing per customer can increase the lifetime value of a customer. Reducing costs to serve means that you need to be more efficient in the yield from your value-creating assets. We are drawn back to the discussion in Chapter 8 about yield management. Costs to serve per customer is reduced when you increase the cost efficiency or the capacity utilization efficiency. To reduce costs of acquisition and remarketing you need to be more effective in your marketing, both to new and to current customers. CRM technology can be used to continually learn from experience and utilize knowledge to reduce operating and marketing costs at the individual level.

ATTRACTING CUSTOMERS

To maximize the total lifetime value of their customers, firms must proactively manage customer relationships. As seen proactive customer relationship management should seek customer appreciation from the heavy user and attract more interest from light users with better value bundles if they can contribute more in their lifetime value to the firm. This is in contrast to the firm that may have good customer service, for example, but in its reactive mode will leave the light user relatively indifferent to the firm and the heavy user susceptible to a competitor.

Most loyalty programs involve some kind of reward for the continued patronage of their customers. Referred to as frequency marketing, continuity programs, awards or points programs, or simply loyalty programs, the goal of these programs is to market and manage relationships with customers. First instituted by American Airlines in the 1970s to get around government regulation that prevented price competition, now many firms' programs attempt to solidify their relationships with its customers. The rewards or awards, as they are called, may come in the form of free products and services at the firm, or sometimes even free products from other firms. The smart firms impose restrictions on the use of these rewards, so that they are used to increase demand when and where needed. For example, the hospitality industry blocks out certain dates so that the promotions are targeted at different segments to entice customer utilization at low demand periods. The problem is that many of these programs are misguided in design and implementation. One obvious omission is evident when the lifetime calculus is compared to the criteria for the rewards.

The rewards focus on revenues for the most part. That costs are taken into account is not clear at all. A recent *Harvard Business Review* article offers data that would be a surprise for managers who have not considered costs of serving the customer. Brand-loyal customers are not necessarily profitable customers. In their knowledge of their own value and indispensability to the firm, the brand-loyal customer could make costly demands of the firm. The firm, in doling out the goodies along with the product and other business favours, may actually be spending more than it recognizes as costs of serving that customer. The only criterion for these (brand) loyalty programs should be that they should maximize the customer equity for each customer, based on the calculus of lifetime value that we have discussed. To be meaningful and powerful in managing relationships with the right customers, these customer acquisition and loyalty programs must specify the following:

- Objectives of the programme
- Market and customer scope of the programme
- Value for customer scope of the programme
- Impact scope (costs, timing, impact on people, process, physical assets, other customers, publicity opportunities, etc.)

The objectives of the programme need to be stated in the context of customer relationship management. What is the expected value of the programme to the firm? What specifically must the programme accomplish? Perhaps it is to shift demand from peak to low periods, to attract new segments, to get light users to become heavy users, to promote a new product offering, or some other specific objective. Without a known objective, no programme can be assessed on merit.

The next specific decision for customer relationship programs is to specify the customer that the programme is intended for. Often, frequency programs are so loosely formulated that the rewards are earned by the wrong customer. Consider this example of the unfortunate consequence of a poorly guided programme. One Mr. Phillips logged 1.25 million frequent flier miles—about $25,000 worth of airline travel—with an investment of 50 hours of his time and $3,140. Mr. Phillips took advantage of an offer he found on the package of a Healthy Choice frozen entrée: 500 American Airlines miles for every 10 UPCs, with early birds receiving a double count of miles! A Mr. Fisher participated in the same programme and got 12,000 Northwest Airlines Miles.

Even if the airlines got an awfully good financial deal with Healthy Choice, one must ask who the loyalty programme attracts—whether the airlines are in the grocery business or in the airline business. How do their returns from this investment compare with the returns that they would have achieved with programs that targeted the frequent flier instead of the frequent grocery shopper? The objectives of the programme should determine the appropriate segment or customer for the programme. The problem with most programs is that they don't take into account the profitability of the customer. Who should be the target of the programme? Not every customer is right for the firm, as we have seen, nor is every customer right for every programme. The best programme is one that tailors the award to the target customer. Thus, giant supermarket retailer UK-based Tesco mails 100,000 variations of promotions to its loyal customers. Further, some customers may be more costly to retain, while others may be increasing their profitability to the firm. As it is evident that firms need to look at the acquisition costs and retention costs of its customer base when determining the focus of their retention efforts.

The calculus of the lifetime value of a customer is clear in its indication of what needs to be factored into deciding to which customer to target the promotion. Low acquisition costs and low retention costs are realized from your most profitable customers. At the other end are your customers who were costly to acquire and cost you a lot to serve. Given the acquisition costs, the firm must keep a close eye on the customer's cost of retention. If the firm misjudged a customer's lifetime value or committed more resources to the acquisition of the customer than the revenue stream would justify, the firm has to either reduce retention costs or stop serving the customer if possible.

For the chosen customers, the firm needs to decide what they would do to motivate the customer to act. Customer knowledge should indicate what the customer is sensitive to, so that the value of the promotion can be appropriate for the specific customer or segment. The value of the promotion may be in the form of additional product, a complementary service, a straightforward price-break, or a discount for future purchases or a gift, among other things. Software firms are able to use lead customers in beta-tests and other benefits about new and innovative offerings before the rest of the market will find out, giving these B2B customers early mover advantage in their value chains in their industry.

Of course, a projected cost/benefit analysis is a must—what additional revenues have been realized and at what cost? For service firms, and where the programme is about service components, it is imperative that the promotion take into account what it would do to the demand patterns of customers. The last thing you want is for customers to strain your operation if your programme ends up drawing more customers during peak times when you are already at optimum levels of served customers. Any programme must consider the impact on other customers, on the staff, physical assets, and the delivery system or process. For example, a shortage of airline seats infuriates frequent fliers who, as brand-loyal customers, having diligently set aside miles for use on family vacations, find they are not able to use the miles because use of awards is limited to a certain proportion of the volume on each flight and are restricted to certain times and dates. Estimates are that about 10 percent of all miles flown on a carrier can be from people cashing in on these rewards. Does it make sense for frequent flier awards to range from personal digital assistants to designer watches? Are the costs and impact of these awards assessed? Another less obvious criterion is the potential for publicity in a promotion. A promotion that is newsworthy could attract the attention of a large number of potential customers and other stakeholders.

Firms must prioritize the management of customer relationships as a firm-wide imperative. Dell Computer, for example, has a "customer experience council" consisting of senior executives from each division or business line and major function that reports to a corporate vice chairman, no less. The council oversees measurement of several aspects of customer behaviour, including the effectiveness of its loyalty programs. Dell even measures all the costs its customers incur in purchasing and using their products, including such things as shopping, ordering, installing, operating, servicing, and disposing of products. The real value of tracking these revenues and costs over the lifetime value of the customer is that it allows firms to understand their brandloyal customers and anticipate their future needs. Such management practices will be able to deliver benefits to the heavy user to maximize their lifetime value.

The lifetime value of the customer must be calculated for each customer—an assessment of revenues and costs over the lifetime of the customer's relationship with the firm. The investment in acquiring and retaining a customer must be made based on the customer's lifetime value to the firm. A continuous monitoring of up-sell and cross-sell opportunities could increase the lifetime value of the customer. The potential customer equity from each segment or customer should determine the extent of value-creating adjustments to be made in terms of delivery process or product outcome customization in terms of value or other benefits to the customer or in terms of adjusting the price and other costs to the customer. These changes in promotion offerings to acquire a new customer or remarket to a current or inactive customer will impact both costs and revenues and their effect on the lifetime value of the customer will determine subsequent investments in acquiring and retaining customers.

Maximizing customer equity requires maximizing customer satisfaction by providing superior customer value. Ensuring product quality as the key driver of customer satisfaction requires checking the links between the firm's assessment of customer expectations and its ability to translate that assessment into product concept, operations design, and execution.

The doorman greeted the guest as the taxi pulled up to the Windsor Court Hotel, a 324-room hotel in downtown New Orleans, one of 120 independent luxury hotels of Preferred Hotels and Resorts Worldwide. Later, the waiter at the restaurant in the hotel accommodated off-the-menu orders—but the waiters did not make eye-contact with the diners. The guest room did not have the current edition of the Yellow Pages. This guest was one of Richey International's hotel spies, who had just conducted the Preferred test for the hotel. He has determined based on his experience as a customer that this hotel had met 88.5 percent of the Preferred standards, passing the 80 percent minimum. Firms such as Preferred want an unbiased assessment of the quality of their product and hire independent quality assessment firms such as Richey International to do the benchmarking of its hotels.

Chapter 6

Customer Defection Management in Hotels

A customer-focused firm with a good customer defection management system can use customer information to monitor customer interaction incidents and preempt customer defection. Customer service is critical. Firms need to give it strategic importance and take a proactive stance with customer service to obtain its numerous benefits for marketing research, product improvements, and customer recovery.

Why would McDonald's create "customer recovery teams?" Internal company documents posted on the firm's intranet revealed that a whopping 11 percent of the firm's customers are dissatisfied and complain to the management. Consistent with the TARP research, this is only the tip of the proverbial iceberg, since only a small proportion of dissatisfied customers ever bother to complain. What is worse for McDonald's is that their internal documents admitted that nearly 70 percent of the complaining customers were even further dissatisfied with the way their complaints were handled. The crowning irony is in the nature of the complaints. They were about the key feature of the core product in a fast food restaurant—slow service. Other issues affecting customer value included wrong orders, dirty stores and, worst of all, rude and unprofessional employees. Earlier that same year, the University of Michigan's customer satisfaction survey

(ACSI) had ranked McDonald's among the poorest-performing retailers.

In contrast, it is not surprising that this classic Nordstrom story is often quoted to exemplify exceptional service. A lady goes to a Nordstrom store and complains that the tires she bought at the store are no good and demands a refund. The store clerk refunds the customer, without asking a question, what she claims she paid for the tires. What is remarkable about the story is that Nordstrom does not carry car tires!

It is usually customer service that gets the rap when a product fails or when a firm fails its customer. With the advent of online brokerage services, customer service complaints from investors are on the rise. In the first half of 2000, the SEC received 2,803 complaints against online firms. These complaints were mainly about operational and service-related failures, as opposed to sales-practice complaints that were the norm prior to the availability of online brokerages. Public service is notorious for poor customer service. When none of the seven customer service employees at the Massachusetts Bay Transportation Authority (MBTA) acknowledged rude treatment of a customer, the MBTA suspended all seven and officials prepared to install a recording system to monitor service calls. The story broke in the local press when a customer experienced a rude MBTA operator who twice hung up on him when he had called to learn why his train was late. This is an example that is probably not uncommon in public transportation. Employee indifference to customer discomfort in the wake of a product failure is a chronic problem with firms that are not customer focused.

The airline industry is frequently chastised for poor customer service. Northwest Airlines got into some real choppy weather when it badly mishandled customer service during a major snowstorm in the winter of 1999. Thirty planes that landed in Detroit during a storm that deposited 14 inches of snow were in trouble when planes already at the landing gates were not able to leave. Some planes with passengers sat on the tarmac for as much as eight hours. One pilot even phoned the chief executive of Northwest from the cockpit asking for help.

Lousy customer experience almost always brings with it severe consequences to the firm. Firms suffer from the drain of customer defection, and when customers feel they were particularly wronged, firms can also expose themselves to lawsuits. Firms must find a way to be proactive to protect the more profitable customer relationships. This chapter covers an important component of managing customer relationships—retaining customers. Since products, especially the service components of products, are bound to fail customers in different ways, firms are vulnerable to customers switching to other firms. It is therefore important to understand switching behaviour of customers. Customer service in recovering from product failures and making amends to the customer is critical to managing customer defection in the customer-focused firm.

A customer defection management system must be designed into the value creation and delivery process.

WHERE WE FAIL CUSTOMER SERVICE

When products fail, customers are aggrieved and will react. What their actions might be is a function of a number of things that are hard to anticipate. At the extremes of satisfaction and dissatisfaction, customers can react with delight or outrage, conceived to originate from the handling of three basic customer needs: security, justice, and selfesteem. Security is the need to feel unthreatened by physical or economic harm; justice is the need to be fairly treated; and self-esteem is the need to maintain and enhance one's self-image.

In a study of about 300 customers regarding how their customer complaints were handled, researchers found that satisfaction with complaint handling is significantly associated with both trust and commitment that customers have toward the firm. They found that their theoretical framework, based on the concept of "justice, " com-prising distributive, procedural, and interactional elements, were useful in explaining customer assessments of complaint handling by the concerned firms. The researchers found that customers related distributive justice to compensation for financial loss and an apology. Procedural justice they found to be related to aspects of customer convenience and firms' follow-up and accessibility. Interactional justice related to several aspects of (un)fair communication and behaviour such as honesty, empathy, and politeness. These relationships reflect the meaning of the terms in the context of customer service. An important finding of this study is that 65 percent of the complaints were received by customer-contact or frontline employees. Firms that have extensive training for customer-contact employees on how to handle complaints will find these investments in frontline education most worthwhile. Where firms fail customer service is when it is not placed in the larger context of customer acquisition and retention, but instead it is seen in its narrowest context as being necessitated by product failures.

ASSESS CUSTOMER SERVICE BY CUSTOMER RECOVERY

Acquiring the right customers is only the first step in managing customer relationships. A large percentage of new customers—up to 50 percent in some sectors—was found to defect before their third anniversary with an e-commerce site. Once acquired, firms must do everything possible to keep that customer or prevent itself from doing things that force or even allow the customer to switch. When a customer switches to another firm, not only do you lose the remainder of that customer's lifetime value, but you also incur the costs of attracting a new one to replace the lost customer. The costs of serving a customer are high in the initial stages, as the firm sets up procedures for the new customer and becomes familiar with the needs and situations of that customer. As time goes by, the costs of serving that customer go down. To replace a lost customer, the firm has to incur all these costs again before costs to serve the customer go down. So adding the cost of attracting new ones and bringing them to the same level of profitability as the old ones doubles the cost of losing a customer. When you consider the *total cost* to the firm in terms of the opportunity cost of lost customers, it behooves firms to pursue the retaining of customers as a relentless endeavor. The first step in retaining customers is to understand why they would want to switch in the first place.

Most firms have established procedures to recover from product failures. Typically, these customer recovery procedures are a part of customer service, a business function that is generally relegated to the status of a necessary evil. It is typically associated with unpleasant situations like product complaints, product returns and refunds. With the way firms are organized, it might fall upon the customer service department to ensure that these processes are in place and that they work properly. Product-focused firms may be focused on their core product and may view complementary services of the product as customer service. But service is not customer service. As we saw in Chapter 6, facilitating services such as customer service is just one of the various services that a firm might offer its customers as part of the total solution.

The customer service function is a significant factor in the efforts to retain customers. Firms may see it as a function to handle customers' special requests or complaints. However, customer service from a customer's point of view is more broadly defined than from the firm's point of view. Some scholars have defined customer service as all customer interactions that enhance the core product other than proactive selling. Even in its narrowest definition, customer service as complaint management is very beneficial for the firm. Not only does it provide the mechanism to make amends to the customer for a botched job, it also provides information to the firm for service design improvements. When the firm goes out of its way to compensate the customer for its failures, it creates an opportunity to obtain a lifelong customer.

Traditionally designed for complaint handling and refund/exchange for product returns, customer service as a function serves other important uses. If one takes the perspective that customer service is at the tactical level of customer retention, there is a very important by-product from these customer retention efforts. It can be a powerful research source to obtain information on the customer and on customer value delivered by the firm. This information can be used as input for product and service design improvements. We know that that the customer service process and what many firms struggle to do with it. The customer complaint management process discussed is generalized for any firm. When a customer complaint is received by the front line in any firm, it is important to take the approach that a dissatisfied customer is an opportunity—an opportunity to alleviate the customer distress and compensate for it in such a way that the customer is impressed with the service recovery and is satisfied with the process. A first step in the whole process of customer service is to acknowledge and apologize to the customer. If the customer is in the presence of other customers, it is important to isolate the complaining customer so as not to disrupt the service delivery process for other customers. Let the unhappy customer vent and explain the nature of the product failure. Fully document the customer's complaint and explore the likely actions that the firm and the customer may have committed to cause the unfortunate situation.

Customer-focused firms will want to gain as much information as possible about the situation and to indicate to the customer that the firm is taking the problem seriously. A commitment to customer satisfaction from a customer-focused firm is also evident in the firm asking the customer for suggestions on how the customer may be compensated and how the product and service may be improved for other customers in the future. The firm then initiates remedial action and promises to rectify the situation for the customer and make product and process improvements such that it will not happen again. Finally, it is important that the firm follow through with its promises and follow up with the customer to ensure that the recovery process met with the customer's satisfaction. It is also a powerful message to the customer if the firm is able to inform the customer about what it has done to prevent such product failures from happening again. Such would be the case when the product failure has indicated a systemic problem with the firm's operation. An important outcome of this whole customer service process is that valuable information has been obtained, recorded, and utilized for permanent product and service improvements to improve customer value created and delivered by the firm.

The TARP study concluded that only 4 percent of dissatisfied customers complain; dissatisfied customers share their story with about 9 or 10 other people. If a complaint is satisfactorily handled, about 70 percent of them will continue to do business with the firm, and if resolved quickly, this figure goes up to 95 percent and they will tell about 5 people about their fair treatment. Thus, it is safe to say that what the firm does in its complaint handling has serious consequences for customer equity. Many firms seem to offer customers avenues to provide feedback. The customer-focused firm will even proactively encourage customers to complain. The Bank of New Zealand, for example, has complaint procedure brochures available at every teller window that show the customer what to do step-by-step if they need to complain. There are instructions on who to call or write to if the problem is not resolved at the first service encounter. If not resolved by senior management, it lists the address and phone number of the CEO for good measure!

Customers will act when they are emotionally charged, either because of the importance of the solution to their need situation or because of the degree of their dissatisfaction. If the product failure was avoidable, customers are more likely to act. Customer action may be in the form of a customer complaint or defection without complaint. The recovery is likely to be effective if the firm has provided the frontline personnel dealing with the complaint or customer action with the appropriate skills and motivation. Effective recovery requires customer knowledge and freedom to exercise the discretion they require to satisfy the complaining customer and remedy the consequences of the product failure. Customers are likely to forgive the product failure if the firm demonstrated a customer-caring attitude in its handling of the complaint and if the recovery options offered the customer were appropriate. Nevertheless, preventing dissatisfied customers from defecting to a competitor is a challenge.

Why do customers switch? A study of 526 responses covering 45 different service industries, using the critical incident technique to explore the question, found eight main reasons for customer switching behaviour. These were categorized under price, inconvenience, core product failures, service encounter failures, failed employee responses to service failures, competitive issues, ethical problems, and involuntary factors. The study found that even satisfied customers switch providers for reasons such as price, competitive issues, convenience, or access. The bottom line is that managers need to develop customer retention strategies or customer defection management programs to preempt customer switching, and to minimize or eliminate systemic reasons for customer switching behaviour. They need to understand why their customers switch. Firms need to be able to identify those customers who are at risk of switching. It is imperative that they set up alerts and remedial mechanisms to reach those customers to prevent them from switching to a competitor. Ensuring a high retention rate must be a treated as a constant endeavor for the customer-focused management. Striving to sustain long-term profitability means ensuring a stable and growing customer base. Growing the customer base by targeting the right customer is only the start of customer relationship. Enhancing the value of each customer to the firm presumes that the customer is retained by the firm. Retaining the customer base requires a close monitoring of how each customer is feeling and behaving in terms of product purchase and consumption. The defection management system should comprise of a means

- To assess customer value changes so that it can alert the firm about the possibility of customer defections,
- To assess the extent of long-term revenues at risk, and
- To determine and execute the appropriate recovery methods for each type of customer.

Customers switch when the customer value they receive at the individual or segment level is inferior to an alternative. Thus, it is necessary to conduct a continual assessment of customer value as the critical first step. Failpoint data on customer experiences is a metric that could serve as a barometer for customer value changes. Customers who have experienced the service when failpoints have failed are at risk of switching. The firm has failed to deliver the expected customer value for these customers. Customer defection management is proactive—its purpose is to identify customers who are at risk of switching and to initiate an assessment of the status of customer value to the firm, followed by an analysis to determine how to increase customer value to those customers. One of the functionalities required in a good customer knowledge system is to alert its users when there might be a problem with a customer, and to provide the information necessary to rectify that problem. Customer defection management begins with designing into the customer information system alerts that are triggered by customer switching indicators. These alerts can be based on thumb rules suggested by the information on successful and unsuccessful customer recovery captured and stored. Thus, any time there is a change in the customer's situation, a thumb rule-based trigger sets off a defection alert that indicates the customer is at risk of switching.

As we saw earlier, customers switch for a number of reasons. Customer-focused firms with good customer information systems would have identified reasons for switching behaviour in their customer base. Causes of switching behaviour can be grouped into firm-induced reasons or environmentally induced reasons. Firm-induced reasons are really customer value changes that could be from price changes, product failures, service encounter failures, or problem resolution failures. Environmentally induced reasons can be those that are customer life events. For the individual consumer it could be events such as change in professional or marital status, income changes, relocation, or change in lifestyle—or in other words, change in need situation in general. For the business customer it could be change in value creation and therefore consumption of productive factors or change in value creation processes, including change in the buying centre, a change in the buying process or criteria, or individuals making the buying decision. Environmentally induced reasons could also include competitor actions that have changed the relative worth of customer value in the firm-such as a price change or a product feature change by a competitor making the firm's own customer value less attractive than the competitor's promise of customer value. Legal, social, or technological factors in the environment could also result in customer switching. Wherever possible, the firm must attempt to integrate alerts into the customer knowledge for system for when any firm-induced or environmentally induced changes occur portending a negative change in customer value.

Once a defection alert is activated, whether related to a specific customer encounter or not, the firm initiates an analysis of whether the customer is in fact at risk of switching. If the customer is at risk, the firm must now determine if this customer is worth the effort, so to speak. If the loss in customer equity outweighs the retention costs, then the firm must attempt to employ the means necessary to alleviate the switching triggers. Incidentally, this thumb rule could apply at the segment level or to a specific customer. When the switching triggers are related to a specific encounter with a customer, it usually involves a critical incident, a product failure of some kind. Either the core product has failed or there was a service encounter failure or a failure to resolve a problem for the customer. For any of these reasons, a service recovery procedure needs to be in place to retain the customer. Customer-focused firms should consider it a functional requirement from investments made in any CRM technology that it is able to power a rich recovery database. The recovery database should yield costs and benefits of the various recovery options for this particular customer either based on segmentspecific information or information related to this specific customer.

A recovery database is utilized to determine possible recovery programs, where specific retention options are assessed along with customer input. Once the retention plan is selected and implemented, it needs to be assessed for effectiveness and employed until the point where customer equity does not exceed retention costs. The recovery database must consist of all the information regarding customer switching behaviour and recovery successes as well as failures. Customer switching behaviour information should contain the reasons for customer switching obtained from customer satisfaction surveys, from exit interviews, and from customer research in general. All methods of recovery that have been tried need to be recorded for their effectiveness. A matrix developed to record what recovery procedures worked and didn't work for each switching trigger should determine a recommended retention programme. To accomplish this, retention reports from each customer recovery experience will need to be recorded, analyzed, and stored in the recovery database. The analysis would deal with the costs of the retention programme and the effectiveness assessment of the programme. Each customer switching trigger needs to be calibrated so that when a segment or customer is at risk the defection alert will move the firm to act with its recovery procedure. A well-planned customer recovery procedure is crucial to a sound customer defection management system. Customer service is considerably enhanced by such a knowledge-based decision support system.

Corporate strategy is about core competencies being leveraged to meet corporate goals. When analyzed into its parts, corporate strategy is about how the core competencies are leveraged in the operations and marketing strategies. Customer service is lost in the shuffle and usually ends up in neither strategy, primarily as a consequence of misplaced definition. Customer service has its unfortunate connotations because of its history and original intent as a business function, and the label does it a tremendous disservice.

Customer service is where most of the interactions with the customers occur for a manufacturing firm, whereas for a service firm not all customer interactions need be customer service. There are interactions whose task is the value creation and delivery of the core product. If firms find that customer service is where most of the customer interactions occur, then customer service should be the most crucial business function for the firm in managing customer relationships. Wherever there is a customer interaction, there is an opportunity to gather information about the customer and how the product meets the customer's needs. The knowledge of the customer's experience with the product in a customer database, if properly utilized, could serve to improve the product. With improved quality and customer value, customer loyalty is nurtured. With the knowledge about specific customers, firms can become intimately familiar with specific preferences of each customer, allowing for customization where possible. Customers can also provide knowledge about how the firm is doing compared to the competition in the customer's eyes. They provide an access to market information not otherwise possible. Firms develop market competence in understanding their competitive advantage and seek the loyalty of the customer by employing this knowledge. As summarized earlier, any manager should be able to look at the good sense in incorporating customer service in the overarching task of managing customer interactions and customer relationships.

Generally, in firms that are not customer focused, customer service has not transcended its image of a necessary evil involving a firm's obligations to take care of the annoyance of product failures. Customer-focused firms elevate customer service to a strategic level by placing it in the context of customer retention and giving it the prominence in the firm that it deserves, alongside customer acquisition, an integral part of customer relationship management.

Elevating the status of customer service function within the firm to a strategic level requires senior managers to practice and perform customer service as well. MBNA requires its senior management to handle four hours of customer service phone calls each month. Folklore in Freeport Maine has it that the founder of L.L. Bean had piped in customer service phone calls to his home! The customer-focused firm makes customer service the responsibility of everyone in the firm. Ritz-Carlton says to its employees, if you are the one to receive a customer complaint, you own it—follow that complaint's resolution process to its conclusion. It is a good practice to regularly involve the backstage personnel in handling customer service. Firms need to construct integrated knowledge management systems that obtain and utilize information from customer service experiences to improve the design and delivery of its value-creating processes. All customer touchpoints in the firm need to be involved in the planning and control functions of the product and service design and delivery.

The customer-focused firm needs to have several things in place to be able to implement a strong retention programme. It needs to have a rich recovery database, the processes to implement the retention programme and the people appropriately trained in recovery procedures. As we will see later, the best-designed processes will not work unless the people involved in the execution of these processes are empowered not only with the knowledge, support, and skills but the motivation and inclination in a customer-focused climate.

Operationally, retention programs and the actual customer service activities must prioritize attention for its most valuable (customers) relationships so that all assets of the firm are dedicated at all times to maximum long-term profitability. The problem is that not all firms are proactive in their management of customer relationships. As a result, customer defections go unnoticed and customer service is the only desk at the firm that handles a customer defect risk. Customer service as an operation of the firm needs to be viewed as within the scope of customer relationship management. It should participate in the firm's retention activities with a much broader scope and higher status. A key consideration is what status the firm has given its customer service function.

Customer-focused quality, when combined with customer-focused productivity, ensures that the firm views operations with a customer focus for an outside-in view of the firm. Productivity is defined differently—not in quantity of customers handled but in quality of their lifetime value. Customer service productivity should not be measured by how many complaints were handled in a certain amount of time, but in terms of how effective it was in retaining customer equity. Costs and efficiencies are measured in terms of customer lifetime value.

A short-term orientation is discarded in favour of acquiring and retaining the more profitable customers for the long term. Short-term losses in a customer relationship are accepted if the long-term relationship with that customer will yield large and sustained profits over the duration of the relationship with that customer.

No customer-focused management decision can be executed without the appropriate customer-focused culture within the firm. The people in a firm, its managers and employees, should be provided with a customer-focused environment. The commitment begins with the CEO. The task of creating and delivering superior customer value must be complemented with the selection of the appropriate employees and the effective management of relationships with those employees. Employee equity, the value of the employee to the firm, should be linked to customer value by valuing an employee based on the individual's contribution to customer value and sustainable profits.

Strategies and tactics that are discussed from the customer-focused perspective are not deliverable unless there is the right kind of environment within the firm. Ultimately, for all of this to work, the people and indeed the corporate culture need to be customer focused and service oriented.

John Chambers runs CISCO Systems, one of the most successful among the largest firms in the world. Rated among the top firms as a "most admired company" and "best company to work for, " by *Fortune* and *Financial Times*, Cisco has grown to over 35,000 employees from about 3,000 when Chambers assumed leadership in 1995. During the same time, sales increased from $2 billion to $22 billion in fiscal 2001. When asked about how he manages growth, Chambers ranked "make your customers the centre of your culture" at the top of his list. To demonstrate the CEO's focus on the customer, Chambers regularly reviews customer satisfaction data and has a daily critical list of customers for whom the firm's products are in jeopardy of failure. He has access to a customer knowledge system that allows him, as he says, to explode critical information on each customer. Chambers focuses on recruiting, developing, and retaining the leadership team that can implement his customer-focused strategy. He ties manager and employee compensation to customer satisfaction.

Over and over again, it is very clear that the successful firm focuses on its people and ensures that new hires fit its corporate culture.

Southwest Airlines' director of field employment says: "We hire for attitude and train for skill." Candidates are put through a rigorous interview process, taking as much as six weeks sometimes. After that, the training period rejects 20 percent of the new hires because they don't fit into the corporate culture. Like CISCO, Southwest has a culture of teamwork and cooperation.

This final chapter is about the glue that keeps the entire firm collectively focused on the customer and on delivering a service-oriented customer value that is superior to the competition. Each chapter in this book thus far has outlined and discussed the critical business decisions and processes in the customer-focused firm. The success of the firm in executing and delivering on the goal is predicated upon the ability of its people, managers and workers, to make it happen. Without the employees, workers, and managers, individually and collectively sharing and believing in a cohesive culture or climate conducive to performing as a customer-focused firm, none of what has been covered in this book would have any meaning.

The CEO sets the tone for the climate within a firm. Senior managers take their cue from the CEO. You can tell how strong the culture is by observing how senior managers refer to their CEO. If you have had the opportunity to hear or watch Jeff Bezos, CEO of Amazon, you will have noted his playful nature and "we can make it" attitude. This attitude is also evident in how the people in his firm approach their tasks. Another CEO credited for his firm's customer-focused culture is Fred Smith, of FedEx, who says: "Customer satisfaction begins with employee satisfaction." Lou Gerstner talked about changing IBM's culture as critical to competing in the information age. By most accounts, he appears to have succeeded. GE's Jack Welch, one of the great CEOs of our time, talked about shared values as critical to realizing his vision. If the culture is not customer focused, the firm cannot be customer focused. The German ERP software company SAP almost disappeared into oblivion until its CEO, Hasso Plattner, who founded the company around an engineering-focused corporate culture, began to heed customers who had been asking for changes in the way its product was configured and were demanding a Web-enabled interface for the product. When CEOs who have been successful in getting a firm to the top or keeping the firm at the top of their industry are asked about how they did it, there is always some mention of the attention they gave to the culture of the firm.

The importance of culture in the performance of a firm comes to the fore following mergers and acquisitions. In a survey of 1,200 adults, Andersen Consulting (now called Accenture) reported that customers of recently merged firms compared to other customers in the three telecom sector players—cable companies, Internet service providers, and phone companies—felt that service was worsening. The telecom industry had been and is still going through some pretty significant series of takeovers, mergers, and consolidations, causing the customers, even the goldplated and special ones, to suffer from lack of customer focus. CEOs who have been successful in leading a firm through a merger are likely very good at also shaping cultures. Such CEOs are much sought after and financially well rewarded by firms going through dissolution, turnaround, consolidation, acquisition, a merger, or some other form of asset reorganization. The clash of cultures is perhaps the most important challenge for this CEO.It takes a capable CEO who understands the importance of corporate culture and renders it prominent attention to successfully lead and shape the culture of the firm.

To ensure a customer-focused culture, the CEO must commit his attention to it. Fleet bank CEO Chad Gifford pledged $75 million in 2002 "to improve the overall customer experience, " recognizing the severity of the customer service problems it had after its merger with BankBoston. Through a number of mergers, Bank of America's CEO, Kenneth Lewis, said he has been insistent on "one culture" and feels that he has succeeded in bringing the previously disparate entities with their respective cultures into one single culture. A major cornerstone of his efforts was the six-sigma programme and the "Spirit to Serve" customer service training at the bank. As of this writing the jury is still out on how successful Carly Fiorina, CEO of Hewlett Packard, is with her reorganization and change, involving everything from strategy, structure, and culture to compensation, following their controversial merger with Compaq in 2002. It had only been a few short years since Compaq itself had acquired Digital Equipment Corp. Even Wall Street has not been kind to its darling, HP. The challenge is tremendous and the rewards are huge. The task of shaping culture is perhaps the most important and fundamental challenge for any CEO. For a successful corporate culture that emphasizes a focus on the customer, the commitment has to begin at the top and be reflected in how the CEO runs the shop.

How an organization behaves depends on what Peter Drucker calls its "theory of the business." He says that the assumptions that a firm makes about its markets, about its technology, and about the strengths and weaknesses of the firm are what define its behaviour. He draws evidence from IBM creating the computer industry in the 1950s, Apple bringing personal computers to the household in the 1980s, and GM inventing lifestyle segmentation in the 1990s. These companies had the right theory of their business because the assumptions they made about the world around them were the right ones. The characteristics that define a customer-focused firm align closely with the assumptions that Drucker is talking about. Drucker's three assumptions centre around markets, technology, and firm. In customer-focused management terms, these relate directly to customers and to the firm's value-creating assets. Firms must understand their customers and be open-minded about the technology of the value creation and delivery in their business to leverage its core competencies toward superior customer value.

The strategic decision making process begins with assessments of markets and firm to determine the customer value that can be created profitably from its productive assets. These assessments serve to define the customer in terms of consumption activities and to define the solution or value bundle it will provide the customer through the core and supplementary product. Value-creating and delivery processes are designed according to these definitions of customer and product. What follows from the definition and analysis of the customer is the estimate of the lifetime value of all customers or more appropriately the long-term profits of the firm. In parallel, the product definition will guide the asset and resource allocation toward the more profitable products. Firms seek to maximize the value to the firm by serving the most profitable customers with the most profitable value bundle that can be produced with its assets.

The strategic decision-making process incorporates a customer focus to guide value creation and delivery decisions. As developed and emphasized throughout this book, the principles of customer-focused management are the following:

- Obtaining and utilizing information about customers, especially with respect to their consumption cycle
- Designing value creation and delivery strategy and processes that are based on that customer knowledge
- Implementing the strategy and processes that provide superior value to customers so as to meet the firm's goals

To make any of this work, the entire firm has to get behind believing in these principles of customer-focused management. To become customer focused, the firm must really change the way it thinks and behaves, such that the customer is always the centre of the value creation and delivery. The firm must have in place the appropriate people with the appropriate attitude. When the goals, structures, processes, and rewards are also in place, the culture and climate should follow for the firm to become customer focused. Two underlying fundamental concepts defining organizational behaviour become evident here in the processes and people requirement: organizational structure and corporate culture. *Organizational structure* refers to how firms define the roles and relationships between the various functions or processes and the individuals responsible for and given the authority to fulfill them. *Corporate culture* refers to the values and beliefs held in the firm that dictate how the firm operates.

Value creating and delivering processes may be designed so that firms can be customer focused. But if the culture does not provide the climate, the firm cannot be customer focused. Just about everything in the firm from the office and building design to social hours can affect the culture of the firm. Nokia, the wireless devices giant from Finland, went so far as to instruct its building designers to design and construct an environment where individuals are immersed in the corporate culture and can interact with the company and fellow employees on a variety of levels. Notice the company's slogan: "Connecting People." Citibank has "pulse lunches" at its banks where managers have a weekly lunch with employees and listen to their concerns and then act on them. These are two examples of how climate can be created for the firm to be customer focused.

ORGANIZATIONAL DESIGN

For the value creating and delivering process to be customer focused as intended, the organization design should follow the way that people who execute the processes need to relate to each other. Traditional organizational structure may not be designed for a customer-focused operation. McKinsey introduced the notion of the "horizontal corporation" in 1996, citing examples of firms that had reorganized around natural workflows rather than conventional functional areas. What is interesting about the principles behind their horizontal organization model is that most of them would translate very well to the customer-focused firm. Among other things, such firms, they say, must focus externally on the customer and realign organizational roles and resources around the processes that deliver customer value. They offered the following as evidence of the benefits of reorganizing into a horizontal corporation.

- A division within Motorola reduced cycle time by 80 percent and late supplier deliveries by 30 percent.
- A GE production facility improved productivity by 50 percent, reduced manufacturing cycle from three

weeks to three days, and customer complaints from 2 to 0.2 percent.

- Ford's customer service division increased productivity by 20 percent and improved customer satisfaction performance by 20 percent to 60 percent.
- Saab Aircraft reduced lead times by 50 percent, value-added costs by 20 percent, and customer complaints by 70 percent.

The point to be made with these examples is that the benefits from an organizational structure that is designed to focus on the customer can be very powerful. A structure that integrates both suppliers and customers and is conducive to a focus on creating and delivering customer value is a prerequisite for customer-focused strategies to work. An interesting support to the logic of making radical changes to the traditional functional, geographic, or product-based forms of organizational structure can be drawn from the following example. The manufacturing chief at Rowe Furniture in Salem, Virginia, disassembled the assembly line and allowed the factory workers to figure out their own processes to get the furniture built. The result? The shop floor seemed to be crazed, but productivity and quality went up dramatically! Organizational structure and design including such things as hierarchy, power structure, and decision making and hiring, training, and rewarding are critical to ensure that the firm is customer-focused.

Organizational design can take various forms depending on the value creation and delivery process. With the recent revolutionary advances in information technology, newer forms are becoming evident. In what is also referred to as the knowledge economy, virtual organizations are commonplace today. A new model has emerged where organizations draw knowledge-based assets from entities outside the firm to create and deliver value to the customer. Clearly, information technology plays the crucial pivotal role in making this possible. Scholars have suggested that in such a virtual organization, three vectors—customer interaction, asset sourcing, and knowledge leverage—are the key components in the strategy and structure of the successful business model. The organization structure must be designed so as to perform its value creation and delivery processes in a customer-focused culture.

CUSTOMER-FOCUSED CULTURE

To understand what customer-focused culture is, it is important to first understand what "culture" means in the context of organizations. One commonly accepted definition of corporate culture among scholars studying organizational behaviour is: the pattern of shared beliefs and values that guide the way the firm behaves. Mrs. Fields would say, "It's the way we do things around here." Culture is deeply rooted in values and translates to "climate" in a day-to-day "feel" of the place. Climate is a manifestation of culture. Schneider and Bowen, two wellknown scholars from the fields of psychology and organizational behaviour who have done a great deal of research on customer-focused culture and service climate, view climate as the "tangible layer on top of the organization's underlying culture."

Culture, along with mission and strategy, is also seen as an important piece for the vision of a firm to work. Corporate culture has been proven to be predictive of the performance of an organization. For example, in a sample of 102 companies, it was found that corporate culture was strongly linked to innovativeness. In this study, investment in technology was found to be influenced by corporate culture when firms provided the climate that fostered innovations. When Snapple, the beverage industry's surprise breakthrough firm, fell on hard times, Michael Weinstein of Triarc Companies, who took over the firm, focused on corporate values to turn the firm around.

Cultures are relatively stable, and it takes a long time to shift core values of a firm. The resistance to change has led to the demise of such former giants such as Polaroid. Polaroid's I-Zone instant pocket camera zoomed to number one status in less than three months after its introduction. This product almost didn't happen. During its development at the firm, the marketers who brought this idea to the table faced powerful resistance from old-line scientists and engineers at the firm who could not imagine what the founder of the firm, Edwin Land, would say about moving away from creating elegant products based on high technology. At one of the design meetings, the chief engineer was said to have asked, "Have we lost our minds?" He wondered why the same firm that Land had founded would produce something that was small, clunky, with a cheap lens, to produce fuzzy, thumbnail-size photographs!

The culture of a firm is its soul, and it resides in its employees and managers. Home Depot founder Bernard Marcus is known for his reliance on employee empowerment to make his vision a success. But, how many firms show a real caring for their employees? The statistical analysis software company SAS is often cited as one of the few information technology companies to have weathered the technology sector-led recession in the last couple of years because of its strong culture and caring for its employees. The firm has won several "best places to work" awards over its 25-year history. The CEO of SAS, Jim Goodnight, says, "I think our history has shown that taking care of employees has made the difference in how employees take care of our customers. With that as our vision, the rest takes care of itself." Unfortunately, it is the exception when a firm is able to say this and execute those sentiments in any meaningful way. The result is that employees are left to fend for themselves and leave unhappy. The Creative Group, a firm that specializes in recruiting creative talent, reported that in their survey, two-thirds of their sample of advertising and marketing executives from the nation's largest companies said the creative professional changed jobs every other year. It is not only important to attract the right employee, it is even more important to retain customer-focused employees.

It shouldn't come as a surprise that firms that are customer-focused are also ones that take care of their employees. When firms minimize their efforts in developing employee dedication to creating and delivering customer value they face high employee turnover. Harvard researchers Schlesinger and Heskett called this unfortunate but common attitude among senior managers, the self-perpetuating "cycle of failure." Among the reasons they offered to explain why firms fall into this cycle is an inability to measure the costs of employee dissatisfaction. They cite firms such as Wells-Fargo, ServiceMaster, Dayton Hudson, Au Bon Pain, and Fidelity Bank of Philadelphia, who have broken the cycle of failure by paying attention to their frontline employees. Recruiting, training, and rewarding practices of frontline employees at these firms are remarkably simple but different from those of the "average" firm. They pay more and reward their employees and managers who are productive and customer focused. The results in the form of employee and customer satisfaction are very compelling.

The direct correlation between employee satisfaction and customer satisfaction is often underestimated. Researchers Schneider and Bowen have shown through a series of studies of bank tellers that satisfied employees deliver satisfying customer encounters that result in employee and customer satisfaction feeding off each other. The key prerequisite is to create an atmosphere that fosters a focus on creating and delivering superior customer value. Such an atmosphere or climate comes from a firm that has a customer-focused culture and instills in its employees the values of customer-focused behaviour. Almost all top researchers in the field of services marketing, operations, and management have called for increasing attention to the culture that promotes satisfying service encounters. A firm cannot hope to satisfy its customers if the employees are not happy themselves. If the employees are not happy they leave. Guess who leaves first? The ones whose skills are most in demand are the ones who are most mobile – usually the best employees.

ATTRACTING AND RETAINING THE CUSTOMER-FOCUSED EMPLOYEE

Turnover at Dallas-based The Container Store is 20 percent compared to the industry average in retail operations, which generally ranges from 80 percent to 120 percent. Full-time employees at the company get 235 hours of training in their first year and are constantly asked what they need to do their job well. The company won *Fortune* magazine's "America's best workplace" honor in 2000. Similarly, at the 60-employee sports apparel company, Athleta Corp., employees set their own schedules and handle personal matters during the workday, backed by a CEO who believes that they will make up the time. To break the cycle of failure, firms have to value their employees. They ought to rethink the way they hire and groom their employees and managers. To do this, firms should be asking, what kind of employee do we need to attract and retain so that we can create and deliver a customer-focused solution? Managers from the functional areas of human resources, operations, and marketing management should jointly help determine the ideal employee for any position that is directly involved in creating and delivering value to the customer. Human resource decisions centre on hiring and training and are critical to acquiring the appropriate human capital in the firm. Study firms such as Disney, Nordstrom, Southwest Airlines, Ritz-Carlton, and American Express, which are known for their customer-focused culture, and you will see that all of them are very careful in how they select and hire their employees. They have in mind specific profiles that characterize the desired skills and personality traits that are necessary for the customer-focused employee in their business. Some of them use quite sophisticated ways of assessing the service orientation of the recruit. With the training and education these companies have in place, new employees are socialized into the corporate culture, whatever that culture might be. In a study within a large firm of five strategic business units (SBUs), 3,500 managers responding to a survey confirmed that the degree of market orientation in the processes of recruiting, training, and reward/compensation were found to strongly correlate with job satisfaction and trust in management.

A very revealing and useful exercise would be to investigate the hiring practices of the firm and check for how well the requirements for a customer-focused employee are reflected in the hiring and training practices. Does the firm have customer-focused criteria in their employee selection process? Do the job requirements and ideal candidate description reflect a customer focus? If the firm is well coordinated and integrated, customer knowledge is likely to be well utilized by the human resources department as well as the operations functions. Knowledge of the consumption activities of the customer should guide the practice of attracting and retaining human capital. If this is in place then the training and education is also likely to be designed to develop the employee for operational excellence contributing to creating and delivering the desired customer value. The operational excellence assumes the appropriate knowledge and attitude of the value creating and delivering role of the employee. Many firms now complement operations skills training with training on customer interaction skills or other customer-focused skills for the frontline employee.

Previously, for example, banks would provide operations training for tellers but not customer skills training. Once hired and trained, the operations and marketing functions take over the direct allocation, motivation, and supervision of the employee. Employees must be able to enjoy their work and find it rewarding not just financially but emotionally as well. How well these functions value the employee will have a major effect on the efforts of the firm to create and deliver the desired customer value. The customer-focused firm ought to be very interested in the welfare of its employees. Otherwise, employees tend to disconnect from the firm and are not committed to their jobs. For example, Dupont began a programme to "re-engage" with employees by helping employees design their career paths in an attempt to win back employee loyalty.

Northeast Delta Dental is one of the major dental care insurance providers in New England. CEO Tom Raffio expresses his main challenge as "how to retain the customer-focused culture that has given us success as we continue to grow." He succeeds by being very close to his employees. He goes to the extent of meeting the families of his employees so that he has an intimate knowledge of his employees' lives. His office is in the middle of the busiest floor of the corporate office. He likes being accessible and close to his employees. Tom brings customer feedback directly to his employees and asks them what they thought the firm ought to be doing. He is genuinely interested in the growth and development of the employee. The employee is empowered with the operational skills and with customer knowledge.

The customer-focused firm is proactive in rewarding employees for being customer focused. As we saw earlier, Commerce Bancorp of New Jersey gives its employees $50 to come up with any practice of the bank's that is not customer-focused. The company almost instantly rewards an employee for specific customer-focused actions in a customer experience or incident. Whoever has wowed the customer gets a "Wow" award hand-delivered the next day from head office. The customer-focused firm ensures that the workplace is a place where people can grow, where they are comfortable at what they are doing.

Several firms have begun to include a measure of customer satisfaction in the compensation and bonus criteria for employees. Here is an interesting example of a culture spillover from a merger that benefits the bigger company. PTC, formerly Parametric Technology, which acquired Computervision, found that their own salespeople were not concerned with managing the customer relationship after the sale while those who came from Computervision emphasized customer service. Today, all salespeople in the company are evaluated on customer satisfaction scores as well, and PTC is focusing on solutions rather than the software product. More than a decade ago, GE began a customer education programme at its Management Development Institute, where customers and employees are educated on the firms' goals and processes. The idea was to get the customers and employees together and explain the goals and strategies of the firm.

In this new economy, knowledge-based employees are very mobile with their expertise. Firms would be well advised to assess each employee's worth, including replacement cost, similar to the analysis in managing customer relationships, to determine the firm's need to retain the individual. Retention efforts should be prioritized according to that worth of the employee. When firms reluctantly started laying off workers during the recent recession, employers were also offering enticements with bonuses so that they would return to the firm when it was ready to rehire workers. Charles Schwab was offering bonuses and $20,000 worth of college tuition money, hoping that these workers would come back to Schwab when the company started to hire again.

Treacy and Wiersema argued that a firm has to have at least one of the three value disciplines they organize their thesis around—operational excellence, customer intimacy, and product leadership. Either firms have to be very good at the customer value that they create and deliver, their values should be built around intimate customer knowledge, or they should be at the forefront of product innovation. The argument that these are separate value disciplines is often commonly accepted. However, in a discussion of the customer-focused firm, the distinction appears to be irrelevant. The customer-focused firm assumes that it has to be good at all these three value disciplines simply because they are interrelated. A customer-focused firm derives its competitive advantage from its service orientation. With its intimate knowledge of the customer (customer intimacy), the firm excels in creating and providing superior customer value (operational excellence), and by anticipating and responding to evolving customer needs it continues to improve its customer value (product leadership).

In the new economy, a firm with a customer-focused culture leverages its people and its information technology to be close to the customer so that it can create and deliver superior customer value. Its people and information technology, as the primary productive factors, have to be employed in such a way as to ensure the firm's ability to understand the customer and to use that knowledge in its value creation and delivery. Thus, the importance of customer intimacy and operations excellence is taken as a guiding element in corporate strategy and performance. This approach requires a culture that is customer focused as a prerequisite to derive a sustainable competitive advantage.

Ensuring that the firm is staying customer focused should be a constant endeavor. It requires assessing the level of customer intimacy that the firm can claim. It requires the continuous assessment of the operational excellence that the firm is able to achieve. Key questions to ask would concern customer knowledge management. The following Table offers the key questions to help assess the customer focus of the firm. How effective is the firm at obtaining, processing, disseminating, and using customer information in guiding the decisions and activities of the firm? Only the customer-focused firm can effectively create and deliver superior value while maximizing returns from its productive assets.

Table: Framing the Customer-Focused Analysis

Impact of Customer-Focused Culture	*Analytical Questions*
Customer Intimacy—How well the firm strives to understand the customer is a measure of how customer-focused the firm is.	How good is our customer knowledge? Do we proactively obtain customer information? Do we analyze our customer information? How well do we deploy that information in creating and delivering customer value? How effective are we in maximizing customer equity?
Operational Excellence—Creating and delivering the desired customer value such that the firm maximizes returns from its assets is the measure of how customer-focused the firm is.	How effective are we in meeting customer needs? Are we creating and delivering the desired customer value? How efficient are we in terms of maximizing returns from our productive assets?

Chapter 7

Fundamentals of Housekeeping

An uncluttered workplace is fundamental to any plant's safety programme. In addition to cleanliness, industrial housekeeping must include other factors, such as orderliness and proper arrangement of materials. It is important to know the benefits of good industrial housekeeping. Let's review the importance and meaning of order in achieving good housekeeping, and discuss some guides for checking your own work area. Sloppy working conditions can lead to a lack of pride in your work. We should not overlook slippery floors, obstacles in aisles, tools on the floors, floors and platforms that are not in proper condition, or other housekeeping hazards.

In addition to encouraging poor attitudes, bad industrial housekeeping can lead to:

- Slips from slick or wet floors, platforms, and other walking and working surfaces.
- Trips from objects or materials that are left in walkways and work areas.
- Falls from holes in walking and working surfaces, uneven flooring, uncovered pits or drains, and boxes and pallets that are used instead of adequate platforms.
- Collisions caused by poorly stored materials, overhanging or protruding objects, haphazard

spotting of pallets, and use of aisles for storing materials and equipment.

Poor industrial housekeeping creates hazards for all employees in the immediate area.

Good industrial housekeeping:

- Eliminates accident and fire causes
- Saves energy by eliminating the need to work "around" congested areas and "deadwood" stored in the work area.
- Provides the best use of space
- Keeps inventory of materials to a minimum
- Helps control property damage
- Guarantees a good workplace appearance
- Encourages better working habits
- Reflects an image of a well-run operation
- Reduces the amount of cleanup and janitorial work

Housekeeping is more than just sweeping the floor and wiping dust off machines and equipment. Cleanliness is only a part of housekeeping. The most critical and most overlooked part of housekeeping is order. A work area is in order when there are no unnecessary objects in the area and when all necessary items are in their proper places.No in this definition means none—not any—not even one! A workplace is not considered to be in order simply because "there is a place for everything and everything is in its place." Do you use your production area for storage? Do you keep supplies in the area because "they'll be needed one of these days?" If there is one item in an area that is unnecessary or not in its proper place, then you do not have order. Order is maintained, not achieved. You cannot put an area in order and then forget about it. A daily conscious effort by everyone working in the area is necessary to maintain order. Order also must be obtained throughout the day. If you wait until the end of the day and then place everything in order, what good did it do you during the day? Disorder wastes time, energy and materials.

A good housekeeping programme must include careful planning, a clean-up schedule or policy, effective inspection, and continuous supervision and enforcement of house-keeping rules. Inspect your area for unnecessary tools, equipment, parts, materials and supplies; items that are not needed should be sent to the storage room or used for salvage. Reorganize the storage area in your workplace. Establish one or more storage areas for holding finished products and daily quantities of raw materials and supplies; storage areas should not obstruct aisles and work areas. Create a daily clean-up policy and programme. Periodically review the housekeeping rules, clean-up policies and procedures.

HOUSEKEEPING RULES

- Walking and working surfaces should be clean, dry and unobstructed.
- Aisleways and exits should be clearly marked and unobstructed.
- Approved trash receptacles should be provided to assure proper waste disposal.
- Splash guards and oil pans should be available for machinery as needed.
- Work area floors should be kept free of pallets, parts, equipment, extension cords and hoses.
- Floors, platforms and stairways should be kept in good repair.
- Adequate platforms should be provided; never use additional platforms or boxes and pallets as substitutes.
- Walls and ceilings should be free of hangings and temporary wiring.
- Materials should be stacked in a stable manner; limit height as necessary to maintain stability.
- Overhanging or protruding storage should be eliminated.
- Storage areas in and around buildings should be free of refuse and debris.

- Stock should be stored in a manner that will not obstruct sprinklers (18-inch clearance for ordinary combustibles, 36-inch clearance for flammable liquids).

Combustible materials should never be stored on radiators, steam coils, ovens or other heat sources; in transformer vaults; or around electrical switch gear.

- Production equipment should be arranged to prevent overcrowding.
- Storage areas should be placed in a convenient location to encourage their use.
- Adequate lighting, both natural and artificial, should be provided to assure good visibility for work activities and to reveal dirt, obstructions and poor housekeeping conditions.
- Leaks from hoses, pipelines and valves should be repaired immediately.
- Racks, shelves and lockers should be maintained for tools, personal protective equipment and personal items.
- Lunch facilities, locker rooms and toilet areas should be clean, orderly and sanitary.
- Order results in greater and safer production of better products at lower costs. Improved production and costs mean increased business and prosperity for our company and you, its employees.

HOTEL HOUSEKEEPING

What Can Happen

Cuts, bruises, sprains, strains, electrocution, Chemical-related injuries, infections etc.

What we Can Do

Watch for things that may cause accidents and report them immediately to your supervisor. Place mops, buckets and other equipment where no one can fall over them.

Practise safe lifting techniques, lift with your legs, not your back. Be careful with cleaning solutions or chemicals read product labels. Store cigarette butts and sharp objects in a separate, metal container. Roll up all linen, rugs and spreads before putting them in the soiled laundry bundle. Wear rubber gloves when using strong cleaning solutions. Push tall or heavy pieces of furniture get help if necessary.

Do not touch light switches or handle electrical equipment when your hands are wet or you are standing on a damp floor Do not stand on the edge of bathroom tubs

Do not mix ammonia and chlorine-based cleaners together, poisonous gas is produced. Do not run up or down stairs, always walk and use the handrail. Do not try to repair machines or equipment, report problems to your supervisor. Do not run your hands along or inside objects unless you have checked first for razor blades, needles, broken glass, etc.

Do not use your hands to compress garbage in a bag, use a stick or plunger. Do not unplug the vacuum cleaner by pulling on the cord, pull on the plug.

Housekeeping in a hotel is a very physically demanding job that includes many, varied tasks. Typically, in this case study, housekeepers were responsible for cleaning 16 rooms per shift. The actual amount of work depends on the size of the room and the number of beds. A housekeeper needs between fifteen and thirty minutes to do one room.

A housekeeper carries out the following tasks:

- Making beds
- Tidying rooms
- Cleaning and polishing toilets, taps, sinks, bathtubs and mirrors
- Washing floors,
- Removing stains, and
- Vacuuming

Housekeeping in a hotel is a very physically demanding job that includes many, varied tasks. Typically, in this case study, housekeepers were responsible for cleaning 16 rooms per shift. The actual amount of work depends on the size of the room and the number of beds. A housekeeper needs between fifteen and thirty minutes to do one room.

The main risk factors for repetitive motion injuries (RMIs) in housekeeping are:

Heavy physical workload and excessive bodily motions which are a high risk for back injuries and forceful upper limb motions in awkward positions which are a high risk for neck or shoulder and arm injuries. Space limitations require workers to use many uncomfortable postures.

These are:

- Standing or walking,
- Stooping,
- Squatting,
- Kneeling,
- Stretching,
- Reaching,
- Bending,
- Twisting, and
- Crouching.

A housekeeper changes body position every three seconds while cleaning a room. If we assume that the average cleaning time for each room is twenty-five minutes, we can estimate that a housekeeper assumes 8,000 different body postures every shift.

In addition, forceful movements while using awkward body positions include lifting mattresses, cleaning tiles, and vacuuming every shift. Housekeeping is a physically demanding and very tiring job. It can be classified as "moderately heavy" to "heavy" work because the energy required is approximately 4 kilocalories per minute (4 kcal/min.)

Hotel housekeepers work in a unique place. Hotels are usually designed for the comfort of their guests rather than their housekeeping staff. This fact makes it very difficult to improve working conditions for housekeepers by means of better engineering. However, some improvements can be made by selecting more appropriate equipment. Lighter vacuum cleaners (preferably the self-propelling type), and lighter service carts with wheels designed for carpeted floors would ease the workload for their operators providing this equipment is always kept in good repair. When new vacuum cleaners are purchased, low noise emissions should be one of the criteria.

Improving the body postures that pose a major risk for musculoskeletal disorders seems an unachievable task. Again, this fact results from the peculiarity of hotels as a workplace. To attract guests and remain competitive, hotel management pursues a policy that everything should be "so clean it sparkles". Floors, walls, windows, mirrors, and bathroom fixtures might be adequately cleaned with some form of an extension tool to reduce bending and over-stretching. However, the demand for spotless cleanliness and hygiene, management often requires their cleaning staff to spend extra time and effort cleaning by kneeling, leaning, squatting, crouching, slouching and stretching. These postures will in time contribute to new musculoskeletal injuries and aggravate old ones.

New approaches, other than strictly ergonomic ones, need to be investigated. For example, action can be taken from the administrative level.

Options for improvement include:

- Job rotation,
- Job enrichment and job enlargement,

- Team work, and
- Education and training on work practices.

Job rotation is one possible approach. It requires workers to move between different tasks, at fixed or irregular periods. However, it must be a rotation where workers do something completely different. Different tasks must use different muscle groups to allow muscles already stressed to recover.

Another approach is job enlargement. This increases the variety of tasks built into the job. It breaks the monotony of the job and avoids overloading one part of the body. Job enrichment involves more autonomy and control for the worker.

Team work can provide greater variety and more evenly distributed muscular work. The whole team is involved in the planning of the work. Each team member carries out a set of operations to complete the whole product, allowing the worker to alternate between tasks. This reduces the risk of RMI.

A well-designed job, supported by a well-designed workplace and proper tools, allows the worker to avoid unnecessary motion of the neck, shoulders and upper limbs. However, the actual performance of the tasks depends on individuals.

Training should be provided for workers who are involved with housekeeping activities. It is important that housekeeping staff be informed about hazards in the workplace, including the risk of injuries to the musculoskeletal system. Therefore, identification of the hazards for such injury at any given hotel is fundamental.

Individual work practices, including lifting habits, are shaped by proper training. Training should encourage employers and workers to adopt methods that reduce fatigue. For example, it is advisable to plan one's workload and do the heavier tasks at the beginning of the workshift, rather than at the end, when fatigue is at its maximum. When a person is tired, the risk of injuring a muscle is higher.

Training should also explain the health hazards of improper lifting and give recommendations on what a worker can do to improve lifting positions. Training should also emphasize the importance of rest periods for the workers' health and explain how active rest can do more for keeping workers healthy than passive rest. The effect of such training can reach far beyond occupational situations because the workers can apply this knowledge also in their off-job lives.

The Housekeeping department must be the most important. It has the greatest proportion of staffing hours to cover, the most staff, the most hours to cover and it is a cost centre. Unlike the restaurant and bar, which are revenue centres, and as long as they are not overstaffed, the more staff you have the more revenue is generated. The housekeeping department is also the one the customers notice most if anything is wrong. You have to have the right number of staff on duty, or it shows.

The housekeeping department can have the following staff depending on the size of hotel. Housekeeper and assistant housekeepers, room maids, cleaners, staffmaids, cloakroom attendants, houseporters, valets, laundry and linen keeper. The staff hours of cover depend on the hotel and type of customer, business people require different time schedules to people on holiday with children. The staff need to be scheduled accordingly and in a ratio to the number of guests staying in the hotel. Fortunately, most people book ahead and the workload is known well in advance, especially during peak periods.

Your staffing requirement will depend on the occupancy of your hotel. It is possible to get quite good estimates of staff numbers based on average times to do tasks, such as cleaning a room. Then you can allocate 10, or 15, or even 20 rooms to each room maid. It is also quite easy to estimate the total number of staff needed in a year for a task. We have a page about annual hours.

For example, cleaning an occupied room takes 30mins/ day, en-suite bathroom 6mins/day, therefore a maid for every 13 occupied rooms. A hotel with 100 rooms(all occupied) needs 8 maids. Then we can sum this up for a year of 365 days, which comes to 2900 maid days per year. We can then divide this by the number of days a maid works per year, say 240, and arrive at a figure of 12 full time maids. Hence we can recruit the 12 maids and start using them on the rooms. I haven't allowed for average occupancy, sickness rates, and a lot of other things which readily come to mind, because at this point, the difficult thing is to find a way of sharing the yearly workload on a day by day basis. This is the difficult part, just how do you allocate the maids so that you have just the right number on every day.

Well, the answer depends on where you are at the moment. An existing hotel staffed, is different to a new hotel unstaffed. If I first deal with a new hotel, then the resultant method is easier. First, don't start from the above yearly totals, use the daily hour totals to tell you how many staff are needed each day. Start Visual Rota, set it up for, say 13 4week periods and name the staff, as RM1, RM2, etc. Then start to allocate shifts according to your occupancy rates(anticipated). At this stage you can use full time or part time staff, working full shifts, half shifts and split shifts. Give the staff days off, usually in the ratio of for every 5 days they work, they have 2 off. Try to use full time staff as much as possible if they are cheaper, and fill in the blanks with part time staff. Then you can recruit the staff in accordance with your requirements and allocate shifts to the staff weeks in advance, possibly months.

At some stage you need to deal with holidays and staff turnover. All staff take holidays but it is difficult to know in advance when this is going to be. That's why we invented dice. If you look back at your records(difficult if you are a new hotel, I know, then you have to guess) you will see the pattern of absenteeism, sickness and holidays, and even staff turnover. This pattern can be replicated by throwing dice. For instance, if you employ 12 maids and your staff turnover is 50%, then six of your maids leave every year, or one every 2 months.

You won't know when exactly and it is difficult for us to be random in our decisions, so throw a dice for each month. If the number is even, a 2, 4,or 6, then a maid leaves that month, if the number is odd, no one leaves that month. Then you can arrange for a new maid to be recruited in line with the throw of the dice. Perhaps not, perhaps what you will do is to include into your budgets the cost of hiring a new recruit and the cost of using an employment agency.

You can use Visual Rota to allocate training days for new staff and existing, or keep records of sickness, absenteeism, lateness, frequency of requests and holidays.

An existing hotel will be using their established working practice for staffing. Visual Rota enables you to analyse this and see if improvements can be made and how much you can save by changing your working practice. Staff need an incentive to change and if you offer part of your savings as a pay increase, that goes a long way to getting the changes accepted. We have regularly improved the way we work by incorporating new pay deals for existing staff and hiring new staff as and when we replaced the staff due to natural wastage on our new terms.

Visual Rota enables you to move your staff around to minimise the effects of peaks and troughs in occupancy levels. You can bring in more staff when needed and give them days off during slack periods. The programme keeps track of their hours and shifts, so everyone gets exactly the right number of hours of work, but your costs are minimised.

Other departments are equally capable of being analysed and scheduled by Visual Rota. It is possible to have one file for the entire hotel, or several files to cover each area, floor or department. Whichever method you use at the moment, you can do the same on the computer, but faster.

There is always a compromise between the number of staff doing a particular job and the cover they provide. If there is only one housekeeper, then the maximum cover would be 40 hours/week, whilst the staff rota would be providing up to 168 hours of cover a week, hence one of the main management functions is to determine how much staffing is provided and at what grade of staff. Fortunately, hoteliers are not subject to staffing levels determined by legislation, and can decide for themselves.

HOSPITALITY SERVICE

The concept of Hospitality Services, also known as "accommodation sharing", "hospitality exchange", and "home stay networks", refers to centrally organized social networks of individuals who trade accommodation without monetary exchange. While this concept could also include house swapping or even time share plans, it has come to be associated mostly with travellers and tourists staying with one another free of charge. Since the 1990s, these services have increasingly moved away from using printed catalogs and phone trees to connect users towards Internet websites. These have grown exponentially since 2000 and today it is estimated that well over 100,000 people are registered users of these networks. These vary in operational structure, place different emphasis on graphical vs. textual formatting, and cater disproportionately to specific geographic regions.

In 1949, Bob Luitweiler founded the first hospitality service called Servas Open Doors as a cross national, non-profit, volunteer run organization advocating interracial and international peace. The next earliest began in 1965 when John Wilcock set up the Traveller's Directory, originally as a listing of his mutual friends willing to host each other when traveling. This later became the Hospitality Exchange in 1988 when Joy Lily rescued the organization from imminent demise. Hospitality Club is the direct successor Hospex, the first Internet-based service, operating out of Poland since 1992. It is currently the largest hospitality exchange network, growing rapidly. CouchSurfing is a newer but also rapidly growing hospitality exchange organization founded in 2004. Just as all the individual services have their own individual creation stories and organizational histories (often including demise and resurrection), many also have specific niche markets that they cater to including students, activists, religious pilgrims, and even occupational groups like police officers. However, the trend in recent years points to a greater consolidation of users in networks without a specific group, value, or lifestyle affiliation.

In essence, these systems employ reciprocity – users gain access to other users' information only by posting their own. Required fields normally include name and contact information, though newer services encourage users to include more detailed personal material, including likes and dislikes, hopes and dreams, and even photographs. Of course, more information included tends to improve the chances that someone will find them trustworthy enough to host or stay with while traveling. It is very much akin to online dating services.

Staying in private homes means that travellers can save lots of money on accommodation that they would usually be spending on hotels or hostels. Used over a long period of time (2 to 4 weeks), this strategy can cut overall travel budgets in half, or even more combined with hitchhiking. These savings can then be passed on towards more generously patronizing local establishments or simply staying abroad for longer periods of time.

Many tourist vacations today are sold in package form, often including flights, hotels, rental cars, sightseeing tours, and coupons for chain restaurants and bars. While this makes purchasing more convenient, it also puts more money in the hands of large multinational corporations exploiting the synergy strategy of marketing their products in the context of their subsidiary companies operating in other markets. Many years ago, this might have been termed collusion; today, however, it is the norm. This comes at the expense of locally owned independent businesses. Accommodation sharing helps to break apart this monopoly and hopefully redirects some of the tourist revenue back to the local or national economy.

While this is especially important in more rural travel venues where hotels are often built in very picturesque, though fragile environments, every night stayed at a local's home means that much less demand for such hotel rooms. Also, if accommodation sharing does in fact increase the length of average stays, it may reduce the amount of trips to and from different locations and back home again, thus reducing the overall fuel expenditures in the process.

Ostensibly, one of the primary reasons we travel is to experience what life is like for people living in other countries. Making interpersonal connections and fostering understanding of different cultures may in the long run also be important to international relations. However, even in our increasingly globalized world supposedly rife with diversity, in many popular travel destinations we find tourists milling around "tourist enclaves" where the companies they patronize back home have set up shop to cater to their desires while they are abroad. Sociologist George Ritzer has referred to this phenomenon as the "McDonaldisation of society" and the more recently, the "globalization of nothing". The location of hotels near these centres only fosters more convenient envelopment of the tourist dollar. During hospitality exchanges, hosts want to show off their local knowledge and exciting "off the map" venues. Not only may travellers get a distinctly different experience, but they will also get a feel for the everyday lives of local residents.

These systems foster richer and more convenient travel experiences not so much on the premise of altruism, but on the basis of social exchange theory. Implicit in the agreement to host travellers is the ability to ask to be hosted by them in the future. If one enjoys having interesting guests in their home, this works out well for both parties. It works comparatively better if you are visited by travellers from a locale you find particularly attractive. Thus, hosting someone from New York City in Gainesville, FL seems to be an unbelievable opportunity. Moreover, if you are a Westerner visiting someone in a developing nation, your stay might be the only way that this individual or family could afford a trip to a rich nation. This may mean more than just a relaxing vacation for such disadvantaged parties.

Tourism has always searched for these two qualities, but much like Midas and his golden touch, the reach of tourism has to a large extent destroyed the opportunity to encounter them in most places. Unluckily, the experience has been thoroughly commodified by everyone who wanted to secure their opportunity to make a buck in the process. Accommodation sharing offers a way out of this bind and a viable alternative to having one's desires manipulated by corporate conglomerates who never had the best interests of the place or the people foremost in their minds.

There is no contractual agreement between users in these systems. Reservations are made, but if they are for some reason broken, there is no higher authority to which one could plead for a refund or other compensation. The only repercussion will be the poor rating you give that user and your only consolation will be that your warning will deter others from visiting or hosting them. For those who feel insecure unless their travel arrangements are written in stone before departure, this system will not be comforting.

There is a chance that guest and host will not get along. Perhaps there will be scheduling or ideological conflicts. Maybe you will find that hosts or visitors have misrepresented themselves. Perhaps the experience will not live up to your expectations. Intense interpersonal communications in advance and a flexibility once you have arrived is your best bet. These experiences require additional planning and courtesy towards the demands of your host. Thus, your living conditions, length of stay, and overall experience will be circumscribed by the living conditions you enter into.

The average user is a young white person who speaks English and lives in a developed nation. While there are many users who do not fit this description, the more different they are, the less likely they will be involved. This is especially true for persons living in the developing world who likely do not have easy access to the fundamental prerequisite for using these services: computers and the Internet. Thus, the sample population found in searches of these databases are really much less diverse than a geographical representation of worldwide users might suggest.

There is a distinct possibility that someone will abuse the system and that innocent users (especially women) will get hurt. All services include disclaimers that require users to waive their rights to hold anyone but themselves responsible for any harm that may come to them in using the system. They advise that the best defence mechanism is to only involve oneself with users that have extensive personal information and interpersonal networks within the system that have been verified by others. It does seem entirely plausible that someone clever and patient enough might be able to invent an entire group of complex user identities and build histories convincing enough to fool even more cautious patrons. Still, the difference between these systems and the other social networking platforms popular nowadays on the web (such as MySpace, Tribe, Orkut, LiveJournal and Ebay) is that any agreement reached through the accommodation sharing medium is contingent on actually meeting other people face-to-face. Other web scams are easier because interpersonal interactions rely so much on putative identities that are never actually verified in the real world. However, this does not diminish the greater risk to physical well being that this kind of traveling by definition must entertain. The best advice is to meet unknown persons in public spaces first, and try to meet some of their acquaintances in person before agreeing to a hospitality exchange.

Chapter 8

Customer Measurement in Hotel Management System

Every company must be able to satisfy and retain customers. That is the key to its business performance. Your job—as an executive in charge of improving quality, customer satisfaction, or loyalty—may be to enable others to act through training and support. Alternatively, if you're in the quality, customer assessment, or development areas of your company, your job may be to do the work directly—to collect, analyze, or use customer data to improve quality, satisfaction, and retention. Whether you are an enabler or a doer, customer satisfaction and retention are your responsibility. Providing high-quality products and services builds strong relationships with customers and ensures future revenue streams.

Even though you may agree about the importance of customers in driving performance, an important question remains. Does your company align its activities to satisfy and retain customers? Too often the answer is either "no" or "not so well." To help understand the problem, consider how a customer focus has evolved in recent decades.

In the 1970s, quality gurus argued that "quality is free." That is, a tireless pursuit of improvement should not only increase efficiency but also increase customer satisfaction in the process, saving enough on costs and bringing in enough new and repeat business to more than cover any expenditures on quality. This was an underlying concept in the success of many Japanese companies. In the 1980s the experts began to focus more directly on increasing customer satisfaction as an explicit goal. Satisfying and keeping customers, it was argued, is simply less expensive than constantly replacing them. More recently, quality and satisfaction have been viewed as not sufficient by themselves. Companies boast of moving "beyond" quality and satisfaction to focus directly on customer loyalty as the key to profitability.

Yet to argue that quality, or satisfaction, or loyalty is what matters misses the point. These factors form a chain of cause and effect, building on each other so that they cannot be treated separately. They represent a system that must be measured and managed as a whole if you want to maximize results.

An example from our teaching experiences underscores the nature of the problem and why companies need to take a systems approach to customer measurement and management. Back in 1993 an executive seminar participant from a Fortune 100 company introduced himself as the "customer satisfaction manager" for his organization. This prompted one of the authors to ask, "What happened to the quality manager?" The participant replied that quality was passé, and that customer satisfaction had become the hot topic in his organization. In fact, being the quality manager had become the "kiss of death" from a career standpoint—a dead-end job! Five years later, a seminar participant from the same company introduced himself as the "customer loyalty manager" for the organization. Again the natural question arose, "What happened to the customer satisfaction manager?" "Oh, him?" It turned out that the satisfaction manager was now the one with the dead-end job.

Many business organizations are beginning to recognize the need to avoid this "Book of the Month Club" mentality and to view customers from a systems perspective. They want explicit linkages that extend from internal processes to customer perceptions to customer satisfaction to loyalty—and ultimately to bottom-line performance. The framework in this book will give executives hard numbers and not just persuasive theories to show that the connection is real and that improving satisfaction and loyalty really does improve profits. And those on the front lines—the quality engineers and service providers—will get specific guidance on what to improve and how to improve it to get the optimal response from customers.

This book will show you how to create an integrated customer measurement and management system that will help you allocate resources and increase profits. To create such a system, you must first understand your company's entire system for generating profit, from internal quality through to business performance. A systems approach acts on the basis of collected and interpreted customer data—but then you have to use the data to allocate resources and create change in the system or else you merely waste time and money.

With an effective customer measurement and management system, you can build organizational value. To do so, you will continually pursue three key activities that underlie a customer orientation: (1) gather customer information, (2) spread that information throughout the organization, and (3) use the information to maintain, improve, or innovate in products and processes.

You need solid information about the concrete product and service attributes or features that customers value, the more abstract consequences and benefits these attributes provide, and ultimately the personal values they serve. The purpose is to understand what your customers want not only in today's products and services but in tomorrow's as well. When you understand your customers at the various levels that motivate their behaviour, you can see their present needs and predict their future needs as well.

To maintain a customer orientation throughout your organization, you need to make sure that customer information gets to everyone who is involved—either directly or indirectly— in improving quality and value and satisfying customers. This both prepares the entire organization for change and provides benchmarks by which to monitor its performance. Finally, you need to prime the organization to act on the customer information to improve product and service offerings so as to increase satisfaction, loyalty, and profitability. This makes it essential to clarify the links among these three factors and understand how your company delivers a compelling product to its customers.

Creating a customer measurement and management system is central to the pursuit of all three of these activities. With such a system in place, you have your customer information in a form that can serve as a basis for both incremental and more revolutionary product and service improvements. The system also makes it easier to share customer information throughout an organization, enhancing its ability to follow through on that information to make product and process changes. It is essential to view customer measurement from a systems perspective that encompasses multiple areas of measurement and expertise (from engineering and design through market research and strategy to finance and accounting) so that you pick up both concrete and abstract details— both what the customers like and dislike and why they react that way—and develop information that will be genuinely useful.

Now you may well be saying, "But we already do a good job of gathering customer information, spreading it, and acting on the voice of the customer." The question is whether you really adopt the "lens of the customer" in this process or fall into the trap of relying on the "lens of the organization."

The lens of the customer shows you your products and services—and the benefits they provide—from your customers' perspective. You see them as they really are in the marketplace, rather than the different and potentially misleading picture you're likely to get from the lens of your own organization. For example, if you run a convenience store chain you may be inclined to view the chain's stores as providing customers with people (service), products (from soft drinks to gasoline), and operations (such as opening hours), each under the management of a different department or business function. The problem is that customers may not share this perspective. Customers view products and services from the standpoint of the benefits they provide and problems they solve, which may not align well with individual business process areas. In this case, customers are looking for safety, convenience, and cleanliness, which are benefits that are not uniquely provided by specific business process areas. Rather, they cut across the people, products, and operating policies of the stores.

Aside from providing a more accurate picture of the drivers of satisfaction and loyalty, adopting the lens of the customer has other advantages. It blurs functional boundaries and provides a common basis and language for communication. The forging of concrete links from area to area within a company is also a key to effective implementation. When an organization reaches a consensus on the importance of customer benefits that are not defined along functional or business process lines, it finds it much easier to engage in the cross-functional activities required to truly innovate and implement change.

We emphasize the word *framework* here. Our aim is to show just what links and models are possible.The actual elements and links in any model vary tremendously from company to company and context to context. After describing the framework, we will illustrate this point using two very different cases in which companies (Volvo and Sears) have developed models to become more customer focused.

The framework includes four general areas: internal quality, external quality and satisfaction, customer loyalty and retention, and financial performance. *Internal quality* encompasses various production and maintenance processes. In the case of a manufactured product, it includes everything from manufacturing processes to the physical characteristics and attributes that describe the product. In a service and retailing context, it includes the service offer, the physical surroundings, and the satisfaction of employees and the resulting service quality they provide.

External quality and satisfaction encompasses what customers see in the purchase and consumption experience: the attributes and benefits that products and services provide and the costs they impose, and the conclusions the customers draw about the company. In the area of customer loyalty and retention, *loyalty* is a customer's intention or predisposition to buy, while *retention* is the behaviour itself (as when a customer returns to a restaurant, comes back to buy the same brand of car, or purchases another financial instrument from the same institution). Although we will use the term *loyalty* at times to encompass both intended loyalty and actual retention, it is important to understand the distinction. When actual retention information is available, it proves extremely valuable in sorting out the drivers of financial performance. When it is unavailable, as it often is, you can use loyalty measures as a proxy for retention.

Quality, satisfaction, and loyalty ultimately affect financial performance, both directly and indirectly. The framework illustrates this point and highlights the possibility that there may be a tension between direct and indirect effects. Consider first the impact of internal quality. Producing a high-quality product or service at an attractive price indirectly affects financial performance through its effect on external customer perceptions of the purchase-consumption experience. But internal quality may also have a direct effect on costs and revenues. According to the "quality is free" argument, improvements in internal quality can increase productivity and lower internal costs and thus directly increase profitability. Recent research suggests, however, that this link is likely to be more positive for products and less positive or even negative for services. Why the difference? Services are produced and delivered at a time and place that is typically dictated by the customer. Thus improving service quality often requires an increase in personnel and operating or contact hours, which raises operating costs.

The external quality, value, and customer satisfaction component of the framework also has both direct and indirect effects on costs and revenues. Indirectly, a positive overall experience predisposes customers to stay loyal toward a product, service, or provider, which generates future sales. Satisfaction thus contributes to financial performance through its effect on loyalty and retention. But satisfaction also has direct effects, independent of loyalty. The cost of maintaining a customer account—or fixing a product—is a direct function of how happy the customer is. Satisfied customers are less likely to demand expensive product repairs or replacements or to invoke service guarantees. Also—even outside the world of TV commercials—people do talk about the products and services they buy, and your company's entry into that stream of word-of-mouth publicity is through perceived quality and satisfaction rather than through loyalty. Satisfaction is *news*—something to talk about—while loyalty is a background state that goes without saying unless something happens to damage it.

The direct effects of loyalty and retention on performance include revenues from repeat purchases, reduction in costs of finding new customers (to replace lost customers), and revenues generated through cross-selling. Another direct effect is the price premium that loyal customers often pay. Because loyal customers are not actively shopping for alternatives, they tend to be insulated from price incentives and offers such as coupons, price cuts, and free merchandise.

The recent turnaround at Volvo Car Company provides a good example of how a durable goods manufacturer views the links described in our framework. In 1991, Volvo was performing poorly in the global automotive market. It ranked as low as twenty-sixth out of thirty-four brands in the J. D. Power Initial Quality Study in the United States, and sales and profitability were suffering. In its comeback effort, Volvo began to develop a customer orientation from a total quality management foundation. Formerly, Volvo had emphasized changing internal quality to improve productivity and reduce costs. Its management realized, however, that just focusing on internal quality was insufficient. Internal improvements had to matter to the customers before they could create improved external quality, customer satisfaction, and loyalty.

Volvo's approach is just one example of the variety of tailored models that are consistent with the framework. Like Volvo, Sears has attempted to radically transform itself into a more customer-focused organization. But since Sears is a retailer that competes primarily on service, its model has evolved quite differently. Internal quality at Sears is primarily about its people and the service they provide. The Sears model draws directly on a service-profit chain that links internal quality (including employee satisfaction and loyalty) to service quality, and the satisfaction generated by service quality to loyalty and financial performance.

In developing its model, Sears has discovered both direct effects of satisfaction on financial performance and indirect effects through loyalty, which is consistent with our framework. A quantitative employee-customer-profit model at Sears has helped the company to establish very specific links that have enabled it to improve financial performance. The model shows, for example, that a 5-point improvement in employee attitudes (on a 0 to 100 scale) drives a 1.3-point improvement in customer satisfaction, which in turn drives a 0.5 percent improvement in revenue growth.

The Volvo and Sears models share a common logic, but each model is uniquely tailored to the organization's own situation. Both models link internal quality through to profitability. At the same time, each reflects the nature of a specific company, its customers and offerings, and the contexts involved. When you look at your own company, you will see that the same logic will work for you when you develop a similar understanding of your own customers and what you can offer them.

The best measurement system can only provide information— it can't make decisions for you. People make decisions, whether it is the convenience store executive who sets corporate priorities, the front-line service manager who translates these priorities into policies and procedures, or the service worker who translates policies and procedures into concrete actions. At all three levels, decision makers are much more likely to choose to do something that will help the store chain succeed if they understand what matters to customers and how the job at hand can enhance that value.

The process of moving from information to decisions draws heavily on *importance-performance analysis.* According to this analysis, the most cost-effective areas of product and service performance to improve are those that are important to customers *and* on which, at the same time, the company is performing poorly. Executives and managers must identify these priority areas of high importance and low performance. As an output of this selection process, they can categorize and display the drivers of satisfaction and loyalty using a strategic satisfaction matrix.

The matrix identifies four categories of performance drivers with different market action implications. Again, the aspects to improve first are those where impact or importance is high and performance is weak. This focuses resources and quality improvement efforts likely to have the greatest impact on satisfaction and thus on loyalty and profitability. Those aspects where performance and impact are both high reflect a firm's competitive advantage. It is essential to maintain if not improve performance on these drivers. When impact and performance are both weak, on the other hand, there is no need to waste resources on improvement.

More interesting is the low impact–strong performance category. This may be an area where resources have been wasted in the past because the benefits and attributes are not important to customers. Alternatively, this category may contain drivers of satisfaction that customers see as basic and necessary—so much a part of the product or service that they ignore it as long as it's there when they want it, like electric power or water on tap. Although such drivers are important in an absolute sense, they have little to no impact on satisfaction because there is little variance in their performance. The danger is that a reduction in performance quality would increase the impact on satisfaction (this danger is often referred to as a "slippery slope"). Another possibility here is to find a new target market segment for the product or service. For example, if the quality of an electrical system is so constant that it has no impact on satisfaction in one application, the system might be used in applications where minor fluctuations in this quality are more important and therefore likely to have a real impact on satisfaction.

There is also a danger that something in this category may become important in the future. For example, few customers considered "environmental friendliness" to be an important factor until recently, but more and more people are beginning to pay attention to this aspect of the goods and services they buy. In a growing variety of fields, companies that predicted the importance of this area and prepared their business accordingly clearly have an advantage over those that did not.

The circular nature of the process reflects the continuous nature of a customer orientation. Customer needs, competitive offerings, and business technologies change constantly, so customer focus is an ideal of constant growth rather than static achievement. The cycle in is thus a continuous process of planning, researching, analyzing, deciding, implementing, and learning. This includes identifying the system's purpose or goals within a more balanced set of corporate performance measures (including financial goals, employee satisfaction goals, process improvement goals, knowledge and learning goals, and so forth). The chapter explores the key customer and market segmentation issues upon which the system is based, including the distinction between internal and external customers.

Chapter Three tells how to conduct qualitative research to guide the development of the measurement system. Conducting interviews and focus groups and observing customers provides you with the lens through which customers view products and services. This lens is the basis for your quality-satisfactionloyalty modeling.

Chapter Four tells how to use the lens of the customer to develop a customer monitoring system. It discusses ways to develop and administer surveys that assess the attributes and benefits your products and services provide and the overall levels of customer satisfaction and loyalty that result. The goal is to customize the measurement of quality, value, satisfaction, and loyalty for a particular customer segment, company, and context.

Chapter Five tells how to analyze satisfaction and loyalty data to provide the information you will need to set priorities for improvement. Again, the purpose is to identify both the relative importance and performance of key satisfaction and loyalty drivers. It provides guidelines for identifying the area or areas where importance is high and performance is low, which offer the most potential return on quality improvement efforts. We develop a statistical approach to help you estimate your system or model linking quality to loyalty and financial performance. We also provide concrete examples.

Chapter Six tells how to evaluate system outputs to make decisions. As emphasized earlier, management must take part in categorizing the output of a customer analysis into a strategic satisfaction matrix. Just where boundaries are set between highversus low-impact drivers and strong versus weak performance depends on a variety of factors, including what you can achieve in the time available, your cost structure, and your overall strategy. Interpreting model outputs also requires appropriate bench for evaluating both performance and importance. We will end Chapter Six by describing how to translate customer priorities into their means of accomplishment.

Who should collect your customer data, analyze it, and use it to set priorities and allocate resources? It often seems logical to delegate the satisfaction and loyalty measurement operation to outside research firms and consultants. This is especially true early in the process of becoming a customer-oriented organization, because outside specialists offer specific skills related to collecting and analyzing customer data that you do not have. Unfortunately, if you delegate the system, your company does not take ownership of it, and you and your people may fail to learn or acquire the skills necessary to measure and manage customer data on your own. The consultant's bills, heavy as they are likely to be, are only a small part of the cost of handing off a customer information system.

Bear in mind that when customer information is the key to strategy, it should reside within the company. Your best teachers about what is right and wrong with your products and services are your own customers. Direct contact with customers and customer data is a critical part of learning what it takes to satisfy customer needs. No matter how good the consultants are, they will always function as filters.

An important part of establishing a customer orientation as a core competency is creating, over time, internal specialists to measure, model, and manage quality, satisfaction, and loyalty. Early in the process, external experts are apt to be a necessity. They can provide the interviewing, surveying, data warehousing, statistical analysis, and interpretation skills that you may lack or not yet want (or be able) to invest in. Over time, however, continued reliance on external specialists becomes costly and also fails to develop customer measurement and management as a core competency. Internalization of the process allows you to adapt to changing market needs and competitive environments in a cost-effective fashion. More important, your organization accepts ownership of the process and the data—and the decisions that emerge.

This is not to say that all parts of the process should be brought in-house in all cases. You may not want to try to run a survey that involves computer-aided telephone interviews or a Web-based system with highly specialized personnel (such as trained interviewers) and potential economies of scale. Even in the most customer-savvy organization, it may be best to outsource certain parts of the process. At the same time, a truly customer-oriented firm should own rather than rent the ability to observe and to talk to customers, formalize survey instruments, analyze and interpret customer data, and use the output to make resource allocation decisions.

Over the last three decades business organizations have evolved from a focus on quality to a focus on customer satisfaction, and onward to a focus on loyalty as a means of creating value. A customer measurement and management system views each of these areas as an indispensable link in a chain of causes and effects that runs from internal quality through to profitability. The goal of this book is to help you and your organization create an integrated customer measurement and management system for making effective resource allocation decisions and increasing profitability. In the process of building a system, organizations develop internal specialists capable of gathering, analyzing, and interpreting customer data. Truly customer-oriented companies should, over time, add these skills to their core competencies.

A systems approach to customer measurement and management also requires that you tailor the system to your unique purpose, customers, and contexts. As an illustration, Volvo's model incorporates the positive effects of improving internal quality on both productivity and customer perceptions of quality, satisfaction, and loyalty. In contrast, a major retailer such as Sears incorporates the central role that satisfied employees play in delivering quality and value to customers.

These measurement systems and models are not substitutes for decision making. Rather, they provide the information you need to make resource allocation decisions and manage the process. The system provides information on how the company and its competitors are performing in different areas and how important the areas are to customers.

When combined with cost and strategy considerations, the system allows both enablers and doers to create organizational value through a continuous focus on customers. To maximize the value generated by the system, make sure your company's own staff perform the bulk of the work of collecting and interpreting customer data, so that you get the full benefit of the insights generated by the effort.

Before you dive in and start conducting customer interviews or surveys, you must know how your measurement system will be used. This chapter focuses on the strategy and planning for such a system. Since a customer orientation builds on internal quality, we'll start with a brief overview of quality management and its role in driving company strategy and customer measures. We'll then discuss two related approaches to translating strategy into action: policy deployment and balanced performance measures. Then we'll focus on the process of getting started on developing a customer measurement and management system—or improving an existing one—which involves taking a look at the breadth and depth of the proposed system and the role of market segmentation in it.

In our customer satisfaction framework, internal quality is the first in the chain of events that drives financial performance. It's important not to underestimate the role of *total quality management* (or TQM, also known as *company-wide quality management,* CWQM, and as *total quality control,* TQC)—nor to exaggerate it. For longterm survival, businesses have been forced to improve their abilities to change and innovate. But internal quality management is not in itself sufficient to assure success. Internal quality improvements must be linked to improvements in external quality, satisfaction, loyalty, and financial performance. And the links must be established in an environment of constantly evolving customer preferences, markets, competitors, and technologies.

The broad principles and methods of quality management apply directly to the development of a customer measurement system. The concept of quality should unify all of a company's activities. After all, only your customers can ultimately define quality for you! In the end, it doesn't matter how well the production system works, how well marketing functions are performed, or how good the company's strategy is. If no one buys, there will be no revenues.

Quality experts emphasize three basic strategies for successful quality management: use reference models or benchmarks, set priorities for quality improvement, and focus your resources.

Do not try to do things completely on your own. Instead, make use of reference models or benchmarks when they're available. Benchmarking is particularly important in developing a customer measurement and management system.

Process benchmarking—finding out how things are done— works as well in developing a customer measurement and management system as in any other area of business. When you can manage it, arrange visits to firms with strong reputations to gauge their practices and learn what they are doing, see how they are doing it, and understand what is possible. Devote some time to reverse engineering their products as well. And don't limit the benchmarking to competitors—in a general area such as customer measurement, you'll find individuals or organizations in many fields who excel in areas that you are interested in improving. Benchmarking on their processes can help you to learn how to conduct better customer interviews, develop and administer more effective surveys, and analyze customer data in more productive ways—and they're likely to be much more willing to share information with you if you're not trying to sell the same offering to the same customers.

For *output* or *performance benchmarking,* you will measure your product or service against direct or indirect competitors on various dimensions such as internal or technical quality, external or perceived quality and value, and overall customer satisfaction, loyalty, and retention. As noted in Chapter Six, external benchmarks will help you interpret your findings regarding your own customers and decide just where to devote your resources to get the most mileage from your improvement efforts.

SET PRIORITIES FOR QUALITY IMPROVEMENT

The second basic strategy of quality management is the universal law of priorities. In a quality context, it is often said that 20 percent of parts, processes, or people account for 80 percent of quality problems (often called the *Pareto principle*). Each customer and each market will react differently to the various drivers of satisfaction and loyalty, so one of your primary goals in customer measurement is to identify the drivers that are most important to improve. As described in Chapter One, you need to find out where the impact on customers is high and your current performance is poor. Your goal should be to set priorities and *optimize* rather than *maximize* your quality and satisfaction improvement efforts.

FOCUS YOUR RESOURCES

Once you have chosen the area or areas to change, the third basic strategy of quality management is to concentrate your resources to maximal effect. The goal is to create a company-wide focus on the things that matter most for performance and survival. This is one of the most important yet also most often neglected aspects of quality management. Increasingly, managers face a common problem in that their customer measurement systems point out specific needs for improvement, but their organizations don't respond. The manager knows what area or areas to attack, but has difficulty getting anyone to do anything about it. This is where the lens of the customer shows its usefulness. Once the concept spreads through an organization the independent actions of each individual and department are much more likely to fit into the overall improvement effort.

TWO WAYS TO TRANSLATE STRATEGY INTO ACTION

Since no amount of information will do you any good if no one will act on it, creating an environment where resources get focused on quality management is in many ways the key element of the process. One basic approach to this problem, called *policy deployment,* has proven very effective where a company has a clear priority regarding what policy to deploy. A variation known as *balanced performance measures* allows a company to determine and deploy a balanced mix of quality improvements.

Policy deployment, or hoshin planning *(hoshin kanri)* as it is sometimes called, is a powerful quality management process that converts a company's strategy into operational change and effectively moves different units within the company in the same direction. Customer policy deployment, in particular, aims to move the entire organization to focus more on customers in order to increase their satisfaction and loyalty.

Policy deployment includes four major steps:

1. *Mission and Vision:* Clearly state the organization's philosophy, mission, and vision (also called the *president's diagnosis*).
2. *Goals:* Understand exactly where the organization is today and where it wants to be in the short, medium, and long term with regard to specific criteria or goals.
3. *Communication Strategy:* Communicate the mission, vision, and goals throughout the organization.
4. *Priority Setting and Implementation:* Set priorities, align the incentives, and implement quality improvement projects accordingly (using project management).

Making customers a priority became a strategy for Volvo's survival in the intensely competitive global automotive industry. Back in 1991, the question was how to create a customer orientation in a traditionally engineering-driven company. Volvo quickly realized that policy deployment was a natural means of building on its quality management foundations to move the company from an engineering focus to a customer focus. Here is a summary of how Volvo implemented the four major phases of policy deployment:

- *Volvo's Mission and Vision:* "To be the world's most desired and successful premium car brand."
- *Volvo's Goals:* "To be number 5 in customer satisfaction (according to the J. D. Power IQS study) in 1995 and number 3 in 1997."
- *Volvo's Communication Strategy:* Stop keeping secrets about customer complaints; give employees an open information system and a broad view of the customer value-added process that encompasses the vehicle sales and service experience throughout the life of the vehicle.
- *Volvo's Priority Setting and Implementation:* Use quality teams to focus on the two hundred highest-priority areas (out of two thousand possibilities identified in an initial review), and reward team members based on the degree to which Volvo met its corporate goals as well as on the degree to which the team met its own goals.

Once mission statements work their way through various levels of management, they often end up reading like the Boy Scouts' oath. Companies want to be all things to all people. In contrast, Volvo's vision was specifically to be the most desired successful specialty car brand. While abstract and forward-looking, the vision nonetheless pointed to a particular segment of the automotive market in which Volvo wanted to excel. Quantitatively,

Volvo's goal was defined in terms of placement in a specific independent survey – to be number 5 in its industry by 1995 and number 3 by 1997. Although any measurement system has its strengths and weaknesses, by defining customer satisfaction using the J. D. Power IQS study, Volvo effectively defined where it was (twenty-sixth out of thirty-four makes) and where it wanted to be at different points in time. Volvo effectively aligned its mission and vision to concrete measures and goals.

Volvo's next step was communication. Stellan Flodin, the senior vice president in charge of quality, and Jan-Olof Nilsson, senior vice president of Business Area 900, led the effort to create a communication process and culture of openness across the company. Volvo abandoned its hush-hush approach to quality and customer data in favour of a more open system in which information was made available to anyone who could influence customer satisfaction. This was critically important at Volvo because its employees perceived their company as doing quite well. Internally, they had been improving products and processes from year to year all along. But externally, relative quality was falling and the company was losing ground to competitors. This decline was a well-kept secret until Volvo decided to change policy and speak freely about its problems.

Many of the problems reported in the IQS studies involved customers' experiences with sales and service, so it was essential that Volvo encompass the entire value-added chain (from production to delivery and dealer service) in its policy deployment process. Over a period of about two years, the company created an environment in which individuals from very different value-adding areas worked together to solve a variety of customer problems. Reported quality problems came to be viewed as opportunities to learn and improve rather than as negative reflections on any particular area, team, or individual.

As noted, Volvo's customer data revealed over two thousand areas in which quality improvements might be made. The final stage of the process, project management, set priorities and put quality teams to work improving approximately two hundred of the most glaring problem areas. On the Volvo 850, for example, customer data revealed that the manual transmission alone generated a surprising number of complaints (about twenty per hundred vehicles). For example, many customers said the manual gear box was too stiff, and people of below average height added that the stick shift was too far away and difficult to reach in some gears. A project team was therefore deployed to improve the quality of the transmission. Additional customer surveys allowed the team to translate customer perceptions into design and part changes that, when introduced, decreased the incidence of complaints by over 50 percent.

A key to making all this happen, however, was that Volvo aligned the project teams' and individuals' goals with overall policy goals. Team members were compensated based on whether their teams met project goals (such as reducing transmission problems per hundred cars from twenty to ten to five over time) and whether Volvo met its overall corporate goals such as reducing overall problems per hundred cars to reach the number 5 position by 1995 and the number 3 position by 1997.

The policy deployment process that Sears is using to create a customer focus is similar to the process at Volvo. The main difference is that, whereas Volvo built on its knowledge of quality management to implement policy deployment from the top down, Sears is using the development of its employee-customerprofit chain (the idea that satisfied employees make for satisfied customers and thereby increase sales and profits, described in Chapter One) to drive the deployment process from the bottom up. The process has been more implicit than explicit.

Retail-service companies have not gone through the same quality management revolution and training as manufacturing companies such as Volvo. But once Sears's employee-customerprofit chain was developed, it became an important tool to drive change in the company's mission, vision, goals, and communication. Everyone from senior managers to store employees had to be taught the logic of the model and its implications, including how the company's competitive environment had changed. The company held town hall meetings and used learning maps to help employees grasp the logic behind the model so that they, in turn, could apply it at the store level. In the end, the deployment process has helped build a leadership model that incorporates the various aspects of the employee-customer-profit chain. The leadership model is to make Sears a compelling place to work, shop, and invest.

Yet the deployment process has progressed more slowly at Sears than at Volvo. The process at Sears has been more data driven, working from the bottom up. Only after the employee-customer-profit chain was developed did Sears executives confront many of the challenges in deploying policy, from a lack of buy-in among top executives to communication problems among their retail employees. And arguably, Volvo has been more successful at implementing its customer orientation and turning the corner on profitability. After some initial success, financial performance at Sears remains weak.

These results aren't surprising, and they provide a useful warning to those in service industries. Product companies tend to have a history of quality management when they begin to implement customer policy deployment, and this gives them a strong head start. Few service companies have gone through the same quality revolution, although there are important exceptions. Disney, Fidelity Investments, and USAA, for example, have long-standing commitments to quality management and its principles. Disney has used policy deployment in the development of its theme parks for many years. But most service firms simply did not get the wake-up call that hit manufacturing firms in the 1970s and 1980s, when they were confronted with competitors producing higher-quality products in less time and at lower cost.

If you manage or work in a service industry such as telecommunication, insurance, or banking, very likely your company is now experiencing or will soon experience the same type of global competition and cost pressures as your counterparts in the manufacturing world. Technology such as the Internet now provides a basis for delivering cost-effective global service. The warning from product companies is clear. If you hope to continue to prosper, establish a culture that emphasizes quality as your foundation for using customer information to drive organizational change.

Balanced performance measures or BPMs share many of the principles of policy deployment. But whereas policy deployment has always been an explicit means of translating strategy into action, BPMs were initially developed as a way of balancing the needs of multiple stakeholders in an organization. Rather than focusing mainly on customers, BPMs recognize that a customer focus must be balanced against the needs of other stakeholders, such as owners, employees, and suppliers. A popular approach to developing BPMs is the balanced scorecard.

Companies use the balanced scorecard to assess their performance and strategy in a highly integrated fashion. The scorecard's four main components are the company's financial perspective, the customer perspective, the internal business process perspective, and the learning and innovation perspective.

The *customer perspective* includes those customer measures that are most important for the company to improve, such as targets for customer satisfaction or account penetration. The *financial perspective* includes targets the company sets with respect to both financial (market value) and accounting (revenue and profit) measures. The *internal perspective* includes internal quality and business process measures, such as the number of hours the company spends talking with customers about current or future projects, or the level of employee satisfaction. The *innovation and learning perspective* include goals and measures for investments in training and new product or service development. For each perspective, goals and measures are developed and drilled down to operational levels for teams and individuals ("personal scorecards").

As balanced performance measurement systems evolved through the 1990s, their relationship to policy deployment has become clear. For example, in more recent versions of the balanced scorecard, a company's vision and strategy drive a management process that includes strategy feedback and learning, clarifying and translating the vision and strategy, communicating and linking rewards to performance measures, and planning and setting targets. These stages obviously parallel the four main steps in policy deployment described earlier. Yet important differences remain. Whereas a full policy deployment moves an organization in a completely new direction, such as focusing more explicitly on customers, BPMs balance various stakeholders' needs. In this sense, BPMs are a weak form of policy deployment. They more or less presume that the organization is headed in the right direction and align its activities accordingly. A balanced scorecard approach keeps an organization on course through an integrated management and budgeting process.

BPMs also lack any guiding framework or model of the drivers of financial performance. The approach focuses generally on synergies among the various perspectives or stakeholder needs. As emphasized in Chapter One, it is important that you build your measurement system on an evolving understanding of the drivers of financial performance that is tailored to your company and competitive environment, as Volvo and Sears did.

Although this book's focus is primarily on the customer perspective, balanced performance measures do serve as a reminder that the measurement and management process described here can be applied to other stakeholders as well. In the Sears model, for example, employee attitudes and beliefs are critically important in driving employee behaviour. The processes and tools described in this book for developing the lens of the customer can certainly be applied to develop the lens of the employee, supplier, or equity stakeholder as a basis for developing and administering surveys, analyzing data, and setting priorities for improvement.

When you embark on a strategy of customer-driven quality improvement, questions will arise about how to set up a system to collect the data you need to work with. Many of these questions can be broadly categorized as relating either to *system breadth*— the range of internal and external customers and market segments that you want to measure—or to *system depth*—the level of detail and nature of the information that you gather.

Companies typically serve a range of very different customers both inside and outside the organization. Internal customers may be in the same physical location, as when marketing and finance are customers of information services, or in different locations, as when manufacturing plants are customers of the home office. External customers range from wholesalers and retailers to end users. The customer chain shows three levels of customers: plant customers, retailing customers, and end users. We have kept this example simple to make the relationships easy to see on paper; in practice any given organization or network is likely to have a much larger number of customer levels, as any individual might be considered someone else's customer. And it isn't enough to track exchanges of funds for goods or services, as even external customers don't necessarily pay to assume that role—regulatory agencies are customers for reports, for example, and people downstream (literally or metaphorically) from traditional end users are the ones likely to be customers for ecological and recycling efforts.

To determine just which customers should be your primary measurement and management focus, refer back to the framework in Chapter One. What links in the customer chain drive your financial performance? Where are the links from quality to satisfaction to loyalty and profitability the strongest? Those are the places where you're likely to get the most mileage out of any investment in improved quality. Even without a detailed measurement system, you probably have some knowledge or understanding of where to start looking.

Think about the nature of the competition and customer choice at each level. The logic of a customer orientation (the idea that quality, satisfaction, and loyalty drive profitability) is based on two critical assumptions. First, the customer is relatively free to choose products and services. This assumption holds for most industries in the developed world today—customers face a dizzying variety of brands of cars, soap, phone service, and most necessities and luxuries, and if one alternative doesn't satisfy there's always another to try. This assumption doesn't always hold true, however—when customers face significant switching costs in moving from one provider to another, or there is only one supplier available, they are essentially hostages. That is, when it's expensive or difficult to find another supplier, only a very dissatisfied customer will switch to a competitor. Airline customers are often held hostage to the hub-and-spoke system of air travel, where flying on other than the hub airline imposes significant costs in terms of time and convenience. However, no company can count on keeping its customers hostage indefinitely. In the gas and electric supply business, for example, many customers still have few options to choose from—but recent deregulation means that the situation is changing rapidly, and customer satisfaction and loyalty are likely to become drivers of profitability soon.

The second important assumption in the logic of a customer orientation is that the important customers are the ones who will generate new business if they're satisfied with their experience—buy replacements for past purchases, buy new offerings, or inspire potential customers to try the company's wares. Investments to satisfy more transient or one-time customers may not generate future revenues or cost savings. The benefits of increasing satisfaction are thus greatest at the level in the customer chain where your customers have both a choice and a potential to reward you with future revenues at lower costs.

Related to the notion of customer choice is the relative *push* versus *pull* of your products and services through the customer chain. Consider a service provider such as Fidelity, which places investment instruments through a variety of independent retailers. In one region, the end users—the individual investors— may have strong brand attitudes and perceptions that have been created over a long period of time through experience, advertising, and word of mouth. In this case, the most important customer in the chain is probably the end user who goes to a retailer (whether an agency or a Web site) in search of a particular offering. The choice in this case resides primarily with end users who pull the product through the chain. Although all customers are important at some level, relatively speaking, the satisfaction of the retailer is not as critical in this case as the satisfaction of the end user. To satisfy and retain their own customers, the retailers need to make the Fidelity offerings available to them.

Elsewhere, investors may be much more likely to follow the advice of the retailer about which brand to purchase. The retailer may be more established and trusted in the end user's mind than any individual brand. If investors are more likely to defer their choice to a trusted retailer, Fidelity is in a position of pushing the product or service through the chain. In this case, the most important thing to measure and manage may be the satisfaction of the retailer and its willingness to push the brand on to the end user. The same logic applies regardless of the product or service—if the offering is seen as interchangeable at the end-user level, you have to give the retailer a reason to favour your brand over others.

At each level in the customer chain, the market segmentation scheme is the key element in your strategic market plan to build a customer measurement system. Market segmentation is the process of identifying and targeting unique populations or *segments* of customers and developing tailored marketing strategies to meet the individual segment needs. To identify and target segments, take the following steps:

1. Group customers into segments based on customer needs, benefits sought, or personal values served.
2. Identify or describe the segments according to their behaviours, lifestyles, or demographics.
3. Evaluate the attractiveness of each segment in terms of, for example, profit potential, risk, capacity utilization, and core competencies required to serve the segment.
4. Determine strategically which segments to target and pursue and, as a result, which segments to measure, analyze, and manage separately.

These steps bring you to a framework for just which customers to measure, analyze, and monitor. Because the drivers of satisfaction and loyalty may be very different from segment to segment, be wary of averaging across segments. Averages can be deceiving. If customer data are aggregated too highly, they provide a profile of an average customer who simply does not exist. If the segments are different enough, they will require separate survey development and analysis. Even when the same survey is applicable to more than one group of customers, be sure to analyze importance and performance levels separately for each group.

SEGMENTATION IN A HOTEL CHAIN

Consider, for example, the needs of business customers and vacation customers at "Wolverine Inns" a fictitious name for a major mid-priced hotel chain we worked with recently. The chain recently segmented its franchisees according to which segment of customers they are most likely to serve, based on the idea that downtown properties cater more to the business customer segment and leisure-area properties cater more to the vacation customer segment.

The matrices are used to set priorities for quality improvement. The company's satisfaction and loyalty survey covers eight general quality areas or customer benefits (reservation process, staff, facilities, grounds, bathroom, room, breakfast, and perceived value) and each area is rated on a variety of attributes. For the moment, just look at the impact and performance aspects of the eight types of benefit. Later we will take up the issue of setting priorities among the attributes that provide each benefit, such as the friendliness, helpfulness, efficiency, and grooming and appearance of the hotel staff.

The vertical axes show how each type of property performs on each of the eight benefits using a weighted average of customers' attribute ratings (on a scale where 1 is poor and 5 is excellent). Both downtown and leisure-area properties, for example, perform very well on the quality of the reservations process. The horizontal axes show the relative importance of each benefit as revealed by its statistical impact on overall satisfaction.

For example, the impact score of.75 for quality of the room for the downtown properties shows that as room quality increases by 10 percent, satisfaction increases by 7.5 percent (10 percent ×.75). (This example is based on standardized scale values.)

The results reveal vast differences in the drivers of satisfaction across the two property types. Business customers who frequent downtown Wolverine Inn locations look for the hotel to simply provide a clean and comfortable room. They use the hotel for a place to get a good night's sleep and have little interest in its other services. In contrast, a much wider variety of factors drive satisfaction for the vacation customers who frequent the chain's leisure-area properties. The quality of the room is secondary to the quality of service and advice that the staff provides. The quality of the grounds, bathroom, and breakfast are also more important for the vacation customer.

As hotel manager at any given property, you would certainly want to know impact and performance levels for your target customers. Assuming the described results for individual hotels, the downtown manager would see improving the quality of the rooms as the greatest priority, given its high impact and currently moderate performance. In contrast, the manager of the leisure-area property would see improving the quality of the staff as relatively more important. Neither manager would have much incentive to do anything about perceived value—the customers' view of the price they are paying for the experience—even though it is far and away the lowest performance area in both cases, because the survey results show that neither group of customers cares much about it. Lowering prices would be costly for the hotel and would make it more difficult to sustain improvements in areas that matter to the customers, so it's best to avoid this step unless the hotel has an incentive to change its customer base to one that regards the current price level as a barrier rather than a minor irritant.

After deciding which customer levels to include in the measurement system and what customers or market segments to include, the next step is to ask what level of generality or detail about the lens of the customer the system should contain. Customer satisfaction is a complex matter, made up of the way the customer perceives the concrete attributes of a product, the benefits the customer derives from those attributes, and the personal values that the product supports. All these elements reside with the customer and are beyond the company's direct control, so we refer to them as *external quality factors*. Measurement systems vary in the amount of detail they provide about external factors such as these.

For example, macro-level measurement systems such as the American Customer Satisfaction Index (ACSI) only include very general differences in external perceptions of overall quality and value as drivers of satisfaction and loyalty. Quality is itself measured using customer ratings of the levels of customization and reliability provided, while value is measured using customer perceptions of the price or prices paid for the quality received. The purpose of measurement systems such as the ACSI is, however, to provide quality, value, satisfaction, and loyalty benchmarks across a very wide range of firms, industry groupings (including products, services, retailers, and government and public agencies), and even countries. Such broad-based comparisons require a measurement system that emphasizes generality and comparability as opposed to depth and detail.

If your goal is to improve or radically reinvent goods and services, you'll need a more detailed and comprehensive information system. It should include information on the range of concrete attributes and abstract benefits that might drive satisfaction and require improvement. Chapter Three will return to the convenience store example and discuss perceived convenience, merchandise quality, and safety as just three of the benefits that directly affect customer satisfaction.

In subsequent chapters we will discuss how to develop these more detailed or in-depth measurement systems for the purpose of measuring and managing customer data for a particular product or service and market segment. Remember that the information in the measurement system is designed to leverage either incremental (evolutionary) or innovative (revolutionary) activities, or both. For example, when Volvo discovered that its customers found its manual transmissions difficult to shift (an attribute-level problem), it translated the problem into one of changing certain parts that immediately reduced complaints. In contrast, when product or service designers are pursuing major innovations, they shift upward from the attribute level to more abstract customer benefits and personal values as input to the design process. Developing a fuel cell or electric vehicle, for example, requires matching the benefits and consequences that the new technology provides (such as zero emissions and moderate performance) with the benefits and values that are important to target customers (such as a willingness to trade off vehicle performance for environmental impact). Product or service design is then a process of developing a whole new configuration of product and service attributes to better serve customer needs.

We are often asked when to engage in revolutionary innovation rather than more evolutionary continuous improvement. The key, of course, is to avoid focusing on one to the exclusion of the other, but rather to balance both activities. Masaaki Imai, who was instrumental in developing the *kaizen* or continuous improvement process, emphasizes the importance of maintaining a balance among three activities: maintaining the quality of existing products, services, or processes; achieving kaizen or continuous improvement; and achieving innovation. The temptation, Imai argues, is to focus only on innovation as a means of making rapid changes and leapfrogging the competition. This ignores the long-term benefits that continuous improvement brings to a company.

When all three activities are balanced, the result is a formidable competitive advantage. Disney is a great example of an organization that consistently manages to balance all three activities. The regular development of new characters for use in movies, television shows, and theme parks is a constant source of innovation. At the same time, Disney works to maintain or keep improving every stage of its customers' experience. The combination has created a legendary service organization that is built on a quality foundation *and* reinvents itself on a regular basis.

Measuring quality, customer satisfaction, and loyalty should be an ongoing, repetitive process. It is difficult, however, to make general recommendations about just how frequently to measure. The frequency varies from company to company and depends on the audience, the stability or volatility of the product or service, and the nature of the market. For instance, if you have relatively few customers it may not be desirable to survey them too often. Needless to say, your customers should never feel that the process is burdensome. And once you do a survey and set some priorities, be sure to implement the changes before you launch another survey. Otherwise, your customers will ask the obvious question: "Why should I bother filling out this survey when you didn't pay any attention to the last one?"

A product's life cycle also affects the frequency of measurement. You need frequent contact with customers early on, when the market is evolving and changes to the product or service can have a great impact on a company's success. Consider the battle between Ericsson and Nokia in the cellular phone market. The early adopters of cellular phones were businesspeople. They simply wanted a reliable phone, which gave Ericsson the edge. But Ericsson did not keep up with the evolution of customer needs in the market and emergence of new market segments that demanded more features and design improvements. This allowed Nokia to achieve a greater advantage as the market evolved.

Later in a product's life cycle, customers are much harder to attract, more valuable to keep, and more costly to lose, so again you want close and frequent customer contacts. And, of course, it is always important to listen carefully to customers when the threat of competition has increased. The general point is that contact with customers should become more frequent during certain critical stages of the product life cycle and market dynamics.

Keeping these contingencies in mind, we recommend a customer satisfaction survey at least yearly. More frequent surveys are likely to have little effect on your improvement efforts when the product and the market are stable. If competition is really active and is moving quickly in a market, it may be necessary to carry out more frequent studies—perhaps even on a quarterly basis. But make sure you have enough resources to process and implement the findings, or the efforts are wasted. It is often a good compromise to measure every six months in times of change.

Finally, remember that there's a difference between customer measures and surveys as the basis of a measurement and management system and more informal surveys or methods designed to take a quick pulse or to identify problems as they occur. The latter methods typically focus on the most recent episode or transaction with a customer (such as the latest stay at the hotel or visit to the bookstore), and are often loosely structured (an informal interview by the manager or an open-ended "opinion" card). Their value toward allocating resources and deciding strategy is limited. At the same time, they may be a valuable source of information for service managers or front-line service personnel to catch and resolve certain classes of problems as they occur.

Providing external quality and customer satisfaction depends directly on the quality of your company's internal processes, operating policies, strategies, and plans. Whether your company provides products or services (or both), quality management provides a solid foundation for developing and deploying strategy and measuring quality through the lens of the customer. As you move through subsequent chapters, you will see the three basic strategies of quality management. We will describe the use of reference models or benchmarks to interpret and analyze customer data. We will show you how to optimize rather than maximize customer satisfaction and loyalty by setting priorities for quality improvement. Finally, we will describe ways to maximize use of available resources to implement the change. Policy deployment and its variants, including balanced performance measures, are important tools for creating a more universal and consistent focus. These approaches provide companies with a means of translating their customer strategies into action.

Just where to begin building the system requires decisions regarding which customers to include, or system breadth, and how much detail to provide, or system depth. You want to include the kinds of customers that drive business performance. To do this, you will need to ask "which of our internal or external customers are both a source of future profits and have a choice about where they take their business?" To drive profitability, produce and deliver high-quality products and services to satisfy and retain these customers. When including customers in the measurement system, remember that customers do not all value the same things and behave in the same way. Build your customer measurement systems on an understanding of how your customer base at any given level (such as retail or end-user) is segmented.

Segmentation is a process of identifying individuals or populations of customers with unique needs and wants. By paying attention to segment differences you will avöid the pitfall of setting priorities based on "average" customers who don't exist. In your planning process, also consider just how much detail you will need to measure and how you will use your measurement system. At a general level, macro-level customer measurement systems provide for broad-based comparisons and benchmarking but give only general guidance about what companies should improve (such as product or service quality or value). In this book, the focus is on measurement systems that are more specific to the company or segment; they provide detailed information regarding concrete product or service attributes as well as information about more abstract consequences and benefits. By continually improving the concrete attributes of existing offerings and finding completely new ways to provide customer benefits, you can leverage your customer data to create a truly exemplary level of performance and competitive advantage.

To link internal quality to profitability, you have to find out how customers see the products and services they purchase and consume. Your first step (and the subject of this chapter) will be to develop a model of how customers view your firm's products, services, and activities—the "lens of the customer" that will guide the rest of your efforts.

As discussed earlier, people inside an organization too often develop customer surveys from their own perspective, or how they believe customers view their products and services.

The result is a survey or measurement instrument that embodies the lens of the organization rather than the lens of the customer. You'll often see airline surveys organized in this fashion, for example, full of questions broken out by organizational activity (check-in, preflight service, food and beverage, flight crews, and cabin environment). A survey that aligns question areas with organizational responsibility in this fashion does have the advantage of producing recommendations that are fairly straightforward to implement. If the survey results and prioritysetting process indicate that flight crews are most in need of improvement, then the responsibility for making improvements within the organization is clear.

Unfortunately, this type of survey may warp or entirely miss issues that cross organizational boundaries, as when flight crews get blamed for being short-tempered about carry-on baggage that should never have been allowed into the cabin in the first place. Customers tend to form opinions regarding such benefits as service, convenience, and safety that cut across the functional areas of an organization. It is essential, therefore, that the measurement system be based squarely on the lens of the customer. In addition, having a survey instrument that better captures the customers' perception of the company makes the data easier to analyze. We are able to explain more variation in key customer evaluations and behaviours, such as satisfaction and loyalty, when the questionnaire is based on the customers' view. For an airline, such a questionnaire might address a whole range of activities from seat reservations through boarding to baggage claim under the heading of convenience, and everything from the gate lobby staff to the seat cushions under the heading of comfort.

The concrete attributes of a product or service and the abstract benefits it generates occupy different levels in the customers' lens. This distinction is very useful but may take some getting used to.

The rectangular objects at the left-hand side represent the concrete aspects or dimensions on which customers can readily report performance via survey measures (such as whether a sales staff keeps its appointments and returns telephone calls and e-mail messages). The circular objects to the right of the attributes represent the relatively abstract or *latent* variables that capture the benefits or consequences that the attributes provide or, at an even more abstract level, the personal values that they serve. For simplicity, we will refer to all the abstract drivers of satisfaction and loyalty as *benefits.*

As in a traditional marketing perspective, the customer satisfaction model embodies the view that products and services compete primarily on the benefits they provide or the needs they fulfill. The concrete attributes of the product or service are only the means to these more abstract ends. Letters, e-mail messages, and faxes all, for example, provide the benefit of communication. You can thus view benefits as the primary drivers of satisfaction in the lens. Notice, however, that benefits may be measured using different numbers of concrete attributes.

Satisfaction in the model is defined as a customer's overall evaluation of the purchase and consumption experience with a product, service, or provider. This definition is quite different from transaction-specific definitions of satisfaction that capture a customer's immediate reaction to a particular episode or experience. Why discard the immediate response in favour of a more cumulative or overall definition of satisfaction? Although it seems more remote, the latter turns out to be more directly tied to customers' repurchase intentions and behaviour. Customers' repurchase decisions are affected by their entire purchase and consumption history with a company or brand, not just the last trip to the restaurant or last shipment from a supplier. Although we list loyalty, broadly defined, as the desired outcome of satisfaction, there are other constructs we could have shown there as well. Customer satisfaction may also lead to an enhanced reputation and greater brand equity for the company, which will in turn attract additional customers who are disposed to develop loyalty of their own.

The also see overall satisfaction and loyalty in circles, treating them as abstract constructs that can be measured in concrete terms. Overall satisfaction is reflected in different concrete satisfaction measures, which might include a satisfaction scale, how the product or service performs overall versus customer expectations, performance versus an ideal product or service in the category, and performance versus "best in class" competitors. Similarly, loyalty may be measured using a variety of behavioural intentions (ratings of the likelihood that customers will return, will purchase other products and services from the company, or will speak positively of their experience to others) or actual behaviours (such as whether customers do return, how often they return and how much they purchase when they do, and whether they bring or refer additional customers).

Note the dotted arrow that runs from an attribute-benefit cluster directly to customer loyalty. This captures the possibility that customers' intentions or decisions to repurchase are affected directly by certain benefits. In a recent study of satisfaction with hair care providers, for example, we found that the quality of the haircut, the relationship with the stylist, and the atmosphere of the salon all affect loyalty via overall satisfaction. However, the timeliness and ease of scheduling an appointment have direct effects on loyalty in addition to their effects on satisfaction. Price can also affect loyalty directly— customers are likely to weigh price or value much more when evaluating loyalty than when evaluating satisfaction. "I love his work, but I can't afford to go back every month"

You can't develop the lens of the customer by sitting around and reflecting on how customers view the world. Instead, you need in-depth, qualitative research to show you the issues from the customers' own perspective. Keep in mind that the goal of conducting qualitative research (such as interviews and focus groups) is not to immediately set priorities for quality improvement— it is to identify a comprehensive range of issues (benefits and attributes) that potentially drive satisfaction, loyalty, and profitability. The customer sample that you use at this stage of the research should represent a good cross-section or range of customers from the population or target market of interest, but it need not be truly random as you're not looking for statistical validity at this point. The lens or model that results from this qualitative research provides the foundation for more systematic survey research, which in turn becomes the primary basis for setting priorities when you get to that stage of the process.

Marketing books offer a wide choice of qualitative methods that you can use to identify product and service attributes and the customer benefits they provide—one-on-one interviews, group interviews or focus groups, protocol methods (having customers "think out loud" while using or evaluating a product or service), and a variety of observation techniques. Here, we focus on one qualitative technique that is particularly well suited to the development of a customer model or lens: the *critical incident technique* (CIT).

The CIT can be used to identify satisfaction drivers for a range of internal and external customers. It typically involves an interview in which individuals or groups of customers are asked to provide a list of the things that they like and dislike about the product, service, or company in question. According to Bob Hayes, an expert on the CIT approach, "A critical incident is a specific example of the service or product that describes either *positive* or *negative* performance. A positive example is a characteristic of the service or product that the customer would like to see every time he or she receives that service or product. A negative example is a characteristic of the service or product that would make the customer question the quality of the company."

The critical incidents themselves should be as specific as possible in describing a single feature of the customer's purchase and consumption experience. Hayes argues that a good critical incident should cover a single behaviour or characteristic, and should either describe the service provider in behavioural terms or describe the service or product using specific adjectives. Consider two examples from the case study in Appendix A, which describes CIT interviews with tire retailers. One retailer noted positively that "the range (variety) of products is good"—pointing to a particular characteristic of the tires (the available range) using a specific adjective (good). Another retailer noted negatively that "regional representatives arrive too seldom"—pointing to a specific behaviour of the local salesperson (waiting too long between visits).

If the critical incidents are too general, the interviewer needs to ask additional questions to clarify what the customer really has in mind. For each specific incident, it is also useful to ask the customer for comments on the significance and consequences of the incident. Such questions will elicit valuable information for the next stage of the process, categorizing the incidents into attributes and benefit groupings. When encouraged to elaborate, for example, the retailer who praised the product range pointed out that carrying a range of tire products allowed him to offer "a tire for almost every customer that walks into my store." The one who said the regional representative arrived too seldom said that "he should come every month ...just to see how things are going."

Overall, the CIT process involves a number of steps that are helpful to describe using an activity-based flowchart. Step 1 is to compile and assess whatever relevant secondary research or knowledge pertaining to the lens of the customer already exists within the company. (One should avoid, of course, any biases from the lens of the organization.) Perhaps similar studies have been conducted in slightly different research contexts that shed light on how customers view the product or service. Step 2 is to make initial visits to different customers early in the process. We have found this important for two reasons. First, the visits will provide firsthand observations of the

QUALITY-SATISFACTION

You'll usually need several sources of data to establish all the links from quality through to profits. Consider the experience at Sears and Volvo. Sears uses one survey to measure internal quality in the form of employee perceptions and attitudes and a second survey to measure external quality and satisfaction from the customers' perspective. Information from both sources is then combined with financial performance information for individual stores to trace the links in the employee-customer-profit chain. Volvo tracks internal quality with engineering-based measures of vehicle performance, and uses customer surveys to track external quality.

Now we focus on ways to develop and administer the survey that measures customer perceptions of quality, satisfaction, and loyalty. The lens of the customer—built from the qualitative research in Chapter Three—will serve as a blueprint for your survey, identifying the attributes to include and the order they should appear. To make the survey results useful, however, you will also need to specify and include measures of satisfaction and loyalty so as to be able to combine the individual customer responses into a meaningful pattern of causes and effects.

Step 1: The Preliminaries

As in any other activity, if you don't know what you want to get out of customer measurement, it's going to be hard to tell if you've found it. So before you develop the survey itself, you need to figure out what information is required—which is a function of what you're planning to do with it—as well as how to segment your customer base, what survey method or methods to use, and how to sample the population.

What Information Is Required?

Start by restating in simple terms what you want your customer survey to tell you, and what you plan to do about it. This might be as generic as "We want to know what our customers want so we can give them more of it—and what they don't want, so we can avoid including it, " or it might be tailored to your particular business. Then look back at the lens of the customer and list the attributes and benefits it identifies as having the potential to drive customer satisfaction and loyalty.

Then list some direct questions about customer satisfaction and loyalty. From a statistical standpoint, these are the primary dependent variables that the model is to explain based on customer perceptions of attribute and benefit performance.

Make sure that the things you're asking about are at least partially under your control, so the results will be meaningful and useful. There is no point in finding out that your customers are uniformly unhappy that every day they get a day older, unless you're in the business of providing some way to preserve youth and prolong life. So consider just how the results will affect areas and individuals in your organization and what actions you may need to take based on the results.

How to Segment Survey Respondents?

The next step is to figure out which market segments to include in the survey—and just how to classify respondents into those segments. The choice of segments should be based on their importance in your strategic market plans. Beyond the choice of key segments (such as "daily" and "weekly" convenience store customers), another important question related to segmentation and sampling is whether to include current, past, or potential customers in the research. Companies are often content to focus only on current customers. Unfortunately, if current customers are systematically different from those you've lost or those you would like to pursue in the future, your results from a currentcustomer survey could be misleading or incomplete.

Market segment classifications may be based on information collected prior to the survey. Existing research may already have determined which customers are classified into which segments. If survey respondents can be identified and classified into segments beforehand, then it is perhaps unnecessary to have segment-related information in the survey itself. Otherwise it will be critical to include information in the survey that allows you to sort or select customers by segment. The sorting or selection criteria may be direct or indirect.

THE INDIRECT APPROACH

Using the indirect approach, you might include descriptive items in the survey such as demographic variables (age, sex, income level, education level, ethnic background), geographic variables (city, country, or geographic area), and experience-related variables (frequency of purchase or consumption of the product or service, confidence in evaluating the product or service, and so on). These measures would then be analyzed *after* the surveys are administered to develop distinct clusters or groups of customers that differ on the variables of interest (such as male versus female or frequent versus infrequent convenience store customers).

This approach is indirect in the sense that the descriptive measures are only proxies for identifying more needs-based segments. A disadvantage of this approach is that it can lead to the inclusion of so many descriptive variables that the survey becomes long and cumbersome. An advantage of the approach is that it provides a database that can be used to develop and identify new segments. This allows you to *cut,* or sort the data, in various anticipated and unanticipated ways. Descriptive variables are typically collected near the end of the survey. If a customer feels sensitive about answering particular questions (such as age, income, or education level), encountering such questions up front may bias the responses to the whole questionnaire or lead the customer to give up on it entirely.

THE DIRECT APPROACH

Using the direct approach, you provide an existing segmentation within which customers place themselves in a needs-based segment. Often companies have some existing knowledge of the major segments or populations in their customer base. If simple descriptions of each of the different segments can be included in the survey, customers can indicate directly which segment they most identify with. For the convenience store survey, for example, independent research conducted prior to the survey helped us define five major segment profiles. We then used the profiles to develop descriptive statements for each segment:

Segment 1: I tend to visit a convenience store several times a day for snacks as well as meals.

Segment 2: I am a parent who occasionally goes to a convenience store mainly to buy fill-in items, emergency items, or things for the kids.

Segment 3: I visit a convenience store daily to buy one or two items such as a soda, coffee, cigarettes, or candy.

Segment 4: I go to a convenience store once or twice a week to buy a snack, soda, or coffee.

Segment 5: I shop at a convenience store less than once a week, mainly to buy snacks and party items or items for a trip.

In the resulting convenience store survey (presented in Appendix B at the end of the book), we asked survey respondents to indicate which of these statements best described their behaviour. The primary advantage of this approach is that it is based directly on an existing segmentation scheme. This greatly simplifies the analysis of the survey data. The responses are simply sorted according to their segment identification and analyzed. The disadvantage of using existing segment profiles is that it assumes that the profiles provide an accurate description of the underlying segments. If the nature of the segments changes between the segmentation study and the quality-satisfaction-loyalty survey, the results of the latter will be skewed in unpredictable ways.

We recommend using a hybrid of the direct and indirect segmentation approaches when possible. Using existing segment profiles simplifies subsequent analysis and bases the analysis squarely on a segmentation scheme. But it is helpful to include some additional descriptive questions. The convenience store questionnaire, for example, augments the segment-level questions with a small number of demographic questions used in U.S. census questionnaires. The hybrid approach allows for some exploratory analysis using the demographic variables to sort or cluster respondents into new segments. The demographics also provide descriptive details of the segment profiles, such as whether "daily" convenience store customers tend to be male, female, older, younger, and so on.

Prior to developing the survey, you also need to decide just how to communicate with customers and administer the survey. The choice of survey methods has important implications for the nature of the questions and scales involved. There are various approaches, the more common being one-on-one interview surveys, telephone surveys, Web-based surveys, and written surveys. Each method has its strengths and weaknesses. The choice of methods should depend on the context.

One-on-one interviews are well suited to business-to-business applications, where the population of customers is relatively well defined (such as those customers who purchase a certain type of chemical or part). Conducting personal interviews is a good way to increase response rates; it shows customers that you are deeply interested in their opinions. This is important if your organization has a reasonably small number of key customers that you want to take special care of. A disadvantage of one-on-one interviews is that they can become difficult to manage when the sample of respondents is large.

Problems also arise when the individual conducting a survey interview has a vested interest in the results of the survey, as when the salespeople's bonus system is tied to the data that they collect from customers. Anyone who has purchased or leased a new automobile in the last few years might remember the pleas from salespeople to "give me 10s on the survey—my bonus depends on it!" It is crucial to maintain independence and objectivity in these cases through the use of a third party within the company (such as a manager or a salesperson who does not serve that customer) or an independent data collection agency to conduct the actual interviews.

Telephone surveys, particularly those using a computeraided telephone interview or CATI system, are particularly well suited to end-user products and services where representative samples of consumers are needed from a large population. The convenience store survey script in Appendix B is taken from a CATI application. The advantages of telephone interviews include their relatively low cost per completed interview and the control the interviewer has over who is responding to the survey (compared, for example, to written or mail surveys). A human interviewer can clarify any misunderstandings or problems that a respondent may have in answering a survey question. And when they encounter respondents who are simply not able or willing to respond to the survey, trained interviewers can quickly say thank you and terminate the interview. The disadvantage of the telephone interview approach is that interviewers may generate unpredictable effects of their own. They must be carefully trained, as the way questions are stated is likely to have an impact on how customers respond.

Through the use of randomization techniques (such as random-digit dialing), telephone interviewing typically yields more representative samples of customers in a population than you get with other methods. Using this approach, time zones and area codes can be systematically sampled. The American Customer Satisfaction Index survey, a large national survey, uses this approach to obtain valid cross-sections of U.S. consumers. The survey samples are checked against census data using demographic profiles to ensure that they are properly balanced with respect to age, sex, income and education levels, and ethnic background.

Internet-based surveys are growing in importance as the population of Web users becomes more representative of specific customer groups. Web surveys offer significant advantages in that data can be collected, transferred, and updated continuously online. And unlike CATI survey participants, Web respondents have a written version of the survey available on the computer screen to help keep the questions and scales clearly in mind—and they all see exactly the same questions, which eliminates the danger of interviewer bias. Web surveys have already become the preferred method of data collection in those industries where Web samples are representative of the customer base (as for certain financial services and online retail operations).

Yet many customer populations continue to contain large percentages of individuals from lower income and education categories that do not have direct access to the Web (such as convenience store and mass merchandise retailer customers). This situation is likely to change in the near future. Infrastructure changes, such as the diffusion of broadband cable, will broaden the population of Web users in the years to come. Even now, creative solutions can be used to give more customers Web access for the purpose of conducting a survey. For example, a kiosk system can be placed in a location that all customers could access (such as a convenience store or an employee lounge). A crosssection of customers could be encouraged to use the kiosk using personal communication or incentives (such as store coupons). Easy-to-read touch-screen displays can be used to collect, transfer, and even analyze the data on-line. Another alternative is to use printed versions of the survey that can be handed out or mailed to customers and later scanned and processed on-line.

Written surveys, particularly mail surveys, remain a popular approach to data collection. An advantage of written surveys is their relative low cost *per targeted respondent,* or survey sent. Written surveys can be mailed or distributed efficiently to a relatively large number of customers. The problem is that response rates tend to be low for this approach. Because of the low yield, direct mail often proves more expensive than telephone or Webbased surveys and the respondents are not as representative of the customer population. The quality of the survey data also suffers in that, compared to phone or interview surveys, written surveys offer less control over the interview itself. Written surveys may be passed along for others (subordinates or other family members) to fill out and there is no easy way to clear up misunderstandings or ensure that the respondent is responding carefully to the questions.

One solution to the weaknesses inherent in any one method of data collection is to combine elements of more than one approach. For example, one-on-one or small group interviews can be used to explain the purpose of the survey and motivate participation. To ensure anonymity, written surveys could then be left with the respondents to fill out and return after the interview. Another successful approach in retail contexts is to use store intercepts in combination with written, telephone, or Web surveys. The store intercepts are used to explain the survey and motivate participants to participate in it, while the follow-up survey (in writing, by phone, or by Web page) allows respondents to participate at their convenience.

Sampling is the process of selecting respondents or customers from a population for inclusion in the survey. Naturally, then, sampling starts with the customer population or populations of interest. Your market segmentation scheme and the specific segments that you have decided to include in the research largely define your customer population. The wide variety of techniques for sampling from customer populations fall into three

General categories:

1. Census samples
2. Judgment samples
3. Statistical samples

Census samples involve gathering information from every possible member of a population, such as all of an organization's customers—or all customers in a given segment. Census samples are perfectly representative because the sample and the population are one and the same. Census samples are feasible primarily when the population size is relatively small (such as potential purchasers of jumbo jet engines or highly specialized industrial tools). If you define your population as all customers who have recently recorded transactions, your own records can supply a census sample of current customers.

When the population of customers is too large for a census sample, judgment or statistical samples are called for. Judgment samples involve—as you would expect—using your judgment to decide who should and should not be included. One common method of judgment sampling is to take a list customers and pick people well dispersed with respect to age, sex, income, education, and so on. The drawback is that the inclusion of respondents in the sample is at the discretion of the researcher. This makes it difficult to generalize any results to the population at large. At the same time, this approach is useful when the goal is simply to identify potentially important issues, as when conducting qualitative research. Recall, for example, that the primary goal of using the CIT (critical incident technique) method is to find out what attributes and benefits to include in a more systematic survey.

Statistical sampling involves using statistical probability to determine a sample. Hayes tells us that the primary differences between judgment and statistical sampling are that statistical sampling involves the use of random selection to include cases or respondents in the sample, the ability to statistically determine an appropriate sample size, and the ability to determine how representative the sample is of the population. Thus statistical sampling allows for greater generalization of the study results to the population as a whole. Examples of statistical sampling methods include random-digit dialing of customers (as through CATI systems) and systematic sampling from a customer list (start at a random point and then pick customers at set intervals, say, every tenth or hundredth name, until you have the number you need for your sample). Respondents in the ACSI survey, for example, are selected using random-digit dialing. Naturally, the choice of a sampling method or methods is a function of both the size and accessibility of the customer population or populations of interest and the purpose of the research.

Once you've cleared away the preliminary survey questions, the next issue that you face in developing the survey is just how to measure benefit and attribute performance and importance. With respect to performance, the survey results should provide reliable and sensitive measures of customer benefits, customer satisfaction, and loyalty. When measuring importance, you must choose between direct customer measures of importance (using, for example, scales or other rating tasks) and derived importance or impact measures based on statistical analysis.

There are two important factors to consider when you measure perceived customer benefits, customer satisfaction, and loyalty.

First is the abstract nature of the constructs involved. Recall from Chapter Three that customers do not obtain satisfaction directly from the concrete attributes and features that describe product and service offerings. Rather, satisfaction and loyalty are a function of the benefits and consequences that the attributes provide. These benefits (such as convenience, safety, and service quality), being abstract or latent constructs, cannot be observed or measured directly using single survey items and scales. The same is true for such overall evaluations as customer satisfaction and loyalty. Abstract or latent variables are reflected in a variety of concrete measures. Benefits are reflected in the attribute ratings that make up the benefit, satisfaction is reflected in a variety of overall performance ratings, and loyalty in a variety of behavioural intentions.

The best way to empirically measure these latent variables is to use multiple concrete *proxies,* or survey measures. For example, qualitative research shows that a convenience store customer's perception of convenience is reflected in ratings of store location, hours of operation, speed and efficiency of employees, and the availability of parking.

A latent variable can be measured using a weighted average or *index* of these survey measures. The convenience index of a convenience store thus becomes a weighted average of a customer's ratings of store location, hours of operation, speed and efficiency of employees, and the availability of parking. Overall satisfaction becomes a weighted average of a customer's ratings on such measures as satisfaction, overall performance versus expectations, and overall performance versus a "best in class" competitor.

The second factor to consider when measuring perceived customer benefits, customer satisfaction, and loyalty is the distribution of the data as it relates to your need for *sensitive measures*—measures that can differentiate among fairly small differences in the underlying conditions. This is an ongoing problem in customer surveys because perceptions of quality and satisfaction almost never fall on a normal distribution. That is, there are typically no bell-shaped curves in the data. In a competitive economy, only those competitors with relatively high quality and satisfaction ratings tend to survive. As we know this results in quality and satisfaction data that is strongly *skewed* (where most of the responses are bunched near the high end of the quality and satisfaction scale and the tail of the distribution trails off toward the low end of the scale).

The measurement challenge is to be able to distinguish among customers that are crowded together at the high end of the scale. To illustrate the problem, consider what happens if you use a very insensitive measure of satisfaction. When asked yes-or-no questions (say, Are you satisfied?), the overwhelming majority of customers answer yes. In a recent study of airline passengers we found 95 percent of customers responding yes when asked to evaluate their satisfaction on a yes-no scale. Unfortunately, yes-or-no questions give you no way to distinguish among customers that range from moderately to very satisfied.

The sensitivity of the scale improves when you move to a 5-point scale (where 1 = poor performance or very dissatisfied and 5 = excellent performance or very satisfied).

Research on quality and satisfaction scales suggests that using a 10-point scale is better still. Going beyond 10-point scales, however, is not beneficial as respondents have trouble using all the scale points.

Most sensitive of all is the use of multiple 10-point scale questions to form an index. Consider that any given survey measure is composed of two sources of variation, that which is supposed to be measured (what statisticians call the "true score") and that which is not meant to be measured (the "error"). The *true score* is what the various items in an index have in common, while the *error* is more a function of the biases or problems inherent in individual survey questions. By averaging the measures into a single index, you can increase the amount of true score and reduce the overall error variance (relative to an individual survey measure or question) as error from the individual questions is canceled out. As a result, in statistical analysis and modeling, when you use indices in place of single item measures, you explain more of the variation in satisfaction and loyalty, and the relationships involving quality, satisfaction, and loyalty are stronger. In state-of-the-art quality and satisfaction modeling, the use of indexing to measure abstract or latent variables has become the norm.

Consider a simple example of the value that indices bring to an analysis. When you assess the financial health of your company, you know that any one marketing, accounting, or finance measure (customer retention, return on investment, return on capital employed, stock price) is an imperfect reflection of overall state of the company. Taken together, however, the measures provide a more accurate picture of financial health than is possible using any single measure.

The next step is to decide whether to use direct or derived measures of attribute and benefit importance. Many satisfaction measurement systems rely heavily on the "gap" model, in which the measure of what needs improvement in quality or satisfaction is the difference between customers' direct ratings of attribute importance and direct ratings of performance (performance minus importance). There are three kinds of direct measures commonly used in marketing research:

1. *Direct scale ratings:* Respondents rate the importance of a product or service's attributes on a scale ranging, for example, from "not at all important" to "very important."
2. *Point allocation methods:* Respondents distribute importance "points" (say 100 points) among a given set of attributes where the proportion of points allocated to an attribute indicates its importance.
3. *Paired comparison ratings:* Respondents rate the relative importance of attribute pairs.

Paired comparison ratings can place tremendous burdens on respondents because of the number of attribute pairs involved. They have also been heavily criticized for producing arbitrary measures of importance.

Direct scale ratings are considered more accurate (less biased) than point allocations and easier for respondents to provide than either point allocations or paired comparison ratings. These factors make direct scale ratings the more popular choice, so the remainder of this discussion will focus on this method of assessing customer responses.

The primary advantage of direct importance scale ratings and the gap model is their ease of implementation. They require minimal analysis (plotting averages and taking difference scores) and can be easily understood at various levels in an organization, from front-line service personnel to CEOs. Yet there are several problems associated with using direct measures. The method assumes that customers understand what you mean by "important" and also that they know just what attributes are important to them—and are willing to tell you about it. In the end, we find that asking customers directly to rate the impact that an attribute has on their satisfaction and loyalty is an extremely difficult task. Direct importance measures often result in socially acceptable or status quo answers and poor discrimination. Using direct scale ratings, for example, respondents have a difficult time differentiating among those attributes that are most important to them. We have rarely found significant differences in importance among the top-rated fifteen to twenty attributes in a survey. Research also shows that the importance measures or weights that people report and those that they use when making a decision often differ dramatically. The insight that direct ratings provide drops off as the number of attributes increases.

We illustrate both the strengths and weaknesses of the gap model using a study in which we examined the drivers of satisfaction for a pharmacy. Approximately a hundred customers evaluated twenty-nine attributes of a retail pharmacy.The mean values of rated attribute importance are ordered from least to most important and plotted question by question (where 1 = not at all important and 10 = very important). The corresponding attribute performance measures are also plotted (where 1 = poor performance and 10 = excellent performance). The key attributes to improve are those where the "gap" (performance minus importance) is lowest.

On the positive side, gap models are relatively easy to implement, analyze, and explain. The analysis simply involves plotting the two dimensions, importance and performance, and examining their differences. This often makes gap models a good option for companies that are just beginning to develop a customer orientation. The models identify the "low-hanging fruit"—the obvious gaps that need to be closed—and get the company into the habit of monitoring customers. The prioritysetting logic is also the same as for the strategic satisfaction matrix. Attributes on which both importance and performance are rated high are core competencies, while attributes with high importance and low performance need improvement.

However, a major problem with the approach is that customers rate most everything as important. The conclusion is that the company needs to improve most of the items with low performance ratings, and it's hard to tell which ones would make the most difference to results. Basically, importance scales are effective at highlighting the *least* important attributes but ineffective at highlighting the *most* important attributes. The direct importance ratings are simply not diagnostic. It is primarily the *performance* measures that drive the priority-setting process.

Another problem with direct importance measures and the gap model is that the survey has a tendency to grow. Because the approach requires at least two ratings for each attribute, the survey becomes nearly twice as long as a survey where importance measures are derived by other (statistical) means, as described in the next section. One question is required to rate an attribute's performance and another to rate its importance. Direct importance ratings may be the only option when the customer population (or the sample size) is too small or ease of implementation is an overriding concern. Where feasible, however, it is much more economical to take the statistical approach and add good dependent variables, such as satisfaction and loyalty, for use in a regression analysis.

Importance measures do not need to be measured directly. They can be derived statistically from attribute performance ratings and ratings of overall satisfaction. Because statistical estimations are more objective and less biased, they are often superior to direct customer ratings. Statistical analysis provides estimates of importance as the impact that one variable has on another. Customers indicate how they perceive a product or service to perform on a number of attributes as well as their overall satisfaction and loyalty. Variation in performance and satisfaction across customers allows the researcher to estimate (using regression or regression-based statistical techniques) the impact that different aspects of quality and value have on satisfaction and loyalty. Statistically determined importance ratings can avoid many of the problems that you encounter with direct importance ratings.

But the quality of the statistical estimates can vary significantly. *The important question is whether or not the estimation builds on the lens of the customer!* The lens should be viewed as a blueprint for both survey development *and* analysis. A major problem facing regression-based estimates of impact or importance centres on the correlation among the drivers of satisfaction. If attribute ratings are too highly correlated, that is, if changes in one rating tend to follow changes in another without regard to outside factors—what statisticians refer to as lacking sufficient *independence*—the statistical estimates of impact may be poor.

The lens of the customer, which is based on thorough analysis of qualitative research, shows just which attributes go together in the customer's mind. By combining multiple attribute ratings together into benefit indices, the lens provides a means of reducing correlation among the satisfaction drivers; it increases their independence. The result is a set of benefit and attribute importance weights that are superior to those that can be collected directly from customers.

Once you go through the background analysis outlined thus far, you'll be in a position to develop a survey instrument you can use with confidence. The process described here follows the flowchart which we have found useful in developing and administering our own quality-satisfactionloyalty surveys. The first part of this chapter covered Step 1 (the preliminary decisions regarding what information to collect and how to collect it), so the discussion here starts with Step 2 and goes through the rest of the process. Appendix B at the back of the book provides a sample output in the form of a finished survey script from the National Association of Convenience Stores (NACS). We refer to this survey throughout the process to illustrate our recommendations.

The primary purpose of the opening statement is to persuade your targeted respondents to take part in the survey.

There are three main messages that can be communicated in an opening statement to help maximize the response rate:

1. Emphasize the importance of the topic or problem area to respondents.
2. Emphasize that the primary purpose of the research is to better understand the problem.
3. Emphasize that the organization or entity conducting the research will use the results to improve the situation.

In the convenience store survey, the emphasis in the opening statements is on the latter two points. The statements point out that the survey is meant to understand what quality areas are important to convenience store customers and that the results will be used to guide quality improvement efforts.

The opening statements may also include screener questions needed to identify customers. The convenience store survey screens respondents to include those individuals who have visited a convenience store within the last three months. The screener in the survey also provides an explanation that convenience stores do not include grocery store chains, drug or discount stores, or mass merchandisers. If asked, the interviewer explicitly defines a convenience store as "typically a small franchised market that is open long hours." These explanations and definitions were added as a result of pretesting and revising the survey.

Once respondents have been screened and agree to participate, their first task is to evaluate attribute performance levels. In some cases the ratings may only apply to the product, service, or retailer of interest (say, stores in the Seven-Eleven chain). In other cases the ratings may apply to multiple competitors (say, Seven-Eleven, Quik Stop, and other widely known chains). Before providing the information, the survey must instruct respondents on how to perform the task. This includes who or what is being rated and how to use the scales.

The types of scales and their explanation depend partly on the method used to collect the data. If, for example, it is important to explain multiple anchors on the scale (such as what a 1, 2, 3, 4, or 5 actually means in the context of the survey), it is easier to do this in a written or Web-based survey where respondents can refer to the written anchors. It is more difficult to do so in a telephone survey. Because the respondent has no written list to refer to, the emphasis is typically on keeping only the two endpoints in mind. In the convenience store survey, for example, it is explained that a rating of 1 means poor performance and a rating of 10 means excellent performance.

Keep in mind that the choice of scales and the need to label scale points depends on the researcher's approach to measurement. Given the abstract nature of the constructs and the need for sensitive measures, we strongly advocate using indices to measure customer benefits, customer satisfaction, and loyalty. The use of indices gets you away from very concrete, individual scales where each point on the scale is ascribed some meaning. Indices resemble temperature scales— they just show that the reported value is higher or lower than some benchmark. The meaning you attach to the index levels is based on how a product or service performs against competitors and over time. By deemphasizing concrete scale points in favour of more sensitive indices, you have less need to ascribe meaning to anything more than the end points. We recommend using 10-point scales, where 1 is poor and 10 is excellent, to evaluate performance across data collection methods.

The next sections of the survey present all of the attributes the lens of the customer research recommended for evaluation. The lens of the customer provides a blueprint as to how the attributes are organized— how they go together in a customer's mind. The survey should leverage this lens and present the attributes in clusters defined by the benefit categories (quality of the service, product offerings, store layout, and so on). Particular to the convenience store survey is the inclusion of two questions at the beginning of this section to assess customer perceptions of store reputation. As described in Chapter Three, these ratings will be used in combination with overall satisfaction to explain customer loyalty.

Satisfaction is the customer's overall evaluation of his or her experiences with a product or service provider. In your subsequent analysis, it will be a major dependent variable that you will explain using your measures of attribute and benefit performance. Satisfaction is a latent variable that will be manifested in a variety of more concrete performance ratings. As we have said, it is critical to combine multiple measures of satisfaction in a satisfaction index. In addition to a simple rating of satisfaction, other measures include evaluations of overall product or service performance against different benchmarks. You might ask customers to evaluate performance versus their expectations, versus an ideal product or service provider in the category, or versus a "best in class" competitor.

Notice that we do not advocate using any one of these as a proxy for satisfaction. Rather, satisfaction as a latent or abstract construct is what all of the various evaluations have in common. The measures simply represent different benchmarks that customers use to evaluate performance and from which an index can be constructed. The convenience store survey has respondents evaluate performance using three different questions. The first asks them to express overall satisfaction, the second asks for an evaluation of performance versus expectations, and the third seeks an evaluation of performance versus an ideal product or service in the category. These questions were modeled directly on those used in the ACSI survey, which have been shown to provide a very reliable and sensitive measure of satisfaction. An added benefit of using the ACSI questions is that it allowed us to benchmark the survey results for convenience stores against other industries and firms included in the ACSI survey.

Whereas satisfaction measures apply more or less universally across industries and contexts, loyalty measures do not. As discussed in Chapter Three, the desired outcomes of satisfaction are highly specific to the nature of the business, product, and service involved. Volvo, for example, has specified a range of desired customer outcomes, from the repeat purchase of a Volvo vehicle to the purchase of Volvo financing, Volvo insurance, the purchase and use of a Volvo gas card, and the spread of positive word-ofmouth advertising. If your customers are retailers who turn around and sell your product to end users, loyalty may take the form of the *push*—the sales effort they make on your behalf—as in the "Råtorp Tire Company" case in Appendix A. If your product is a once-in-a-lifetime purchase (a piece of jewelry or a collector's item), loyalty may involve the customer's willingness to buy other products or services from you (cross-selling) and to tell other potential customers about your offerings. In an industrial context, the level of satisfaction may have little effect on whether a customer buys at least some of your products and services. At the same time, it may have a great effect on just how *much* they buy (account penetration). Another desired outcome may include the trust that customers place in you and their resulting commitment to maintaining a relationship.

Our point is simply that, whereas satisfaction measures are more or less universal, loyalty measures must be customized. In the convenience store survey, the desired outcomes for the store chains and franchisees are rather straightforward. They include enhancing the customers' likelihood of visiting the store again in the future and their likelihood of recommending the store to others. The measures used in the Råtorp Tire Company survey were quite different. As in the convenience store survey, they included the likelihood that the customer (in this case a retailer) would continue to purchase, but they also included whether the proportion of products ordered from the manufacturer would likely increase or decrease in the future (account penetration) and the degree to which the retailer would recommend the manufacturer's products to its customers (push).

Descriptive questions (including market segment profiles and demographic questions) are typically added near the end of the survey. As noted earlier, the main reason for this placement is that the questions, being more personal in nature, are apt to lead a respondent to terminate the survey if asked early on. Once the interviewer has developed some rapport with the respondent and the interview has the momentum provided by answering the performance, satisfaction, and loyalty questions, descriptive information is often easier to get.

The primary purpose of the descriptive questions is to group customers by characteristics such as age and income level for later analysis, so as to track their representativeness and discover possible new segments. Recall that the convenience store survey contains both a direct question regarding segmentation and a group of indirect demographic questions that can be used to segment or describe customers. The direct question presents 'he five segment-defining statements listed toward the beginning of this chapter and asks respondents to select the one statement that best describes their use of the convenience store. As noted earlier, the primary benefit of having respondents selfselect into preexisting segments is the ease of subsequent analysis. The drawback is that it presumes that the segments do not change or evolve significantly over time.

A golden rule of survey research is to conduct one or more tests before you put any survey into the field. The primary purpose of preliminary testing is to identify and resolve whatever problems respondents might have in answering the questions. Pretesting tells you whether the survey is able to collect the desired information, and where you need to reword questions to make them simpler and easier to understand. If the pretest is weak and major revisions are required, the revised survey should be tested again before being put into the field.

Pretesting is not just the domain of those who administer the survey; it can raise questions of strategic relevance to top management as well. Another rule we like to follow is to involve both those directly involved in the survey process and those who will use the information to make resource allocation decisions. In pretesting the convenience store survey, for example, we learned several lessons. One was that many people were unclear as to just what a convenience store was in the first place. Does it include gas stations that sell some other merchandise? Grocery store chains that sell gasoline? This led to the inclusion of more specific screening questions and definitions that the interviewer could use as needed.

Pretesting also raised questions about what benchmarks the customer should use to evaluate the competitiveness of a convenience store's prices. Should the benchmarks be limited to other convenience stores, or should they include other stores that sell similar merchandise (such as grocery stores for bread, milk, and soft drinks). Based on top management input, it was decided to let customers compare prices to other stores at which they may buy similar merchandise. The reason was that executives at the various chains were very interested in the gap between perceived and actual price differences between convenience stores and other types of stores. Whereas convenience stores are often perceived as having relatively high prices, actual price differences are often small or nonexistent.

Just how the survey is arranged and conducted is largely a function of the method of contact. Telephone surveys often involve random-digit dialing or random selection from a customer list.

The interviewer makes a pitch for participation and, if the time is not convenient, can arrange for a better time to call back. Before collecting survey data in a one-on-one interview, the respondent is usually called and an explicit appointment is made. Recall that store intercepts are also a valuable tool for selling the survey—persuading people to take part in later administration either by phone, Web, or mail. Web surveys may use an e-mail message to introduce and gain interest in the survey and then instruct the respondent on how to access the survey. Customers may also self-select to participate in surveys that are available on a company's Web site.

Just who administers the survey is a function of both the sheer number of respondents and the need for objectivity. We suggest that people within the sponsoring company administer the survey themselves as long as the number of respondents is not too large and administrators can remain objective. As argued in Chapter One, a truly customer-oriented company should not routinely leave the job of collecting customer data to outsiders. But for a large-sample survey, it will be more cost-effective to use a professional data collection firm. If the interviewer's compensation is a function of customer responses (the number of "10s" on the survey), the objectivity of the responses and resulting data will be compromised. If a more objective interviewer cannot be found within the company, it would again be best to use a third party to collect the data.

The development of a quality-satisfaction-loyalty survey builds directly on the lens of the customer. Survey development should not be a process in which people from different parts of a company sit around and decide what they would like to see on the survey. Rather, the lens of the customer provides a blueprint for deciding which attributes to include and the benefit categories to use for organizing them. Even before developing a survey it is important to understand what populations or market segments to survey, what data collection method or methods to use, and how to sample from the target populations.

In leveraging the lens of the customer, the construction of a quality-satisfaction-loyalty survey should follow certain guidelines. Benefits, satisfaction, and loyalty are abstract constructs that cannot be measured directly using any one concrete survey item. They are best measured using an index of multiple measures or proxies. Indices also provide for more sensitive measures than single survey items, so they can explain more of the variation in satisfaction and loyalty and are better at identifying important satisfaction drivers.

The importance that customers place on attributes and benefits has traditionally been determined by two different approaches: direct measures of importance and those derived from statistical analysis. Among the different direct measures, direct scales (ratings from "not important" to "very important") are often preferred. They are straightforward to collect and as good as or better than other direct approaches (such as point allocation or paired comparisons). Yet, when done properly, statistically derived measures of importance are better than direct measures at objectively capturing the impact attributes and benefits have on satisfaction and loyalty. It is important for statistical analyses to leverage the lens of the customer when grouping variables for analysis. Otherwise, even the most rigorous statistical estimates may be a poor reflection of reality.

With the lens of the customer in mind and the data collection methods chosen, you can complete the survey instrument in a systematic way. First, assess attribute performance by benefit category. After that, obtain overall evaluations of satisfaction. Then select loyalty measures and customize them to fit the product, service, or context. To some, loyalty is simply a matter of whether a customer comes back to buy the same product or use the same service. To others, loyalty is a matter of how much more customers will buy (account penetration) or what else they will buy (cross-selling). After adding descriptive questions to help identify market segments, pretest the survey to identify any unforeseen problems. Arranging and conducting the survey yields the data that serves as input to the next phase of the process. In Chapter Five we focus on using this data to derive the information needed to set priorities and improve product and service quality.

W hen it comes to analyzing your customer survey data, you have a lot of options. We recommend a variation on *principal-components regression (PCR)* that is relatively simple to use and provides as much detailed information as you need to make quality improvement decisions. It combines two statistical methods: principal-components analysis and regression analysis. *Principal-components analysis* is a data reduction tool that shows what any group of survey measures have in common, so you can develop the benefit, satisfaction, and loyalty indices. *Regression analysis* relates these indices to each other and lets you determine the benefit, satisfaction, and loyalty impact scores.

As in earlier chapters, we present a flowchart to illustrate the necessary steps used to apply PCR to the lens of the customer. To support our recommendation, in Appendix C at the end of the book we compare results achieved using this method against the results of other approaches.

We begin by describing just what information you can and should be obtaining from your analysis. After describing our data analysis method, we end the chapter with a discussion of how to link survey data to financial performance measures, illustrating the links with examples from Volvo and a major hotel chain. These financial links, which highlight the payoff from investments suggested by customer measurement, will help you inspire people to make real quality improvements based on the information the survey process develops.

When you analyze satisfaction and loyalty data, you're really looking for answers to two relatively simple questions. Where does your company need to improve quality or value to increase satisfaction and loyalty? And once satisfaction and loyalty are improved, what are the payoffs? The basic assumptions are that improved quality leads to increased satisfaction, which in turn makes customers more loyal, and that you get more profit from loyal customers than from those who don't care where they get the product or service you're selling.

Now, how do you quantify the links? The prerequisite is that your measurement system should provide sensitive *and* reliable measures. Your goal is to provide managers with truly diagnostic information—with levers they can push to improve quality and satisfaction. You don't want results that suggest that everything (or nothing) is important, or results that show differences (as among competitors) or changes (over time) that are not valid and meaningful. In other words, you want a system that produces results you can trust. Finally, you want to be able to predict what happens when satisfaction increases. How likely are customers to come back and how much more revenue or profit will they generate?

To make your measurement system a reality, you will need to analyze your survey data to produce multiple levels of information in the system. The circles labeled "satisfaction" and "loyalty" are the key to understanding your customers' overall consumption experience. Best measured using indices made up of multiple concrete measures, these abstract constructs are important in benchmarking performance versus competitors and tracking performance over time.

These benefit-level indices are the heart of the lens of the customer. They provide an overall view of how you are performing in quality areas as defined by your customers. But because these indices are abstract, they cannot be acted upon directly. Action requires moving down to the level of the underlying concrete attributes.

Attribute values are obtained directly from the quality-satisfaction-loyalty survey ratings. Each is measured using a 10-point scale like the ones in the convenience store questionnaire in Appendix B. For the benefits and attributes, 1 is poor performance and 10 is excellent performance. But setting priorities requires you to measure impact as well, that is, the extent to which a change in an attribute will lead to a change in satisfaction, loyalty, and other desired customer outcomes. As there are attribute and benefit levels of performance, so there are also attribute and benefit levels of impact. The benefit-level impacts (obtained from the regression analysis described later in this chapter), indicate how much impact each benefit has on customer satisfaction. It is helpful to focus initially on these benefit-level impacts to gain an understanding of the consumption experience. Looking at the attribute or question level impacts (obtained from the principal-components analysis also described in this chapter) will help you relate your improvement efforts to the everyday activities of the company that have the highest payoff. Attribute impacts are more the focus of continuous improvement efforts, while benefit impacts are the focus of innovation efforts—attempts to find completely new ways to deliver the benefits that customers value.

A benefit-level impact of 0.5 shows that a 1-unit change in that benefit index is associated with a 0.5-unit increase in the satisfaction index. Once you have impact information at every level of the model, you can quantify the change that improving an attribute or benefit would make in loyalty (and subsequent profitability, once this data is added to the model). The impact of changing an input to the model (an attribute) on the output of the model (loyalty or profitability) is simply the product of all impacts in the chain of causes and effects. (Where there is more than one path or chain of cause-and-effect relationships, it would be the sum of the different impact chains.)

If you are familiar with traditional PCR, you will see that our approach to principal-components regression has some unique features. Traditional PCR factor-analyzes all the attribute ratings simultaneously to produce a set of independent components or factors. It ignores benefit clusters of the type we recommend you develop using qualitative research to create the lens of the customer. The problem is that the approach is too data driven; the factor analysis dictates the lens. In contrast, our approach uses the benefit groupings or clusters in the lens as a theory or model to structure the PCR analysis. This approach provides the technical sophistication and diagnostic information that your analysis requires.

The main alternative to using our version of PCR is *partial least squares* (PLS). Both our PCR approach and PLS use the lens of the customer as a guide to structure the analysis. PCR is a two-step approach in which the benefit, satisfaction, and loyalty indices are first estimated using a series of principal-components analyses. The researcher then uses these indices or latent variables in a series of regression models to estimate a causal chain of events (as from quality through to financial performance). PLS performs both of these steps for the researcher. It estimates an entire causal chain or model using an iterative estimation procedure that integrates aspects of principal-components analysis and multiple regression. Researchers in the areas of quality, marketing, and consumer research regard PLS as the state of the art in customer satisfaction modeling.

The disadvantage of PLS is that it requires special software and training, and the software is neither user-friendly nor easy to find. If you have mastered PLS, by all means use it. At a conceptual level, our flowchart and procedure for evaluating the quality of your analysis still applies. Otherwise, we recommend that you use PCR, which is straightforward to do using easily available and user-friendly software packages. In Appendix C we demonstrate just how similar the results are with PCR and PLS. Comparing the two approaches we find a 0.99 correlation in estimated benefit-level impacts and a 0.98 correlation in estimated attribute-level impacts. In other words, the results are virtually identical. The following sections describe how to analyze a customer satisfaction model using our PCR method.

The sole purpose of analysis is to make sense out of the data you collect. This section includes a step-by-step guide to analyzing data sets that you can use if you're in charge of performing or managing the data analysis. Even if you're remote from the actual research and your responsibility is to create an environment where customer data will be developed and used, the guide will still be useful as it will demystify the process and, as a consequence, make you more constructively critical when evaluating the output of an analysis.

The first major accomplishment will be to create the latent variables for benefits, satisfaction, and loyalty. Then the process will go on to derive the actual values for the impact of one level of the model on the next, and to establish benchmark values for the benefit, satisfaction, and loyalty indices. The combination of impacts and indices will provide the cause-effect chain.

Once you've built the lens of the customer for your products or services and seen the valuable information it can help you produce, it's tempting to sit back and ask, "Well, now what do the numbers say we should do?"

But it's not that simple. The critical next phase of the process is to use the information to set priorities for improvement. And don't underestimate the importance of obtaining top management input to your action plans at this point. This may require some persistence. Too often managers view measurement systems, including the quality-satisfaction-loyalty model we present here, as a means of avoiding tough decisions—but "the numbers" don't pay the bills, and they don't make decisions, either.

Managers who are in charge of implementing their company's strategies and hold the authority to budget and who allocate resources to improve quality and satisfaction cannot absent themselves from the process. The numbers simply help managers base their decisions on facts.

Here in this chapter we close the loop. We first discuss management's role in using the output of the measurement system to set priorities for improvement. We then discuss how to implement the priorities. We bridge the gap between the customer benefits and product or service attributes that need improvement and the internal changes they require.

As we said in Chapter One, setting priorities requires both impact and performance information for the various drivers of satisfaction and loyalty. But to set priorities, you must make some critical decisions regarding just what constitutes high versus low impact and high versus low performance. These decisions require you to consider a number of factors beyond the information in your impact-performance chart, including your strategy and competencies as well as relevant benchmarks, costs, and market dynamics.

Recall that the basic logic is to categorize the various benefit and attribute drivers of satisfaction into one of the four cells of the matrix, each of which is associated with its own market action implications. Generally, the essential areas to improve are those where impact or importance is high and performance is low. Customers are essentially telling us that we are falling short in these important areas. Improvements to these areas will effectively focus resources where they have the greatest impact on satisfaction and subsequent loyalty and profitability. This is also the cell in which you are most competitively vulnerable. If competitors do an excellent job in these areas, they will lure your customers away.

Those areas that are important to customers and in which your performance is strong represent your core competencies and competitive advantages. It is essential to maintain if not improve performance on these drivers. The implications for the opposite cell, where impact is low and performance is weak, are also clear. Generally, there's no reason to waste resources on improving these areas. According to the customers, performance here just doesn't matter.

The implications for the remaining cell, in which impact is low yet performance is high, are less straightforward. This may be an area where resources have been wasted in the past because the benefits and attributes are not important to customers. In one recent application, for example, we found that customers at an IKEA furniture store in the United States rated traditional Swedish amenities – a child-care facility and a Swedish bake-shop – very positively. Nonetheless, these amenities had little to no impact on satisfaction and loyalty.

From a cost-benefit standpoint, we concluded that having the amenities was not costeffective for the U.S.-based store.

Alternatively, benefits and attributes in the low impact-high performance category may contain drivers of satisfaction that customers consider to be basic and necessary (as in Kano's model described in Chapter Five). Customers may find these benefits and attributes everywhere they look and take them for granted. Although important in an absolute sense, these features offer no differentiation because there is little to no variance in their performance across customers and competitors. Airline safety is a classic example here—as long as the planes aren't falling out of the sky, passengers tend to regard one airline as much the same as another. That doesn't mean that any airline can afford to ease off on safety! The same sort of consideration can apply in less dramatic circumstances as well. In the IKEA project, we found that "ease of assembly" was also rated highly and had little impact. Our conclusion here, however, was to make certain that we assure continued high performance on this benefit. Withdrawing resources and reducing performance would only serve to put us on a "slippery slope" and decrease satisfaction. The area would quickly return to the high impact–low performance category. Another possibility in the high performance–low impact quadrant is to find a new target market segment for the product or service. It may well be possible to find new customers who would especially value these benefit areas (such as customers who would value the child-care and bakery facilities in the IKEA store).

But data analysis does not determine where to draw the cell boundaries. Managers must draw the lines and decide just where the improvement should occur. Again, the impact-performance charts are a primary input to this decision process, but there are several other factors that you need to consider.

Your strategic market plan leads you to focus on particular segments of customers to leverage core competencies. But what if your customer data analysis suggests that you improve in areas that are inconsistent with your basic strengths? Management must decide whether or not the areas that need improvement are those in which core competencies and a competitive advantage can be achieved. If not, you may be pursuing customers you can't please with your strengths, at the risk of alienating customers who currently value your offerings. Perhaps you should reconsider your entire strategic market plan instead.

At the same time, the information may be very valuable in deciding on network partners who can help provide customers with the benefits they need. Think back to the convenience store survey, which revealed that safety is the primary driver of satisfaction for customers. In practical terms, safety is not something that a convenience store can completely control, so the implication may be to network and collaborate with those who can have more effect. In some cities, for example, convenience stores provide an area where local law enforcement officers can take a break, make phone calls, and do paperwork. This win-win solution saves the officers time and creates a greater atmosphere of safety than the stores could provide on their own.

It is also critically important to benchmark both impact and performance when using this information to set priorities. In the Råtorp Tire Company case (Appendix A at the back of the book), impact-performance charts are supplied for three main competitors in the market. As the reader quickly finds out, making decisions for Råtorp requires a careful consideration of impact and performance levels for the competitors as well. In an absolute sense, impact may be high and performance low in a given area, suggesting the need to make improvements. But what if your closest competitor shows even lower performance and higher impact? It may be a mistake to improve that area if there are others that also call for attention. Relatively, it may be a competitive strength, at least in the short run.

At the same time, do not ignore the absolute levels of impact and performance. Over the long haul, the absolute levels of performance and impact highlight your vulnerabilities, as well as those of your competitors, and suggest where new competitors may enter or improve to take customers away.

In Chapter Five we briefly discussed how to incorporate cost considerations into the analysis. When you tie your model and analysis to increased profit per customer, you then have some idea that the costs typically incurred to improve quality are covered. But in most cases, managers must consider the relative costs of making improvements when deciding which areas to improve. Remember that the goal is to optimize rather than maximize satisfaction and loyalty. If two areas show equally low performance and high impact, managers should ask, "Which is more cost-effective to improve?" One source of cost information is management itself. Another is through the use of tools such as QFD (quality function deployment, described later in this chapter) that translate product improvements into internal change and explicitly consider cost information.

Finally, consider where your market is headed over time. Just what factors will become more or less important? For personal computers, will processing speed become less of a differential advantage going forward? For convenience stores, will prepared foods become a greater source of differentiation and impact? Both social and technological forecasting are important bases for predicting these market dynamics, but are beyond the scope of our discussion.

Appendix A at the end of the book concludes with a prioritysetting exercise that makes use of the Råtorp Tire Company information discussed in Chapter Three. The exercise provides the output of a survey and data analysis for Råtorp and its two main competitors. We strongly encourage you to work through the data in the case and set priorities for Råtorp. Based on the data, consider what you expect the competition to do as well. The case will force you to consider several factors, including what Råtorp's strategy should be, how the benchmarks influence interpretation of the results, how the competition is likely to evolve over time (such as the role filled by import brands), and what the improvements might cost. The case emphasizes that the task of moving from information to decisions is far from trivial. It requires significant reflection and input from managers in a position to set and implement a strategic market plan.

Once you have targeted which benefits and attributes to improve, you have to figure out just how to improve them. In effect, you need to build a bridge from your model of customer perceptions and behaviours to your internal metrics, parts, processes, and people. When you do this, you'll soon find that—as with any bridge—the traffic on this one flows both ways.

The framework integrates aspects of two leading approaches to improving quality and satisfaction: *quality function deployment* (QFD) and customer satisfaction modeling (as detailed in Chapter Five). Together, the two approaches illustrate qualitatively different steps in the overall process of translating satisfaction into its means of accomplishment. Our satisfaction models translate overall satisfaction down into the customer benefits that drive satisfaction and into the product and service attributes that provide the benefits. These are the uppermost stages of the framework. The lower stages, taken from QFD, translate these attributes further down into their means of accomplishment or production.

It is important to consider what we mean by *translation* in the framework. Consistent with the arrows is a process of moving from the most abstract information of interest to the most concrete. Customer satisfaction is customers' overall evaluation of their purchase and consumption experience. Moving downstream in the framework from satisfaction to production is, therefore, a process of translating abstract, subjective evaluations into concrete, objective means of accomplishment.

In contrast, the process of moving up in the framework from concrete processes and attributes to abstract benefits and overall satisfaction is more of an inductive or *change monitoring* process. After determining what changes to make, it is important to track the changes back upstream in the process. Did, for example, the changes we made internally have a subsequent effect on customer perceptions and satisfaction? To what degree did our improvements to production processes improve process operations, parts deployment, engineering or design characteristics, and ultimately attribute and benefit performance? As we see, the combination of translation and change monitoring forms a two-way traffic that is essential to close the loop on the quality improvement process.

A central point of the framework is that QFD picks up where satisfaction modeling leaves off. The product and service attributes that are the output of the priority-setting process represent the input to QFD. The four houses or phases of QFD thus represent phases four through seven of an overall translation process. The translation is, however, different for pure products than for pure services. For products, targeted attributes must be translated into engineering or design characteristics, parts characteristics, process operations, and finally production requirements. Because services are co-produced by customers and employees at a time and place of the customer's choosing, service production is a different beast. In service applications of QFD, targeted attributes for improvement must be translated into service qualities (for example, hotel arrival), service functions (airport shuttle service), service process designs (number of shuttles, routes, and personnel), and operating policies and procedures (daily schedules and contingency plans).

An important implication of the framework is that for a given product or service, there are at least seven conceptually distinct stages in the overall translation and change monitoring process. It highlights the difficulties and challenges that we face even after a satisfaction model is analyzed and priorities are set. Our goal here is not to exhaustively discuss the implementation phases, but rather to introduce you to QFD as one tool that has helped thousands of companies around the world to link their customer data to product and service improvements. A thorough treatment of how tools such as QFD are used to implement product-driven product and process changes is beyond the scope of this book. It is, in fact, the subject of our next book in the UMBS Management Series.

The work is usually documented in a series of matrices. Its primary benefits are reduced design costs and development time. Other benefits include improving communication and cohesion within a product development or improvement team and solidifying design decisions early in the development cycle.

Generally there are two variants of the QFD methodology. The first is the four-phase system captured and presented in more detail later. In this approach, QFD starts with an input list of customer-desired attributes. These attributes are often ordered hierarchically to handle the large number required to describe a product (such as an automobile door system). At a higher level of abstraction are the benefit categories similar to those used in our satisfaction model (such as that a door system "operates well"). At a lower level of abstraction are the more concrete attributes (such as that a door system is "easy to close from the outside").

The QFD translation process begins in Phase 1, the "House of Quality, " where attributes are translated into engineering characteristics. In subsequent phases – often called *houses* – engineering targets are translated into parts characteristics; targeted parts characteristics are translated into key process operations; and key process operations are translated into production requirements or work instructions. As mentioned, this system is altered when applied to services.

The second variant of QFD recognizes that the four-phase system that only fulfills a portion of the planning that is needed for a new product. Separate matrix systems are required to incorporate product quality deployment, technology deployment, cost deployment, and reliability deployment throughout the planning, design, trial, manufacturing, and service phases of product development and launch.

Index

C

D

E

F

G

H

I

O

P

Q

R

S

T

U

V

W

Y